MW01593157

Colorado Vanguards

Colorado Vanguards

Historic Trailblazers & Their Local Legacies

PHYLLIS J. PERRY

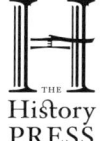

THE
History
PRESS

Published by The History Press
Charleston, SC
www.historypress.net

Copyright © 2015 by Phyllis J. Perry
All rights reserved

First published 2015

Manufactured in the United States

ISBN 978.1.46711.937.5

Library of Congress Control Number: 2015949880

Notice: The information in this book is true and complete to the best of our knowledge. It is offered without guarantee on the part of the author or The History Press. The author and The History Press disclaim all liability in connection with the use of this book.

All rights reserved. No part of this book may be reproduced or transmitted in any form whatsoever without prior written permission from the publisher except in the case of brief quotations embodied in critical articles and reviews.

For David and Casey, who make the impossible possible.

Contents

Contents

Foreword

We see their names everywhere, and not just in Colorado: Baby Doe Tabor, Kit Carson, Zebulon Pike, Chief Ouray, Nikola Tesla, and Florence Sabin. And who doesn't recognize the name of Adolph Coors? But what many people don't realize is just how important these individuals and many others, who arguably are less well known, were to the development of Colorado.

One definition of *vanguard* reads, "the foremost or leading position in a trend or movement." And Colorado's leaders were as grand as the Rocky Mountains, from Zebulon Pike, who more than two centuries ago spotted a mountain that he called Grand Peak that now bears his name, to Enos Mills, known as the Father of Rocky Mountain National Park, whose lectures, photographs and books ensured that land was set aside for national parks.

Their motivations for taking on the challenge of exploring or living in Colorado, mostly in the 1800s, varied widely. Some, such as Zebulon Pike, Stephen Long, Jim Bridger and Kit Carson, were seasoned explorers. Jim Beckwourth, Charles Bent and William Bent sought adventure and fortune. Today's entrepreneurs would admire the restlessness of Uncle Dick Wootton, who couldn't resist establishing new businesses from stores to a saloon and a hotel, eventually establishing a tollgate for the toll road over Raton Pass right in front of his home.

Because of the times, many of the trappers and explorers also became competent fighters, whether serving in the army or defending a fort or settlement during various hostilities. At the same time, many worked hard to have strong, peaceful (and financially beneficial) relationships with Native Americans. Black Kettle, Chief Left Hand and Chief Ouray worked tirelessly against insurmountable odds and heartbreaking circumstances to keep peace in a quickly changing landscape.

And then there were the women of Colorado. Lady Isabella Bird wasn't about to let her long hiking skirt get in the way of climbing Longs Peak or exploring the Estes Park area. Helen Hunt Jackson, an accomplished writer, came to Colorado Springs for her health and stayed to write about the shameful treatment of Native Americans by the government. Don't miss that chapter about the Tabors for a glimpse into the social and political mores of the time.

Readers of *Colorado Vanguards: Historic Trailblazers and Their Local Legacies* will recognize the fine scholarship that supports each chapter. They will also relish the grand storytelling that brings these people to life. Author Phyllis Perry's voice and her attention to detail set *Colorado Vanguards* apart from other offerings of its like. Each story is peppered with those kinds of facts that readers will be itching to share in social situations or around the water cooler: Did you know that Tesla Motors honors an inventor named Nikola Tesla? Did you know that Nikola Tesla's father wanted him to join the clergy? That he had to sneak candles so he could read at night because his father thought reading wasn't good for his eyes? That he got involved with gambling as a young man? That he built the largest Tesla coil ever…in Colorado? That is the kind of irresistible reading found in this book.

Today, you can drive up to the Stanley Hotel in a Model X Tesla, have a Coors beer and toast your good health, thanks to F.O. Stanley, Nikola Tesla, Adolph Coors and Florence Sabin. In fact, that would be the perfect setting for reading this intriguing collection of stories about Colorado's vanguard. And if you can't get to Colorado's mountains right now, this book will take you there anyway.

–SUZANNE BARCHERS, EdD

Introduction

Few driving along today's Colorado highways—whether going to visit the Great Sand Dunes National Park near Mosca, to a Broncos game in the mile-high city of Denver, to the annual Peach Festival at Palisade or to the Shakespeare Festival on the University of Colorado campus in Boulder—would stop to reflect that only a few hundred years ago, there were no Americans in this vast land. It was empty except for Native Americans and the animals and vegetation that supported them.

The first chapter in this book details the explorations of Zebulon Pike that took place in 1806, when, for the first time, the American flag was raised within the boundaries of Colorado. Many other men and women would follow. Some blazed trails, trapped and traded, while others sought gold and silver. More and more came, creating towns and cities; establishing a state government; building railroads; working farms and ranches; developing mining, timber and other industries; or contributing through teaching, medicine, invention and the arts.

Although these remarkable people might not have been born in the Rocky Mountain Region, each of the men and women discussed in this book made a significant contribution to the Rocky Mountain West and is best remembered for an association with a specific geographic place. Pike was the first to gaze up at the peak that today bears his name, and another of Colorado's towering mountains is named for Major Stephen Long, who in 1820 set forth on his Rocky Mountain expedition. Long's group was responsible for collecting, sketching and describing the plants and animals of this remarkable piece of the Louisiana Purchase. Towns began to flourish. El Pueblo, founded as a tiny fur trading center by James Beckwourth, grew into the city of Pueblo.

Charles and William Bent are associated with the trading fort that they both built and destroyed, the same fort where Kit Carson served as a scout and hunter. Uncle Dick Wootton—although a trapper, trader, freighter and farmer—is best remembered for charging a toll from those who traveled over his Raton Pass. John Gregory and George Jackson are typical of the miners who sought their fortunes in gold and silver in Clear Creek Canyon. Chief Niwot astonished the first visitors to present-day Boulder County by speaking to them in English. Through her writings, Isabella Bird immortalized her climb up Longs Peak with Rocky Mountain Jim. Helen Hunt Jackson not only wrote about the plight of Native Americans in California but also extolled the beauties of Colorado Springs.

Chief Ouray and Chipeta at the Los Pinos Agency worked for peace between Native Americans and new white settlers. Although he was one of the few to escape, Chief Black Kettle is linked with the infamous Sand Creek Massacre. All three of the Tabors provided stories of wealth and drama in Leadville and Denver. In 1873, three years before Colorado became a state, Adolph Coors founded his brewery in Golden. John L. Routt led the state as its first governor, while Casimiro Barela served as representative from Trinidad, speaking up for the needs of minorities.

David Moffat is remembered for the Moffat Road railway, and Otto Mears for opening toll roads throughout the San Juans. William Jackson Palmer of Colorado Springs built a railroad empire. F.O. Stanley brought visitors to his Stanley Hotel in Estes Park in his Stanley Steamer automobiles, while the inventions of eccentric Nikola Tesla found a practical use in Telluride. Dr. Florence Sabin devoted her efforts to medical research and to the city of Denver's public health. Naturalist Enos Mills's untiring efforts were a huge factor in the successful creation of Rocky Mountain National Park.

Each man, woman and place in this book is representative of a stage in the history of the West and of the variety of backgrounds and areas of expertise that contributed to its growth. Although they deserve and, indeed, already have inspired many books about them, it is hoped that their short profile here illustrates some of the colorful threads that make up the rich tapestry of the history of the Rocky Mountain West.

Zebulon Pike

1779–1813 • Pikes Peak

In late July 1806, Lieutenant Zebulon Pike led a small group of men on a historic expedition from St. Louis into the unexplored Rocky Mountains. They often moored their keelboat along the bank of the Missouri River, made camp and sent out a hunting party for food. Game was plentiful, and Pike was a good shot who brought back deer, turkey, geese and sometimes buffalo meat.

A member of Pike's party, Dr. Robinson, described what happened while he was out with Pike on one of these hunting expeditions. Pike nearly stepped on a huge rattlesnake. Instead of striking, the snake pulled itself in and avoided being stepped on. Dr. Robinson, who was walking behind Pike, saw this, sounded the alarm and jumped aside. Robinson reported that Pike stopped, turned back to study the snake carefully and was curious about it.

The doctor wrote that when he urged Pike to shoot the snake, Pike refused, saying, "It could have killed me a minute before and didn't…It spared my life. Why should I be so ungrateful as to kill it in return? A man must surely be at least as generous as a snake."

Dr. Robinson was left to wonder about what sort of a man was leading this expedition—one who had already completed a major wilderness exploration, one with a reputation as a stern disciplinarian, one who was unbending when a principle was involved and yet a man who would spare the life of a rattlesnake.

Zebulon Montgomery Pike was born in Lamington, Somerset County, New Jersey, in 1779 and grew up on farms in Pennsylvania. His family moved

Zebulon Pike. *By Thomas Gimbrede, 1781–1832, engraver. Library of Congress.*

often, which caused Pike's education to be interrupted. He attended country grade schools and was tutored by his mother. Pike enjoyed sports, fishing and hunting and proved himself an excellent marksman.

Pike's father had served in the Continental army, and his grandfather distinguished himself in the Revolutionary War. After the Revolution, Pike's father struggled to support his family as a farmer. When President George Washington asked for experienced military men to serve in a campaign against Indians of the Northwest Territory (then in the Ohio-Indiana area), Pike's father quickly signed up and was commissioned as a captain in the Pennsylvania militia. In 1793, Pike Sr. took his family with him to Fort Washington on the Ohio River.

General James Wilkinson was second in command at Fort Washington, and young Zebulon Pike, aged fourteen, greatly admired the general. The boy's greatest desire was to be a soldier. At age fifteen, young Zebulon joined as a cadet in his father's company and acquitted himself well.

After the Treaty of Greenville in August 1795, the Native Americans gave up their lands in Ohio and parts of Indiana. There was no longer a real threat in this area from Native Americans, but young Pike continued on in the army, mostly transporting supplies overland and up the various rivers to the forts in the new territories. Although considerable theft was common in such situations, Pike quickly earned a reputation for absolute honesty. Pike grew proficient in using keelboats, and he learned to speak a number of Native American dialects.

During this time, Wilkinson became commanding general of the army. Pike's father was promoted to major and transferred to Fort Pickering, an easy assignment prior to retirement. Zebulon Pike saw his father frequently, and his father could watch his son moving up the ranks. Young Pike was promoted in 1799 to second lieutenant and eight months later to first lieutenant. These speedy promotions further endeared General Wilkinson to Pike.

Pike served at Fort Massac and at other stations along the Ohio River. Now a commander, he held his men to strict discipline but won their respect since he never gave them duties that he himself did not share. He was considered gentlemanly and somewhat reserved. Committed to life as a soldier, Pike continued to learn as much as he could about the military and along the way also gained some proficiency in French.

From 1795 to 1801, as Pike went up and down the Ohio River purchasing supplies for various forts, he got to know several of the farmers and planters in Kentucky and Ohio. He sometimes visited their homes. A regular stop was the Brown Plantation at Sugar Grove, Kentucky. Here Pike met his cousin, Clarissa, or Clara, Brown, the eighteen-year-old daughter of his maternal uncle, Captain James Brown. Captain Brown had considerable wealth and did not want a young soldier courting his daughter. Since Captain Brown refused to sanction a marriage between the two, Pike and Clara Brown fled to Cincinnati, married and established a home in Fort Washington.

When Spain ceded its territories west of the Mississippi to France, Secretary of State Madison instructed the United States minister in Paris to look into purchasing this land for the United States. Negotiations went on for months, but eventually, Napoleon, the Emperor of France, sold 530 million acres to the United States for $27,267,622. This new territory needed to be explored, and Meriwether Lewis and William Clark were sent by President Jefferson to cross overland to the Pacific. Their famous journey is very well known. What is not so well known are the two explorations of the West made at approximately the same time by Zebulon Pike.

After his marriage, Pike moved about a good deal, first to Washington, D.C., and then to posts in Indiana, Illinois and Fort Knox. To provide a home for his family, Pike brought his wife, Clara, and their daughter, Clarissa, to St. Louis and found quarters for them there. In 1805, while he was commanding the post in Kaskaskia, Illinois, he received orders from General Wilkinson to go to St. Louis. There he handpicked a group of men and made preparations to lead an exploration up the Mississippi.

Pike gathered a few simple scientific tools such as a primitive sextant, a thermometer and a watch to take with him in a seventy-foot keelboat with the twenty soldiers he had selected. Within three weeks of receiving his orders, Pike set out on August 19, 1805, from St. Louis to explore the headwaters of the Mississippi. Pike's expedition had several assignments. He was to find locations for military forts and get permission from Native Americans to build them; note the direction, flow and navigability of rivers; record latitudes and longitude of shoals and islands; and warn all trappers and traders that they were now on United States land and must obtain licenses from the United Sates government and pay taxes.

Pike's group had its share of troubles. Their keelboat was always in one difficulty or another requiring repairs. In dealing with Native Americans, Pike found it hard to discuss land rights. The Native Americans had no understanding of individual land ownership, believing rather that this wilderness belonged to the entire tribe and that no chief was in a position to negotiate away any part of it. Pike reached Prairie du Chien, located at the confluence of the Wisconsin and Mississippi Rivers, in early September. Late that month, seven chiefs were brought together, and Pike negotiated for land on each side of the river on which to build a military encampment.

Continuing up the river, Pike and his men sometimes made only six or seven miles a day. Quail, pheasant, deer, buffalo and raccoons were plentiful, and the men stopped to hunt frequently. It took over one hundred pounds of meat a day to feed the men, and Pike was also trying to lay in extra stores for winter.

Snow began falling in October, and many men became ill. Pike stopped and spent several weeks building a fort surrounded by a stockade at what is now Little Falls, Minnesota. Sick and weakened men would stay there with a good food supply. Healthy men not only built the stockade and hunted but also constructed a large canoe, well stocked with food. After many delays, Pike finally left the stockade, dividing his men into two groups. One group went in the canoe, and the other rode in sledges along the river bank. Both groups found it hard going, and they made only a few miles a day. By January, many of the men had frozen fingers and toes, but they continued through what is now northern Minnesota, near the Canadian border. It was February 1, 1806, when Pike reached Leech Lake, which he believed was the source of the Mississippi River. (The actual source was Lake Itasca, some twenty-six miles away.)

At Leach Lake, Hugh McGillis ran a trading post of the Northwest Fur Company, which flew the British flag. Pike quickly ordered the flag be shot down and replaced with the stars and stripes, demonstrating to the trappers, traders and Native Americans that this was now territory of the United Sates of America.

Having reached, or at least come very close to, the source of the Mississippi, Pike and his men then headed toward home, returning to the stockade, where they found that the sergeant left in charge had done a poor job. Supplies were short, and some of Pike's personal possessions had been sold to Native Americans. Pike promptly demoted the sergeant to a private. In April, when the ice in the river had broken up sufficiently, Pike led his men back to St. Louis along the same route they had taken the year before.

Only three days after he returned from this major Mississippi expedition on April 30, 1806, Pike was asked by General Wilkinson to prepare for a second journey, this one into the Rocky Mountains. In spite of all the hardships he had endured, Pike was eager to go but worried about his family. Pike did not feel he could resign from the army, because he had no other profession and had no savings to support his wife, who was still estranged from her father. Pike signed on to lead the new expedition, knowing he would receive a promotion and that a successful trip would bring him fame and advance his career. He knew it would also please his friend General Wilkinson.

So in 1806, twenty-seven-year-old Lieutenant Zebulon Montgomery Pike set out on his second expedition with a small group from St. Louis. His mission was to escort captured Osage warriors and their families safely back to their tribes in southwest Nebraska and northwest Kansas and to try to establish good relations with the Osages, Pawnees and Comanches. In addition, he would explore the Osage, a tributary of the Missouri, to its source and then head south to the Arkansas River. Pike's group would be the first party to explore the Middle West as it sought the source of the Arkansas River, found the Red River and descended to the Mississippi.

At the time Pike received his orders, General James Wilkinson was both governor and commander in chief of American military forces in the Louisiana Territory. The Louisiana Territory had belonged to the United States for only three years, and Spain and the United States had conflicting claims about boundaries. Pike would be entering parts of the Louisiana Territory involved in boundary disputes between the Spanish and United States governments, and he was under strict orders to avoid any conflict with the Spanish. Spies abounded, however, and news of Pike's impending trip had no doubt been sent to General Don Nimesio Salcedo, governor and commander in chief of the Spanish provinces at the seat of government in Chihuahua City.

With provisions for only four months, Pike and his twenty-two men left on July 15, 1806, in a keelboat. They escorted the Osages back to their lands and then continued their explorations, arriving in October at the Arkansas River in mid-Kansas. Pike split his group in two, dividing their supplies equally. One group descended the Arkansas River to its mouth, where it

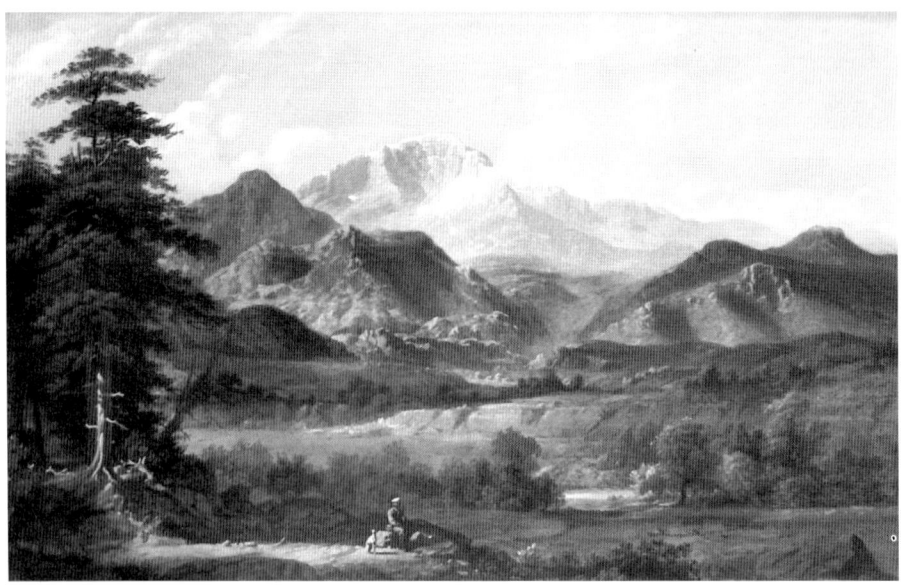

View of Pikes Peak, a painting by George Caleb Bingham, 1872. *Wikimedia Commons.*

flowed into the Mississippi, while Pike led the second group of about sixteen men into what is now Colorado.

Pike and his group camped somewhere near present-day Pueblo, Colorado, building a small stockade and raising the first American flag in November 1806. Pike kept a detailed journal, and his entry for November 15 is the first mention of the Colorado mountain now called Pikes Peak. "At two o'clock in the afternoon I thought I could distinguish a mountain to our right." Like many before and after him, he misjudged the distance to this great mountain. By November 27, the mountain to which he referred to as Grand Peak still appeared about fifteen miles ahead of them. It was a beautiful sight, and in subsequent years, many famous artists would paint the peak, including Albert Bierstadt and George Caleb Bingham.

Pike took a small group to try to climb the mountain, but it was much farther away than he had thought. He gave up the idea of an ascent, not because it seemed impossible, but because his men were ill equipped for a winter climb. They wore thin cotton uniforms, were low on provisions and had half-starved horses. It was two degrees below zero, and his men were beginning to suffer from frozen feet. Pike led his men up the Arkansas River from the Pueblo campsite. In his journal on December 5, 1806, he mentioned seeing Royal Gorge and going across South Park to the upper

Arkansas River. He set up camp on December 10, in what is now the location of Cañon City.

Believing he had come to the Red River, Pike divided his men into small groups to explore. They fought their way downstream through a gorge until they looked out and recognized they were back at the outlet of the Arkansas River, which they'd left a month earlier. They had traveled in a great circle. Pike reported "great mortification" and wished fervently, since this was his birthday, that he would never spend another "so miserably." As they spent Christmas Day 1806 near what is now Buena Vista eating only unsalted buffalo meat, their supply of flour long since exhausted, Pike wrote, "The hardships and privations we underwent were on this day brought more fully to mind…Here 800 miles from the frontiers of our country, in the most inclement season of the year; not one person clothed for the winter, many without blankets (having been obliged to cut them up for socks, etc.) and now laying down at night on the snow or wet ground."

By January 9, when all the stragglers from the small groups had reunited, they found themselves exactly where they had been on December 10, back at what would become Cañon City, Colorado. Pike built a small stockade there, left two men and some supplies and again turned south. But things only got worse. After a few days' rest, the men headed up Grape Creek toward the Wet Mountains Valley. Many of their horses were dead or injured, so the men were on foot. Finally, several men could not continue because of frozen feet. Those who dropped out were assured that Pike would send supplies and help to them. It was January 29 when Pike arrived on the banks of the Rio Grande del Norte, which again he mistakenly thought was the Red River. Here the men were successful in hunting deer.

After a march of twenty-eight miles, nine of the group were left behind with frozen feet, while Pike continued with his small party, shuffling along with the aid of sticks through drifts of snow three feet deep. Pike's group had only eleven men when they walked up Mosca Pass and into the San Luis Valley. Eventually, they reached the Great Sand Dunes. It was January 29 when they arrived near what is now Alamosa, Colorado, where they were again able to successfully hunt deer for food. Pike built a stockade in present-day Conejos County, next to the Rio Grande, and sent several of his party back to rescue the clusters of men they'd been forced to leave behind.

Ten days later, a group of fifty Spaniards arrived at the stockade. Their leader was Don Ignatio Saltelo, who, according to Pike's journal said, "Sir, the governor of New Mexico being informed you had missed your route, ordered me to offer you in his name, mules, horses, money or whatever you may stand in need of to conduct you to the head of Red River; as from Santa Fe to where it is sometimes navigable, is eight days journey." Pike was amazed to learn he was only at the Rio Grande del Norte and was still a long way from the river he had sought.

Pike did not want to violate Spanish Territory or to leave for Santa Fe until all the men he had left behind had rejoined him, but he agreed to go. He left two men behind to tell the others to follow him as soon as they got back to the stockade. Pike was escorted to Santa Fe on April 26, 1807, where amazingly every other man who had been left behind caught up with him again. Pike was taken to meet with the Spanish governor and was told he and his men would be released back in United States Territory. They traveled south to Chihuahua and then across Texas to Natchitoches, on the Red River, arriving on July 1, 1807, two weeks short of a year from when they had begun their expedition.

Pike received some fame and a promotion. He published reports of his travels with a company in Philadelphia, and these were translated into several languages. Because some of his papers and documents were stolen when the Spanish took him into custody, Pike had to reconstruct parts of his trip from memory, leading to some inaccuracies. Pike earned little money from his publications because the explorations of Lewis and Clark overshadowed his journeys.

Brigadier General Pike saw his final command during the War of 1812. In April 1813, he headed for the eastern end of Lake Ontario. Before starting out, Pike wrote to his father, "I embark tomorrow in the fleet to Sackett's Harbor at the head of fifteen hundred choice troops, on a secret expedition. If success attends my steps, honor and glory await my name—if defeat, still shall it be said we died like brave men; and conferred honor even in death on the American name."

Pike was part of a fleet of fourteen armed American transports. They took heavy fire from the British on shore, and Pike got into a boat to direct the assault on land. As they withdrew, the British exploded one of their own powder magazines, killing 52 and wounding 180 Americans. Among the wounded was Pike. He died in a few hours but not before hearing shouts of victory and learning that the Stars and Stripes had gone up over the British fort at Yorkville (now Toronto).

Clara Pike outlived her husband by many years. Her father, Captain Brown, died in 1824 and left his plantation to her. Clara Pike and her daughter and son-in-law returned to Sugar Grove, where she managed the estate until her death in 1847.

Pike's name in history is clouded. He had the misfortune to serve under General James Wilkinson. Wilkinson and Aaron Burr were implicated in a conspiracy to establish an independent nation west of the Alleghenies. Some believed that Pike, on his expedition into the Rockies, was little more than a spy for Wilkinson. There appears to be no evidence to support this claim, and much to suggest that Pike was in fact a brave and loyal officer committed to serving the United States.

Pike is also often belittled for being frequently lost and ill equipped. But it must be remembered that as a young lieutenant, the "lost pathfinder," didn't have the clout to demand sufficient supplies and that he was heading off on a journey into unexplored territory where no one knew exactly where he was going or for how long he would be gone. Though often lost, he did not lose any of his men. He followed orders, survived danger and hardship and made his way back safely from two dangerous expeditions, keeping an excellent journal that proved to be the first guidebook to Pikes Peak, the Royal Gorge and the Great Sand Dunes of Colorado. And finally, Zebulon Pike gave his life for his country in the War of 1812.

Stephen Long

1784–1864 • Longs Peak

A wall of armed and hostile Native Americans stood squarely between the small expeditionary force of two dozen soldiers and scientists and the narrow path they must follow. "Outnumbered three to one" was what Major Stephen Long later recorded in his journal for Monday, July 18, 1823. In the uneasy silence that had fallen over the group, the sound of guns being cocked on both sides could clearly be heard.

When the first members of this Native American hunting party had arrived on the scene, they appeared friendly, but as they were joined by more and more of their tribesmen, the Indians turned surly, demanding whiskey and presents and eying the horses of the small expedition force as if they might try to steal them. Once the large group of Native Americans grew threatening, Major Long ordered all his men to mount, took his place at the head of the line and led the way down the trail. The Native Americans quickly formed a crescent-shaped wall in front of them to block their progress.

Instantly and unhesitatingly, Major Long chose his course of action. He immediately rode straight toward the natives, making it clear that he and his men would move forward or fight here and now. Clearly the badly outnumbered explorers would lose in a battle, but it was obvious there would be heavy losses on the other side, too. No one spoke or even breathed as the little expeditionary force rode single file right through the band of hostile Native Americans.

Safe for the time being, Long made camp a few miles away and urged his men to eat and rest. Expecting that the band of Native Americans

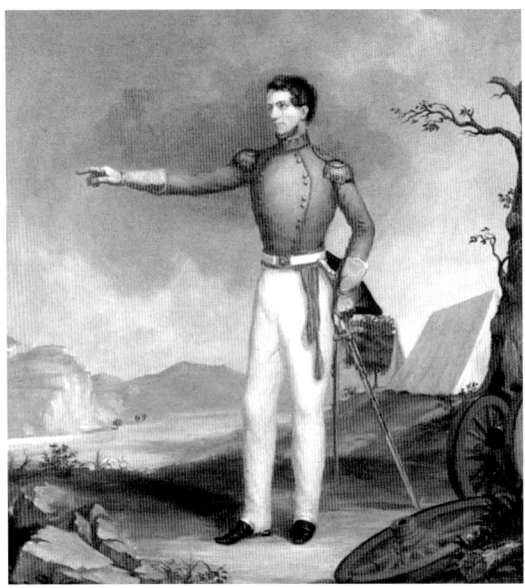

Major Stephen H. Long on the Rocky Mountain Expedition by Titian Peale, circa 1835. *National Park Service.*

would attack them at dawn, Long hobbled the horses and put all his soldiers on guard in two relief shifts. At midnight, he awakened everyone and ordered that camp be broken. As silently as possible, the men rode away by moonlight. Long's experience and leadership probably saved his small expeditionary group from a disastrous conflict.

Stephen Harrison Long was born on December 30, 1784, to Moses and Lucy Long, their second child and eldest son. Moses Long had served in the Continental army during the Revolutionary War. After the war, he married and settled in Hopkinton, New Hampshire, where he farmed and also worked as a barrel maker. Moses Long was active in public affairs, serving as town selectman and tax collector.

As a boy, Stephen Long worked on his father's farm and was able to attend school only during the winter months. A good student, he read a lot and wanted a future other than farming. He borrowed money to apply to Dartmouth College, where he was accepted as a freshman at the age of twenty-one. Long proved to be an able student and was elected to Phi Beta Kappa. His marked interest in music led him to join the Handel Society.

After graduation from college in 1809 at the age of twenty-five, Long accepted a teaching position in Salisbury, New Hampshire, not far from his hometown. He taught for only one year before leaving to become principal of a public school in Germantown, Pennsylvania, located ten miles from Philadelphia. Long thrived in his new environment, meeting members of the American Philosophical Society, joining the Harmonic Society and making many friends, including the family of Martha Hodgkiss, his future wife.

By 1812, Long felt some dissatisfaction with his job situation. He told a friend that he was considering an offer to apprentice to a physician. He was hesitant because he didn't want to appear "fickle and unsteady," and he knew he still had debts to pay. While working as an educator, Long made use of his strong mathematical aptitude by doing part-time survey work, and he invented a device that he called a hydrostatic engine for which he received a patent. This invention attracted the attention of a major of the army topographical engineers.

Long was introduced to General Joseph Swift, who was impressed with the young man. Swift tried to persuade Long to resign his principalship and become an engineer, offering to secure for him a commission as a second lieutenant in the army. Although Long declined the offer to join the army, he did hire on as a civilian engineer charged with strengthening the Brooklyn Harbor defenses during the War of 1812. Long did well on this assignment, and he was commissioned a second lieutenant in the corps of engineers in 1814. The following year, he was appointed as an assistant professor of mathematics at West Point. This eventually led to his receiving a brevet commission as a major in the army and being assigned to the topographical engineer unit, a position for which he was remarkably well suited. In his new assignment, his commanding officer noted that his "character for science, industry, and perseverance is not surpassed by any topographist in the American army."

During this time, the War Department was assessing its defenses in the aftermath of the War of 1812, and Long received several interesting but modest assignments. He selected a site to replace Fort Clark at Lake Peoria, Illinois, and he explored and mapped the Chicago and Fort Wayne region and gathered data for canals to be constructed between Lake Michigan and the Illinois River. In 1816, Long proposed to President James Monroe that he be commissioned to build a steamship to explore the main tributaries of the Mississippi, the Great Lakes and the rivers flowing into them.

In the spring of 1817, Long was commissioned to explore. He was not outfitted as he would have liked and had to set out in an old six-oared skiff borrowed from William Clark rather than in a new steamboat. Instead of well-educated West Point cadets, Long was assigned a sergeant and six privates, three of whom could not even write their own names. Long carried out his mission anyway. He charted the Mississippi as far north as present-day Wisconsin, and he recorded information on the Native Americans and the countryside encountered. He even extended the trip into what is now Minnesota, examining sites for new military posts. Although he had almost no scientific instruments, Long made what observations he could about rock formations and animals and, on his return, submitted a variety of reports.

Long then returned to Philadelphia, and on March 3, 1819, he married Martha Hodgkiss. He and his wife took up residence in Philadelphia.

Although he moved his family close to where he was stationed when he could, he was often away on military trips. Eventually, Long and his wife had five children, and the dedicated father made sure that each was well educated, including his only daughter, Lucy.

Long was still eager to go on explorations and asked General Swift to use his influence with the president to let him organize a new expedition that would include scientists and topographical engineers. Shortly after his marriage, Long got his wish. He was chosen to lead an expedition different from all previous ones. In addition to soldiers, half the men in the group would be scientists. Secretary of War Calhoun's orders to Long stated, "The Object of the Expedition, is to acquire as thorough and accurate knowledge as may be practicable, of a portion of our country, which is daily becoming more interesting, but which is as yet imperfectly known. With this view, you will permit nothing worthy of notice, to escape your attention." The expedition was charged not just to chart a path or trace a river, but to observe all types of flora and fauna.

Long selected for his group some extraordinary people drawn from several scientific fields. Thomas Say would serve as zoologist. Edwin James served as botanist, geologist and surgeon. Samuel Seymour, a middle-aged, British-born engraver and landscape painter, was included as an artist, as well as eighteen-year-old Titian Ramsay Peale, who was not only an artist but also a naturalist trained in natural history at his father's Philadelphia Museum. Long also added two other officers and a West Point cadet.

At the same time as this exploratory group was setting forth, another expeditionary force was being readied, made up entirely of troops charged with going up the Missouri to establish a fort at the mouth of the Yellowstone River near the present-day border of North Dakota and Montana. Both the military and scientific groups were referred to as the Yellowstone Expedition. The military contingent left Pittsburgh in five steamships in the spring of 1819. Long's group of twenty-four military and scientific members left shortly after and included a six-man crew for the steamship the *Western Engineer*. Long had designed the *Western Engineer* specifically for this trip. It was seventy-five feet long, thirteen feet wide and had a paddlewheel in the rear. Narrower and more able to handle shallow water than most steamships, it succeeded in going farther up the Missouri than any of the five ships of the military expedition.

Each of the scientists in Long's group distinguished himself. Samuel Seymour is credited with being the first artist to sketch the Rocky Mountains. Titian Ramsey Peale painted remarkable watercolors of the birds and other animals that he saw. Dr. Edwin James, in addition to finding and naming new plants, became the noteworthy chronicler of the expedition. Thomas Say carefully identified numerous new mammals and birds. The scientists made notes and drawings of fascinating trees, plants, insects and animals as they took a month to descend the Ohio River. The *Western Engineer* arrived in St. Louis on June 9, where officers and scientists were treated to a banquet. On June 21, they left St. Louis and entered the Missouri River. Because of muddy water, they moved slowly, and it was July 13 when they reached Franklin, at that time the most important town west of St. Louis.

Long's group would typically pull up on the riverbank and go ashore in swampy areas while sketching and collecting specimens. Several members of the group became ill, and one died. In addition to illness, Pawnee raiders descended on the group and stole some of their horses and equipment. The military contingent also ran into major problems. Considering that all was not going well, Congress decided to cut short the military exploration and send the scientific group off in another direction. Long's group was now advised to go overland across the prairies to the headwaters of the Red, Arkansas and Platte Rivers.

Following these new orders, Long led his expedition west in June 1820. We learn from Edwin James's *Account of an Expedition from Pittsburgh to the Rocky Mountains* that, after locating what later came to be called Longs Peak (the highest mountain in what is now Rocky Mountain National Park), Long's group went southward to the headwaters of the Arkansas, where they stopped and made camp. This allowed James and four others to ascend Pikes Peak. The group knew this was the same mountain described in some detail but not climbed during Zebulon Pike's earlier expedition.

James and members of his small climbing party each carried with them a blanket, ten pounds of bison meat, some parched cornmeal and a small kettle. They left two men and horses at a base camp while the other three began the climb to the top. James and the two men with him made a second small camp where they left most of their blankets and provisions. Unencumbered, they continued upward, noting as they went the rock formations, wild flowers, trees and animal tracks. They took measurements from a variety of spots as they went.

The men climbed above the tree line to the summit of the mountain, where they remained for about half an hour. Although the day was clear, the temperature in the sun was only forty-two degrees atop the high mountain. At the main camp, where they had left Major Long, it was ninety-five degrees. James and his party spent a cold night but made their way back,

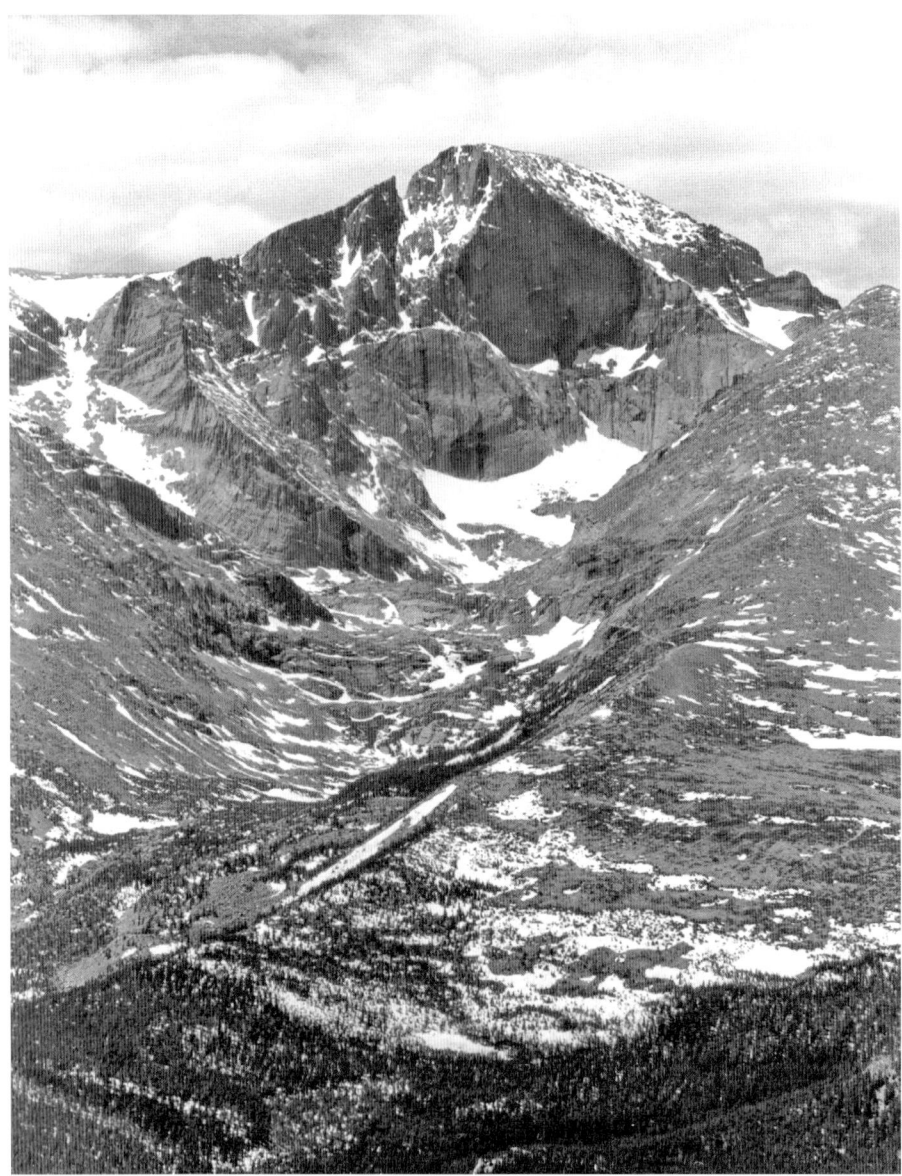

Longs Peak. *David L. Perry.*

heading for some smoke that proved to be caused by a fire they had left at their own small campsite. It had gotten out of control and burned up most of the supplies they had cached there. They felt lucky that the smoke did not attract an Indian raiding party. Eventually, the three men made their way back to the base horse camp and finally back to Major Long and the full party. In honor of this climb, Major Long named the massive mountain James Peak. Instead, the name Pike's Peak stuck and is what appeared on Captain Frémont's later maps of the West and the Oregon Trail.

Major Long next led his party to the Royal Gorge on the Arkansas, where it divided into two groups. Captain James Bell turned east and descended the Arkansas, while Major Long led his group south in search of the Red River. Captain Bell wrote in his journal in July 1920, "We are where imagination only has traveled before us—where civilization never existed."

Long reached the Canadian River and was not at all impressed with the southern plains, describing them as "almost wholly unfit for cultivation." Major Long is credited with naming this area the Great American Desert. He wrote that he thought it "might serve as a barrier to prevent too great an extension of our population westward." Long wrote that the land was "uninhabitable by a people depending on agricultural [sic] for a livelihood" and said it would best "remain an unmolested haunt of the native hunter, the bison, and the jackal."

Long busied himself with mapping the area and allowed Edwin James to write the official report of their expedition into the Rocky Mountains. Unfortunately, many of the expeditionary notes were taken by two men who deserted Captain Bell's party, and these notes were never recovered. Major Long kept his notes, and Edwin James had with him the detailed journal he had kept throughout the expedition. It was James's narrative that was published in 1823, along with Seymour's sketches.

Major Stephen Long's final scientific exploration occurred in 1823, when he was sent up the Mississippi to the forty-ninth parallel and east along the international boundary of Lake Superior. Two of the scientists who had been with him on his earlier trip joined him on this expedition as Long explored the area that the United States had acquired from Great Britain through the Convention of 1818. Long decided to start at Philadelphia and travel west to Wheeling, Fort Wayne, Chicago and Fort Armstrong on the Mississippi. Then he would move to the Minnesota River, on to the Red River of the North and follow this to the forty-ninth parallel. Finally, his route would take him east along the border to Lake Superior and back by way of the Great Lakes. Long was charged with making a topographical description as well as gathering information about minerals, plants, animals and any Native Americans they met.

In addition to Major Long and army men, this expedition included a mineralogist, zoologist, landscape painter and astronomical observer. Edwin James was supposed to come again as a botanist and doctor, but he did not learn of this invitation until Long had left and it was too late to overtake him.

The group left Philadelphia on April 30, 1823, riding on horseback and using light wagons. At various points, they made use of Native American guides, replenished supplies and had military assistance from forts along the way.

After reaching the Wisconsin River on June 19, the men left Fort Crawford on June 24, 1823, and separated into two groups. One group went up the river, while Long led the other group overland. Long thought in this way they would double the information gathered. The overland group visited several camps of Native Americans. Both the river and land groups met with difficulties and took longer than expected to reach Fort St. Anthony. They remained at the fort for several days and got new horses and provisions in addition to an attachment of men to assist them.

At the fort, the explorers met Giacomo Beltrami. This Italian, who was obsessed with finding the source of the Mississippi, had been at the fort since May 10 and thought that Long's party would help him go on into the wilderness. Although Long tried to persuade Beltrami not to come along, he eventually consented to let Beltrami join them. This proved unfortunate because the two men clashed, and Long considered Beltrami a troublesome companion.

When they left Fort Anthony, they again split into two groups. This time Long took the river group, which included what he called the "Italian gentleman." The two detachments tried to stay close and camp together in the evenings. Both groups had difficulties. Game was scarce. Canoes tipped over. Rains poured down. Eventually, the water party abandoned its boats, and the united group traveled overland, enduring temperatures in the nineties and plagued by insects. Long wrote in his journal on July 17, 1823, "At our encampment of last evening we were exceedingly annoyed by musketoes. Our horses appeared to suffer exceedingly by them, and were hovering around our camp in order to protect themselves from the attacks of these blood-thirsty insects in the smoke of our fire."

In spite of difficulties, the group gathered information about the river valley and made reasonably accurate estimates of distances. Near Big Stone Lake, they met a group of friendly Sioux. They went on, stopping briefly at an American Fur Trading Company post on Lake Traverse. It was shortly after this that the explorers met the threatening band of Native American warriors who tried to stop their forward progress and barely avoided a deadly confrontation.

On August 5, 1823, the explorers marched into Pembina on the Red River. Once he determined that the village did lie south of the forty-ninth parallel, Long had completed his last official assignment. He raised the American flag and fired a salute. When Beltrami tried to turn some Native Americans out of their own lodge, Long interfered, and in a huff, Beltrami left the expedition at that point. Long and his little group headed home, learning only later that the Native American guides who went with Beltrami deserted him only a week and a half later.

When Long finally reached Philadelphia again on October 27, he had traveled 4,500 miles in six months. Long and three other men from the expedition prepared a manuscript of their exploration for publication. William Keating was the primary author, while Long spent much of his time drawing a detailed map. Keating's report included appendices with Long's topographical report, a listing of zoological items, a catalogue of plants, astronomical findings, meteorological tables and several Indian vocabularies.

Long was made a colonel in the corps of topographical engineers and was assigned to projects such as improving the navigability of rivers and planning railroads. He published a manual of railroad construction in 1829 and a booklet on bridge building in 1836 that contained several bridges of his own design. He also was involved in hospital and steamboat construction. With the outbreak of the Civil War, Long was promoted to chief of the corps of topographical engineers. He retired from the army in 1863 at age seventy-nine and died a year later.

While Long's expeditions did not stir up the excitement of those of Lewis and Clark or Zebulon Pike, they did succeed in gathering data about the Native Americans and the physical and natural resources of the West. His travels from all of his expeditions covered an estimated twenty-six thousand miles from the Atlantic Coast to the Rocky Mountains and from New Mexico to Lake Winnipeg in Canada. Undervalued and mocked because of his description of the area as the "Great American Desert," Long actually accomplished a good deal. He established, in 1819, an American presence in the Mississippi Basin, and his 1823 expedition added considerable knowledge of the Minnesota and Lake Superior area. Long filled in major gaps left by the earlier explorations of Lewis, Clark and Pike, and his map is considered a landmark of American cartography. He laid the groundwork for the later and better-equipped explorations of John Frémont and John Wesley Powell.

Perhaps most importantly, Long committed the federal government to scientific explorations. The men in his group provided information about geologic features, land forms and weather; they described new mammals, birds, reptiles, amphibians, arachnids, crustaceans and insects; and they described 140 species of plants. These were important first steps in learning about the fauna and flora of the High Plains and the Rockies. A few of these specimens remain in Harvard's Museum of Comparative Zoology and in the Herbarium of the New York Botanical Garden.

James Pierson Beckwourth

1798–1866 • Pueblo

Young Jim Beckwourth galloped home as fast as his old farm horse would carry him, racing away from the terrible scene he'd just spied at his neighbor's house. Even with his eyes closed tight, Jim could still see his playmates and their mother and father lying dead in the yard and in the doorway of their house, killed in an attack by a band of hostile Native Americans.

Minutes before riding up to his friends' home, Jim had been planning in his head exactly what he'd call out to them as he rode by on his way to the mill with a sack of corn. Only nine years old, Jim was proud of being trusted with this important grown-up task, and he'd looked forward to showing off in front of his friends. Now, no longer feeling the least bit grown up, Jim was racing back to the protection of home and family to sound the alarm among their neighbors.

It was 1807, and St. Louis, Missouri, about twelve miles away from Jim's home, was still a small town. Jim Beckwourth hadn't lived here very long. He was born in April 1798, in Fredericksburg, Virginia, to a black mother and a white father. He was one of thirteen children. Jim was seven years old when his family moved to Missouri, where his father farmed a section of land between the forks of the Mississippi and Missouri Rivers, about twelve miles south of Saint Charles.

On this awful day when Jim rode home in a panic, his father quickly organized a party of men to hunt for the attackers. The death of his friends was a vivid reminder to all of them that they lived in a wilderness that held many dangers. Among those dangers were bands of angry Native Americans who resented people moving into their hunting lands. At this time, there was no way that Jim could have guessed that one day he would come to be a chief in a Native American tribe.

Fortunately, such hostile attacks were rare at that time and place. Jim and his family grew more comfortable as days passed peacefully, and they settled into life in Missouri. Jim went to school for a few years and then was apprenticed to a blacksmith in St. Louis, where he worked until he was nineteen years old. He was a hard worker, but Jim knew this was not the life for him.

Even as a teenager, Jim Beckwourth was not the kind of person who liked to stay in one place. He wanted travel and adventure. He ran away in 1822 to go to the lead mines in the Fever River area of Mississippi, and then he continued traveling all the way to New Orleans. He came back home to St. Louis again but didn't stay long. In the fall of 1824, Jim joined a beaver trapping expedition heading into the Rocky Mountains. He was hired on as a blacksmith and a horse wrangler, although he soon learned to be a hunter and trapper, too. In time, he also grew skillful in using a gun, a bowie knife and a tomahawk.

Jim Beckwourth's group was led by explorer and fur trader General William H. Ashley, who, with Andrew Henry, had founded the Rocky Mountain Fur Company. On their journeys with horses and pack animals, Ashley's men, including Beckwourth and others like him, opened new trails along the Platte and Green Rivers.

In 1803, President Thomas Jefferson purchased, for the United States from France, the land stretching from the Mississippi to the Pacific Ocean. During the forty years that followed, this new western frontier was opened up by trappers and traders. Mountain men like Jim Beckwourth went up the Missouri and followed streams to their mountain sources, climbed over high passes and crossed plains. As they searched for beaver, they became pathfinders and trailblazers. Many years later, covered wagons, railroads and eventually super highways would follow these same early trails.

Beckwourth must have enjoyed his first wilderness adventure as a young man, because he signed on for other Ashley expeditions. He and other famous trappers, such as Jedediah Smith, were employed mainly to trap beaver. There was a high demand for beaver fur to make fancy hats for gentlemen. The trappers lived a lonely life in the mountains, trapping and saving up their beaver pelts. They eagerly looked forward to what was called a "rendezvous," or meeting of trappers and traders.

Jim Beckwourth took part in the first Mountain Man Rendezvous at Henry's Fork on the Green River in 1825. At the appointed time for one of these summer rendezvous, arranged by Ashley and other trading companies, the company men and other independent trappers, as well as Native Americans, came together in a big encampment that sometimes lasted for two weeks. They would exchange their animal pelts for money or for various items that they wanted or needed.

Much feasting, drinking and celebrating took place at these events. One activity around the campfire was storytelling, and at this Jim Beckwourth excelled. He won the name of "gaudy liar" among his friends. He could spin wild tales, one after another, partly based on fact and partly fictitious. When the rendezvous was over, the mountain men would return to the hills for another year of fur trapping. The fur traders would take all the furs they had collected at the rendezvous to St. Louis. Sometimes they made this long journey by wagon, but often they traveled the river with their load of furs.

In his life as a trapper and at the many rendezvous he attended, Beckwourth often came in contact with Native American tribes. He knew that sometimes fights broke out among these different groups, especially between the Arikara and Blackfeet tribes. Other groups got along fine. Jim was respected by all for his skills as a hunter and trapper.

In 1828, while trapping, Jim was captured by a party of Crow warriors and taken to their camp. According to Jim's account of this event, one old Crow woman welcomed him as her "lost son." Whether or not that was true, it is fact that instead of trying to escape mistreatment, Jim Beckwourth was adopted into the Crow tribe in 1829 and happily lived with them. The Crows were traditionally friendly to trappers and traders, and Beckwourth fit right in. Beckwourth was six feet tall, dressed in buckskins and beaded moccasins and wore his waist-long dark brown hair in braids. Around his neck on a thread of sinew, he wore an amulet of a perforated bullet with a large oblong bead on either side of it.

Over the next six to eight years, Beckwourth lived with these nomadic people along the Yellowstone and Bighorn Rivers, fought in their battles against the Blackfeet, accepted their customs, took several Crow women as wives and represented the Crow tribe in their fur trading business.

Jim Beckwourth was renamed "Morning Star" by the Crows and eventually became one of the Crow sub-chiefs. His account of how he was given this honor involves a fight with a bear in which he demonstrated great strength and courage. The description of this event was told to G.C. Leland, who prepared an edition of Beckwourth's autobiography in 1891. On page 11 of *Mountain Man, Indian Chief*, by Betty Shepard, one man who knew Beckwourth was reported as saying:

A very large grizzly bear had been driven into a cave and Beckwourth asked of a great number of Crows who were present whether any one of them would go in and kill the creature. All declined, for it seemed to be certain death. Then Beckwourth stripped himself naked, and wrapping a Mexican blanket round his left arm, and holding a strong knife, entered the cave and after a desperate fight, killed the bear. I came up to the place in time to see Beckwourth come out of the cave, all torn and bleeding. He looked like the devil if ever man did. The Crows were so much pleased at this that he was declared a sub-chief on the spot.

Since childhood, Jim Beckwourth had always craved adventure. Even life with the Crows was too tame for him. He finally left the tribe to roam through various parts of Colorado Territory until he got back to St. Louis, Missouri. Soon after his return, a trapper/trader friend introduced him to General William Gaines, who was recruiting men for a war on the Seminole in Florida. Being in the thick of any action appealed to Beckwourth. Jim was one of six hundred men who went by boat to Tampa Bay to engage in the Seminole War. He served as a scout for Zachary Taylor, and then, in 1838, he came back to St. Louis again.

During the next several years, Jim Beckwourth continued with trapping and trading and was agent-in-charge of several trading posts for Andrew Sublette and Louis Vasquez, often operating out of Fort Vasquez on the South Platte in northeastern Colorado. He established good trading relationships with the Cheyenne. He went to work for a time with the Bent brothers at Bent's Fort, and he also traded out of Taos.

Beckwourth helped to build and, for a time, operate his own trading post in Colorado. It was a very crude fort that was called El Pueblo. Mountain men who didn't want to travel all the way to Taos or back to St. Louis for the winter came and stayed there. Rent was free, and whiskey could be purchased for beaver pelts. The little settlement that he helped found eventually grew into what is now the town of Pueblo, Colorado.

Beckwourth went on at least two expeditions to California and herded horses from California across the plains to Bent's Fort in Colorado and Fort Bridger in Wyoming. While in California, Beckwourth told his many adventures, with facts and embellishments, to Thomas D. Bonner, who has been variously described as a "journalist" and an "itinerant justice of the peace." Bonner edited *The Life and Adventures of James. P. Beckwourth, Mountaineer, Scout, and Pioneer, and Chief of the Crow Nation of Indians.*

Whether this biography was all fact, or whether it contained considerable fiction, it proved successful. First published by Harper & Brothers in

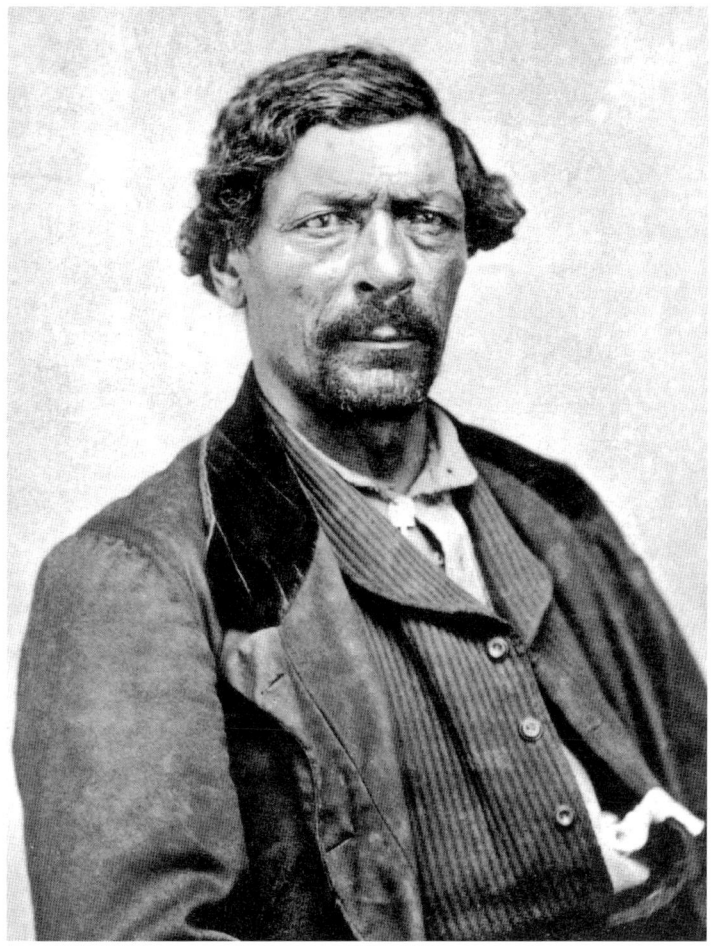

James Beckwourth. *Wikimedia Commons.*

1846, it came out in later editions in England and France. Scholars think it contains quite a bit of exaggeration about Beckwourth's part in many events, but nonetheless, they consider it a great source of information about the times.

While out in California, Beckwourth, always the adventure seeker, joined California's Bear Flag revolt against Mexico in 1846. He returned to California again during the gold rush of 1849, where he prospected along the Feather River. In the spring of 1850, he discovered an important mountain pass that went over the Sierra Nevada Mountains northwest of Reno, Nevada. This was a much easier way for settlers to reach Marysville,

California, and eventually, Sacramento. According to Jim's account of Beckwourth Pass, the officials of Marysville offered to pay him to establish this trail that would help in building their city. Beckwourth worked on the trail in the summer and fall of 1850 and again in the spring of 1851. He led the first wagon train of settlers over Beckwourth Pass late that summer. Unfortunately, a big fire destroyed a large part of Marysville that summer, and there is no record of Jim Beckwourth being paid for work on the pass. Still, his name is well known in early California history.

Jim Beckwourth also continued to be involved with the U.S. Army in a variety of duties, including carrying dispatches and working as a scout in New Mexico and California. When he was sixty-nine years old, he served as a guide to Colonel John M. Chivington on his trip from the Pueblo area to Fort Lyon.

Beckwourth was scheduled to continue on as a guide and take Colonel Chivington and his troops to what turned out to be the massacre at Sand Creek. But records show that Beckwourth was not the guide. It is possible that he simply did not want to be part of this expedition that would bring death to many Native Americans. Or it may be that at his age and after a long ride, he was not up to continuing. Whatever the case, Beckwourth reported being so stiff and cold that he could not lead the troops on their late night march, and Beckwourth was replaced by another guide.

Even with adventures from coast to coast and travels that crisscrossed the country, Jim Beckwourth kept returning to his Crow tribe. He went back to it again toward the end of his life. Accounts of his death are as wild as the many accounts of his life. Some records state he died peacefully at home back with "his people." Others report that he was poisoned at a feast where he was asked, but declined, to try to lead the tribe back to greatness; this was apparently a Crow ceremonial attempt to keep his "spirit" with them.

It is known that Jim Beckwourth died in 1866. He was laid to rest on a traditional Crow Indian tree platform in the northern Plains in Montana.

The Bents

Charles Bent, 1799–1847 • William Bent, 1809–1869 • Bent's Fort

It was 1832 in the Colorado Territory as William and Charles Bent, brothers and successful fur traders, sat around a campfire, discussing the permanent trading fort they would like to build. As they talked, they heard the sound of approaching horses. Warily, the Bents stood, guns at the ready. With relief, William realized it was the small group of friendly Cheyennes they had been expecting and put away his rifle. He had already established a good trading relationship with them. The Native Americans stopped a short distance away, and three warriors, Wolf Chief, Little Wolf and Yellow Wolf, approached the Bents on foot.

Using words and hand signals, William Bent welcomed the chiefs and invited them to sit down and have coffee. When everyone was comfortable, they began to discuss establishing a fur trading post. The chiefs liked the idea and promised that their people would bring many buffalo furs and deer hides to trade. The chiefs even suggested that the Bents build the fort at the mouth of the Purgatory River not far from a Cheyenne camp. Pleased and satisfied with the way the talks were going, one chief pulled out a peace pipe and handed it around the circle.

Because they had been treated in a friendly and respectful way, Yellow Wolf wanted to honor the Bents by giving them good Cheyenne names. William, who was short, was called Little White Man. Charles Bent was given the name of White Hat. The friendship and trust between the Bents and the Cheyennes would be a major factor in the eventual success of Bent's Fort in Colorado.

Charles and William Bent were two of eleven children born to Judge Silas Bent and his wife, Martha Kerr. Charles was born in Virginia in 1799, and William was born ten years later on May 23, 1809, in St. Louis. They grew up on a farm overlooking the Mississippi River. A newspaper item alerted Charles to the fact that William Henry Ashley was recruiting one hundred men for an 1822 fur trading/trapping expedition to Missouri. Charles Bent decided to head west and trap beaver in Sioux country as a hired hand for the Missouri Fur Company. When the company reorganized two years later, Charles became a partner, and a few years later, his brother, William, joined him.

In the early 1800s, a lot of trapping and trading was going on in the central part of the United States. Trappers—or mountain men, as they were known—rode on horseback, carrying their supplies on pack mules. Native Americans first hunted on foot and later used horses. Many of the hides taken by mountain men and Native Americans were sold to traders for money or goods. Sometimes the traders came into Native American camps to conduct business. At other times, a great rendezvous was held, and everyone gathered to trade. The traders made trips back and forth between St. Louis, Missouri, and Santa Fe, New Mexico. This life of trapping and trading in the West appealed to adventurous men including the Bent brothers.

Charles and William went on a nearly disastrous trapping expedition during the 1827–28 season. Hostile Crows stole the horses of the traders, who then had to hide their trade goods by burying them. The traders spent a hard winter hiking through the Wind River mountains to Green River. They eventually managed to buy horses from some Shoshones and sent some of their party back to retrieve their buried trade goods. The spring trading rendezvous was a failure for them, however, because, while buried, their goods had rusted and rotted.

Instead of quitting after this experience, Charles refitted for another trading trip to Santa Fe and soon formed a successful business relationship with Ceran St. Vrain, a Santa Fe trader and former mountain man. William decided to do something a little different. He joined a group of men who were independent trappers. They headed west to trap beaver in the Upper Arkansas and its tributaries.

On one of his trapping expeditions, William Bent saved the lives of two Cheyennes who were being chased by some Comanches. Bent hid the Cheyennes in his camp, and when the Comanches arrived, he bravely walked out to talk with them and sent them off in the wrong direction. This act started a lifelong friendship between William Bent and members of the Cheyenne tribe.

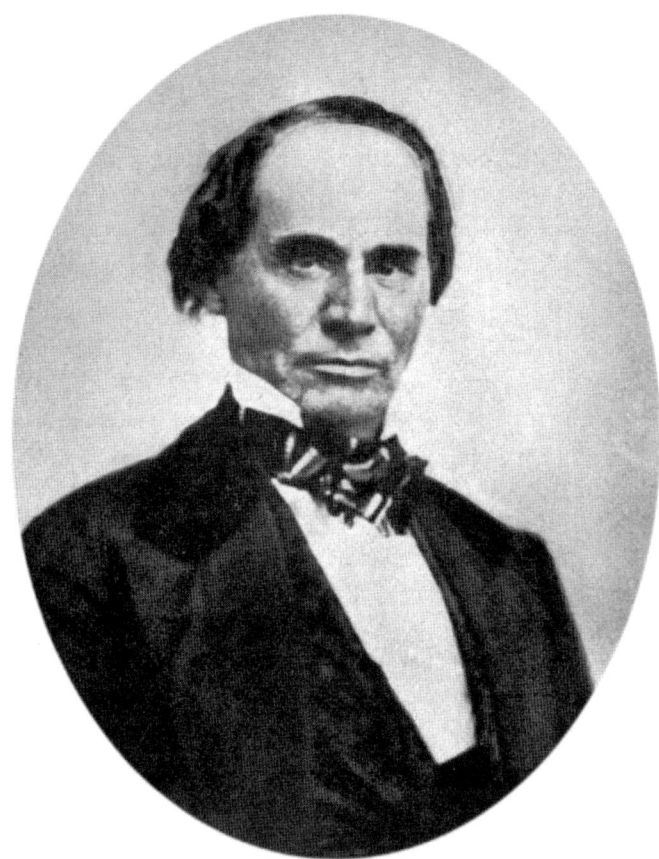

William Bent. *From* Kit Carson Days (1809–1868) *by Edwin L. Sabin.*

William built a headquarters for his trapping and trading operations at the mouth of Fountain Creek, a spot that today is the city of Pueblo, Colorado, where he traded with mountain men and Native Americans.

Both of the Bent brothers did well in the fur trade. Charles Bent became a very successful businessman, while William was recognized as a fine trapper and trader who had forged strong bonds with various Native American tribes. William learned to speak fluently with the Cheyennes and Arapahos and could communicate in Comanche, Kiowa and Apache as well, using some of their words and sign language.

On one of his trips to Santa Fe, William Bent talked to his brother and to Ceran St. Vrain about his idea of establishing a large and permanent trading post. He believed that mountain men and Native Americans, especially the

Cheyennes, would come to the post to trade their buffalo, deer and beaver skins for trade goods. By 1832, Charles Bent and Ceran St. Vrain had assets exceeding $100,000, so they were looking for more business opportunities. The trading post idea appealed to them.

That summer, Charles and William Bent arranged to meet with several of the Cheyenne chiefs to discuss the plan. The trading post idea met with approval, so in the spring of 1832, the brothers employed Mexican laborers using hand tools to construct what they first called Fort William but eventually came to be known as Bent's Fort. The spot they chose for the trading post was at a bend in the Arkansas River, about forty miles from Big Timber, where there was good grass and soil for making bricks. At that time, Mexico owned the land to the south of Colorado, so the Bents chose to build on the north bank of the Arkansas River on American soil. The site was between the two towns that are now known as Las Animas and La Junta, Colorado.

Ceran St. Vrain lined up the laborers and supplies in Taos. The workers at the site of the fort set out tens of thousands of bricks to dry in the sun. They used wool to bind the mud together to make the bricks extra strong. Work was delayed when smallpox struck, and many people became ill and died. William Bent caught a mild case, and Ceran St. Vrain became very ill and had to be carried to Taos to recover. When he was well, he returned with more men, and they soon completed an adobe fort, which some called "the mud palace" about four hundred miles from the nearest American settlement.

When completed, Bent's Fort was a rectangle that faced eastward toward approaching caravans of western travelers. Up to two hundred men and three hundred animals could be kept there. The front wall was 137 feet long, 14 feet high and 3 or more feet thick. Inside the fort, the laborers built a square made up of twenty-five rooms. The doors of these rooms faced an inner court called the *placita*. Another set of bedrooms was on the second floor. For safety against possible hostile attack, the main gate was 6.5 feet wide and 7 feet tall. It was made of heavy planks of wood covered in iron. A brass cannon was placed in front of the main gate each day. In addition to bedrooms, the fort had a kitchen, dining room, storerooms, wagon house, blacksmith shop, round towers outfitted with cannons for protection and corrals for the animals. Settlers coming by on the Santa Fe Trail were amazed to see this adobe palace in what appeared to be the middle of nowhere.

Trading business began at the fort in the fall of 1833. Charles Bent was granted an official trading license from the U.S. government. Although beaver hats were going out of style, there was a demand for buffalo hides. The Bent–St. Vrain partnership with the Cheyennes and the Arapahos was very successful.

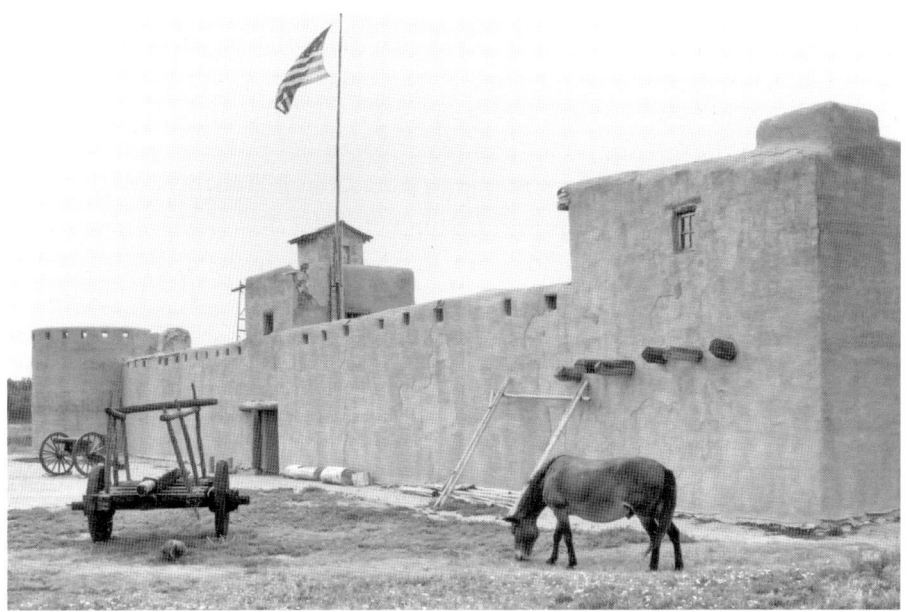

Bent's Fort. *David L. Perry.*

Ceran St. Vrain took out Mexican citizenship, married a Mexican woman and worked the trading business from Santa Fe. Charles also married into a prominent Mexican family, was given a land grant and built a huge hacienda near Taos. He handled the business at the St. Louis end and managed the caravans going back and forth between there and Santa Fe.

William Bent knew all the Cheyenne leaders, and with the completion of the fort, many bands of Cheyenne moved closer to make trading easier. One of these prominent Cheyenne chiefs, White Thunder, had a beautiful daughter, Owl Woman. William Bent married Owl Woman, and a two-day celebration at Bent's Fort marked the occasion. In honor of the event, William gave away guns, blankets, beads, knives and kettles. These two powerful men, one white and one Native American, had forged a strong alliance by this marriage.

Owl Woman and William Bent sometimes lived in a corner room in Bent's Fort, and sometimes they stayed in a buffalo-skin lodge in the nearby Cheyenne village. Though he conducted business with many tribes, William Bent gave the Cheyennes a favored position and traded most often with them.

William was the resident field manager at the fort. The greatest danger at Bent's Fort came in summer, when various Native American war parties crossed the plains and stopped by the fort to demand guns and ammunition.

William had to decide when to set up armed patrols around the fort, when to offer gifts and how many Native Americans to allow at one time inside the walls.

In January 1838, there was an uprising in Santa Fe involving the Mexican army and the Pueblo Indians on one side and the merchants on the other. Charles Bent and other Americans were captured and imprisoned by the Mexican army. Word reached Ceran St. Vrain and William Bent at Bent's Fort. They began to organize a rescue party. However, before the rescuers rode all the way to Santa Fe, Charles Bent came galloping up to them. With money, he had won his own release.

Rumors of war with Mexico began, and in the summer of 1846, there were mobs in Santa Fe calling for the murder of American residents. Troops under the leadership of Colonel Kearney began arriving at Bent's Fort. William Bent put together a group of scouts. When Kearney was made general, he appointed Charles Bent to govern the Territory of New Mexico. William Bent was named an honorary colonel for scouting the way for the army to reach Santa Fe. Supplies, including arms and ammunition for the troops, came into Bent's Fort, which became a depot and staging area for the war effort.

The American army marched to Las Vegas expecting a battle, but no one came to fight or negotiate with them. The American troops went on and easily took control of Santa Fe without firing a shot. Things seemed peaceful, so a month later, Kearney and his men left and marched to California. Without an army there for protection, Charles Bent wrote to Secretary of State James Buchanan, outlining for him New Mexico's immediate needs.

Soon after Kearney's troops left for California, Navajos began raiding the Las Vegas area, and Mexican troops were involved in these skirmishes. A plot for a Christmas uprising in Taos was discovered and prevented, but in January 1847, a mob of Pueblo Indians went to the home of Governor Charles Bent, shot and killed him with arrows and scalped him. Twenty miles north of Santa Fe, 1,500 Pueblo Indians and Mexican troops held the hills above the town.

News spread of the uprising and the murder of many government officials. A force of about three hundred American troops from Santa Fe, joined by sixty-five volunteers led by Ceran St. Vrain, moved into the area and defeated the poorly organized force of Mexicans and Indians. Leaders of the uprising, tried by a jury of which William Bent was foreman, were found guilty and executed.

Because trading was completely disrupted by the battles and the soldiers had all but taken over Bent's Fort for their own purposes, Bent offered to sell his fort to the U.S. Army. He was insulted by the small price they offered him. While U.S. troops and the Mexican army battled, various Native American tribes took this opportunity to attack migrants whom they felt were ruining their lands.

In the spring of 1849, a cholera attack wiped out many of the Cheyenne. William's wife and children survived, left the Cheyenne camp and came into Bent's Fort. Comanches and Arapahos gathered nearby and threatened to attack. William realized that the good days of peace and trading at his fort were over.

Rather than have his fort taken over by the army or hostile Native Americans, Bent hatched a plan. His fort would go out in a blaze of glory. He loaded twenty wagons inside the fort with everything of value and led them five miles down the river to a camp. He returned to the fort alone, rolled kegs of powder into the main rooms, set a fire and raced out. A huge explosion marked the end of Bent's Fort on August 21, 1849.

In 1853, William Bent built his second fort about thirty-eight miles downstream from the original Bent's Fort. He tried to resume trading but gave up and sold out in 1856. He was named Indian agent in 1859 and tried unsuccessfully to keep the peace. Discouraged with the dealings between the government and the Native Americans, Bent resigned as Indian agent in 1860.

In 1865, Colonel John Chivington marched his troops to the Cheyenne camp at Sand Creek, intent on destroying all the Native Americans there. Chivington posted a guard on William Bent so that he could not inform the Cheyennes of the impending attack. At Sand Creek, Owl Woman and one of Bent's sons were killed.

A discouraged William Bent had outlived the time of trappers and traders. Days of Native American and whites trading peacefully together were gone. Promises and treaties had been made and broken. William moved to Westport, Kansas, but in a couple years moved back to Colorado and lived on his Purgatory River ranch. It was there that he died of pneumonia on May 19, 1869. He is buried in the Las Animas Cemetery. The original Bent's Fort was reconstructed between 1974 and 1976 and is now open to visitors as a National Historic Site.

Chief Black Kettle

1801–1868 • Sand Creek

Fourteen-year-old Black Kettle tried not to show his excitement as he rode out on his first war party. Two years ago, he had gone on a successful buffalo hunt. But this test was far more important. If he did well, he would be closer to being a full-grown member of his Cheyenne tribe. Today, he would show what he had learned about being a warrior. Would he be able to capture a weapon or a shield? Would he touch an enemy with a coup stick or with his bare hand, which was the bravest feat a warrior could perform? If so, this would be a great honor for him and his family.

Black Kettle proved his strength that day in battle and showed the type of skill and bravery that would one day lead him to become an important Cheyenne chief but one who would be remembered not for feats of war but for working for peace.

Black Kettle was born around 1801 to his mother, Sparrow Hawk, and his father, Swift Hawk. He had a sister named Wind Woman and two brothers, Gentle Horse and Wolf. Black Kettle's tribe was known as the Sutaios, or Buffalo People. They shared a language with the Cheyennes. By the time Black Kettle was three, the Buffalo People had become part of the Cheyenne tribe. They lived near the present-day boundary of North and South Dakota.

Although he no doubt had a family nickname, Black Kettle would not receive his formal name until he was older. The babies spent much of their early days strapped to cradle boards. The cradle board could be carried on a mother's back or propped up where the women were working at their daily tasks. It could also be hung down from a horse when his tribe moved from camp to camp.

Like other baby boys, Black Kettle would have his ears pierced when he was between three and six months old. This special ceremony symbolized a lightning strike and was thought to make him an invulnerable warrior. By the time he was seven or eight years old, Black Kettle was already an accomplished horse rider.

In his teens, Black Kettle joined a Cheyenne society known as the Elkhorn Scrapers. Members of this group carried a rattling instrument carved from elk horn and painted yellow and blue. The leaders of the several societies reported to the council of chiefs. This Council of Forty-four, all of whom were respected warriors, made the final decisions about alliances, disputes and wars. When he was recognized as a full-grown Elkhorn Scraper warrior, Black Kettle married a woman named Little Sage.

Black Kettle took part in Cheyenne ceremonies. His tribesmen held sacred a bundle of four arrows that they thought kept them safe from enemies and starvation. Their medicine hat, made from the fur of a buffalo head with the horns attached, was thought to have power over their health and welfare. Each year, Black Kettle watched the Sun Dance performed over an eight-day period just before the summer buffalo hunt to ensure the tribe's good fortune. The Cheyennes lived by following herds of buffalo. An old legend promised this would be their way of life until buffalo were replaced one day on the prairies by a new kind of horned beast.

During the 1830s, Black Kettle and Little Sage and their band drifted south and from the Black Hills to the eastern plains of what would become the Colorado Territory. The tribe settled along the Arkansas River and became known as the Southern Cheyennes. For the most part, the Cheyennes got along with the trappers and mountain men at Bent's Fort, near present-day La Junta, Colorado, but they constantly fought with the Kiowas, the Comanches, the Utes, the Crows, the Shawnees and the Pawnees.

Throughout the early 1840s, few conflicts erupted between Native Americans and the wagon trains that were crossing the plains. With the California gold rush of 1849, more settlers came west, and forts were built to hold soldiers who patrolled the migrant trails to protect the western settlers. Some immigrants brought with them the disease of cholera. Large numbers of Native Americans died from cholera, but Black Kettle and Little Sage lived through it.

Black Kettle saw the lives of his people changing because of these new settlers. He believed the cattle of these white men were the ones mentioned in the ancient prophesy, signaling an end of the time when the Native Americans peacefully hunted buffalo. Black Kettle decided survival depended on making peace with the soldiers and settlers, and he resolved to do everything he could to bring this about.

In September 1851, ten thousand members of Plains tribes gathered at Horse Creek, near Fort Laramie, Wyoming, and made a treaty of peace with the U.S. government. Even so, the Cheyennes still had the Pawnees for enemies. On one raid on a Pawnee camp, Black Kettle was chosen to carry the sacred arrows at the end of his war lance and to ride at the head of the Southern Cheyenne warriors. He later led a group of men deep into Mexican territory to seek revenge for the killing of two tribesmen. In a battle on their way home from this expedition, Little Sage was taken captive during a Ute attack. Black Kettle never saw her again.

After a period of time, Black Kettle took another wife, Medicine Woman Later. She was a member of the Wotapio band. In 1854, when the Wotapio chief died, they chose Black Kettle to be their new chief and a member of the Cheyenne Council of Forty-Four.

The decade of the 1850s saw troubles arise between Native Americans and immigrants and soldiers. Killings and raids took part on both sides. The Native Americans trusted William Bent, with whom they had traded at Bent's Fort. When Bent became Indian agent for the Upper Arkansas tribes in 1860, he helped draw up a new treaty with the Cheyennes and Arapahos. Black Kettle and the other chiefs present at the peace council did not sign the treaty but promised to discuss it with the absent chiefs.

In February, six of the chiefs, including Black Kettle, signed the agreement. But other members of the Council of Forty-four did not sign. With the outbreak of the Civil War, Union soldiers worried whether the Native Americans would support them or the South. Black Kettle's tribe and most of the other tribes stayed out of Civil War matters. They also largely ignored the treaty land boundaries and followed the movements of the buffalo as they always had.

Those in power in the Colorado Territory, including Governor John Evans and his friend John Chivington, thought military might should be used to force the Native Americans onto their assigned reservations. In June 1864, they issued an order that Native Americans were to report to Fort Lyon (just east of Bent's Fort), Fort Larned (Kansas), Fort Laramie (Wyoming) or Camp Collins (present-day Fort Collins, Colorado). Some tribes, including Black Kettle's Cheyennes who were in central Kansas, didn't even hear about this new order.

In September 1864, Black Kettle and other chiefs met with Governor John Evans at Camp Weld (near present-day Denver). Black Kettle pleaded for peace. Evans and his friend Colonel Chivington insisted Black Kettle's

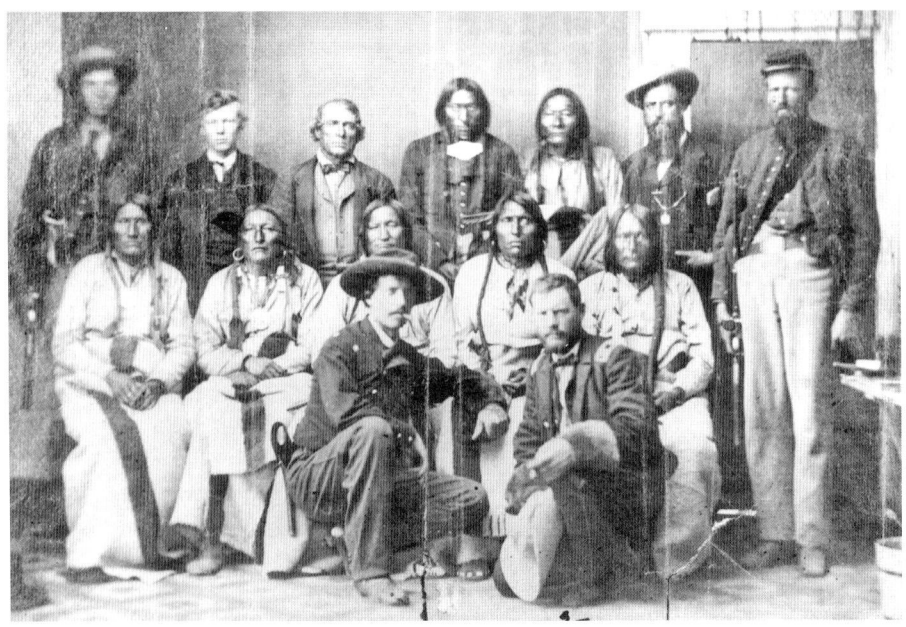

Chief Black Kettle seated in the middle of the second row at the Camp Weld Council. *Colorado History.*

people had stolen livestock, committed war-like acts and made an alliance with the Sioux. Black Kettle denied the charges.

Black Kettle led his people to Sand Creek about forty miles northeast of Fort Lyon. Bull Bear and his Cheyenne tribe headed up the Republican River, where they raided along the Platte Road and were chased by Colonel Chivington's cavalry.

Black Kettle left his people at Sand Creek and journeyed to meet with Major Anthony, commander of Fort Lyon. He assured the major that his people were not involved with the recent raids of Bull Bear and would camp peacefully at Sand Creek until they moved to a reservation. Anthony promised Black Kettle that his people would be safe there. Black Kettle returned to his tribe, and Chief Left Hand led his Arapahos, who were also at the fort, to join Black Kettle at Sand Creek.

On the night of November 28, 1864, the Native Americans at Sand Creek slept in lodges arranged in a circle that spread about a half mile in diameter. Early the next morning, between 750 and 950 cavalry led by Colonel Chivington suddenly appeared on the horizon. As the cavalry rode toward the camp, Black Kettle seized a long pole and raised a large American flag to show his tribe was peaceful and respectful. A few of Chivington's officers refused to let their men fire on the Native Americans, but the majority began shooting. Approximately 180 Native Americans were killed at Sand Creek. Soldiers scalped and mutilated many of the dead.

Black Kettle stood for a long time in front of his lodge waving the American flag while some of his surviving people fled for the safety of the creek bed. Then he and Medicine Woman Later ran for the creek, too. As they ran, his wife was shot, but Black Kettle made it to the creek. Since his eyesight was no longer good enough to shoot, he assisted his warriors by loading guns for them.

The small number of Cheyenne at the creek held off their attackers until dark when the soldiers left to loot the camp. Under cover of darkness, the surviving Cheyennes made their way up the creek toward safety. Black Kettle crept back to where his wife had fallen. Although she had been shot nine times, she was still alive. He carried his wife up the creek and joined the rest of the escaping Cheyennes. The next morning, they were rescued by a party of Cheyennes and taken to the nearby Smoky Hill camp.

Word of what happened at Sand Creek spread to other Native American bands. The Lakota Sioux and the Northern Arapahos declared war on the white man and pledged revenge. About one thousand warriors assembled at Cherry Creek (which runs through present-day Denver) on January 1,

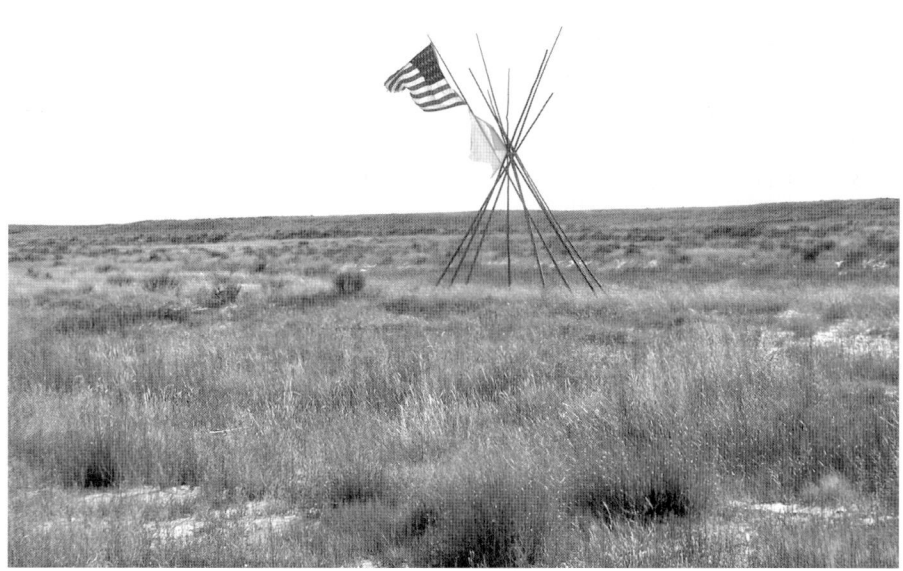

A marker at Sand Creek National Monument. *National Park Service.*

1865. In spite of all that had happened, Black Kettle still argued for peace, but the majority of the council of chiefs voted for war. A large band of warriors attacked Fort Rankin and Julesberg in northeastern Colorado, killing soldiers and taking supplies. These warring groups made plans to continue their attacks to the north along the South Platte. Black Kettle and a few others opposed this plan. Black Kettle led a group south of the Arkansas River, hoping in time to again establish peace.

Fact-finding committees investigated what had happened at Sand Creek. The Senate and House Committees blamed Chivington for "acts of cruelty and barbarity," but no one was fined or imprisoned. Colonel Chivington and Governor Evans were forced to resign.

Over the next four years, Black Kettle continued to attend peace meetings. He was the first Cheyenne to sign the new peace treaty of the Little Arkansas. Many other chiefs were not willing to agree to the treaty, because they believed previous treaties and promises had not been honored. Bands of Native Americans continued to go on raiding parties. The U.S. Senate was slow in ratifying the new treaty, and promised payments to the Native Americans were not made.

Black Kettle and his people spent a peaceful winter of 1867 and 1868, but attacks on whites by small war parties of Native Americans continued, and the governors of Colorado and Kansas demanded protection from the U.S. Army. After several small skirmishes, General Philip Sherman sent Lieutenant Colonel George Custer to assume field command of the Seventh Cavalry.

Black Kettle and other council chiefs and members of the Arapahos, Comanches and Prairie Apaches gathered for their winter camp in the Washita River Valley (in present-day Oklahoma). There were six thousand people in the group. Black Kettle had first sought safety at Fort Cobb but was told he had to move to reservation lands. Black Kettle returned to his camp, which was a short distance from the others in the valley, telling his people they would need to move the next day.

But on the morning of November 23, Custer and his eight hundred men rode south to the valley of the Washita River with orders to kill hostile warriors, destroy their village and ponies and bring back the women and children. Within ten minutes, Custer's troops took control of the camp. A few Native Americans found safety, but the majority of men, women and children were shot and killed. Fifty-three women and children were taken captive. Custer burned the village and all the supplies in it.

Although Black Kettle spent a lifetime waging peace and not war, he and his wife were among those shot and killed by soldiers on November 27, 1868, in his Washita River Valley camp.

Jim Bridger

1804–1881 • Gore Range, Berthoud Pass

Jim Bridger peeled off his moccasins and waded upstream through the icy water. From his pack, he pulled out a steel trap, spread the jaws and set the trigger. After placing the trap under the water and fastening the attached chain by slipping a stake through the ring at the end of the chain, he pounded the stake deep into the bottom of the shallow creek. He unstopped a vial of castor that he carried in a horn at his belt, dipped the top of a bait stick into the vial and then plunged the bottom of the stick firmly into the river bottom above the trap. To make sure that he left no human scent, Bridger walked downstream. When a beaver was attracted to the castor scent and put its foot in the trap, it would be caught and drowned. Bridger would pick it up in a few days when he came back to check his trap line.

Trapping was hard, lonely and dangerous work, but it was the life of many mountain men in the 1820s and 1830s in the Rocky Mountains. Jim Bridger, however, was not an ordinary trapper and trader: he was also a born explorer who had the ability to hold in his mind and remember details of every path he ever walked. With his enormous store of knowledge of the peoples, rivers and mountains of the Rocky Mountain West, the end of the era of trapping and trading simply meant that Bridger took on a new career of guiding emigrants, army regiments, hunters and railroaders as they sought routes through the West. His extraordinary skill of finding his way made Bridger far more than a mountain man; he was a true pioneer.

Jim Bridger was born on St. Patrick's Day, March 17, 1804, near Richmond, Virginia. His father, James, worked a farm and was also a land

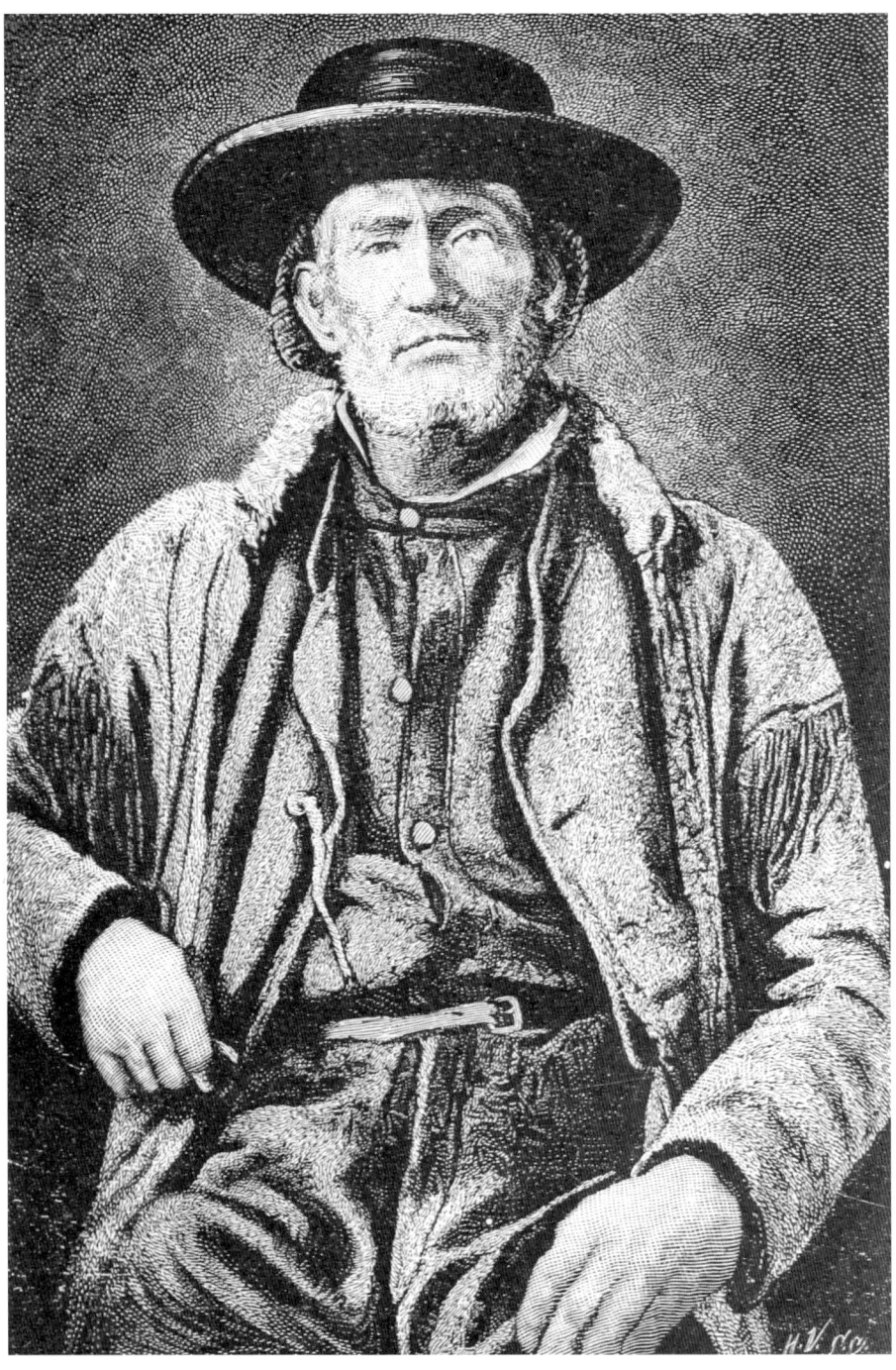

Jim Bridger. *From* Famous Frontiersmen and Heroes of the Border: Their Adventurous Lives and Stirring Experiences in Pioneer Days *by Charles Haven Ladd Johnston.*

surveyor, while his mother, Clarey Tyler Bridger, ran the family tavern. When Jim Bridger was a child of eight, his family moved by covered wagon and flatboat to a spot near St. Louis, Missouri, called Six-Mile Prairie. Jim was only fourteen when his mother died. Not long after, his father and brother died, too. Orphaned, Jim and his younger sister were cared for by an aunt. Jim supplied food for the family by shooting game and raising corn. He did his first trapping for muskrats and mink in the bayous near their home and sold the pelts to buy other items the family needed. Although Jim never learned to read or write, he made sure his sister went to school and got a good education.

As a teenager, Bridger worked as a boatman on the river from Six-Mile Prairie to St. Louis ferrying pigs, sheep, cattle and machinery. Later he apprenticed to a blacksmith. After serving four years in the blacksmith shop, Bridger moved to St. Louis, then a bustling city of two thousand. Through a newspaper advertisement in the *Missouri Republican* on March 20, 1822, Bridger learned that "enterprising young men" were being sought by William Ashley to join an expedition going up the Missouri River to its source, "there to be employed one, two, or three years." Having had some experience with horses, guns and trapping, Bridger thought the job seemed perfect, and he hired on by signing an "X" on his contract, beginning his long career in the West.

As part of this expedition, Bridger traveled up the Missouri River past the military post of Fort Atkinson and the Missouri Fur Company's Fort Recovery and then through Native American country. The expedition faced danger and hardships from Native Americans, wild animals, raging rivers, towering mountains and changeable weather.

When in mid-August the expedition arrived just above the mouth of the Yellowstone River, some men, including Jim Bridger, remained and built Fort Henry, while others retraced their steps back to St. Louis for additional supplies and men. Once Fort Henry was built, Bridger had time to learn to trap beaver. In October, when the fall trapping was complete, he worked at the fort as a blacksmith.

Bridger found many groups of Native Americans were peaceful and helpful if they were respected and treated fairly. While spending the winter with a friendly tribe, he met up with another mountain man, Jedidiah Smith. Tribe members told Smith and Bridger about an easier route through the mountains than the path they usually took. This led Bridger and Smith to explore and find South Pass and cross the Continental Divide. After trapping in the Bear River Canyon that summer, Bridger built a boat and sailed down the Bear River in 1824. He came to a large body of salty water. At first, he thought he had reached an arm of the Pacific Ocean, but in fact, he had discovered Great Salt Lake and perhaps was the first white man ever to see it.

Mountain men always sought new and richer beaver territory. In 1826, Bridger signed on with Bill Sublette, Jedidiah Smith and David Jackson, who had bought out Ashley, and joined in an expedition to the head of the Yellowstone River. Here he was amazed at finding boiling springs, geysers and petrified forests. So bizarre was the area that some of the more superstitious on the trip thought they may have stumbled upon the gateway to Hades. Bridger knew better than that, but after that trip when he related what he'd seen, he sometimes said, "Boys, I've been to Hell and back."

Jim Bridger was a great storyteller, but he found that when he shared with others what he had actually seen, many people did not believe him, and some accused him of lying, so Bridger began exaggerating his stories. He told one about a race of giants living on an island in the middle of the Great Salt Lake who rode elephants as ponies. Perhaps his most famous tall tale was telling people he had come upon "a petrified forest with petrified trees, and petrified birds, that sang petrified songs!"

Each year in the summers between 1825 and 1840, Bridger took part in a major fur trading event called the rendezvous. Native Americans and trappers like Bridger gathered together for two or three weeks and sold their pelts to traders for supplies such as traps, gunpowder and flour. Bridger was popular when they relaxed and exchanged stories. The men also participated in various kinds of contests including horse racing and shooting.

In the 1830s, Bridger led Jedidiah Smith's party through Blackfoot territory, south of the Yellowstone River. Bridger's solemn face apparently reminded Smith, who was religious and always carried a Bible, of the angel Gabriel. He started calling Jim Bridger "Old Gabe," and even though Bridger was only thirty, the name stuck. Bridger and his partners now bought the old Ashley outfit from Sublette, Jackson and Smith and renamed it the Rocky Mountain Fur Company.

At a rendezvous in 1837, Bridger put on a fancy suit of armor given to him by Sir William Drummond Stewart in recognition of his service as a guide on several expeditions. The Scottish painter Alfred Joseph Miller captured this strange moment in a most unusual western painting called *Rendezvous*. It showed Native Americans on horses in feathered headdresses and Jim Bridger right in the midst of them wearing his suit of armor.

At a rendezvous in 1835, Bridger met and married a Shoshone woman, the daughter of a chief. Together they had two children, Josephine and Felix. Bridger's Shoshone name was Peejatowahooten.

Upon the death of his first wife, Bridger married again. His second Native American wife died in childbirth, but their daughter, Virginia, survived. Bridger married a third time. He and his third wife, Little Fawn, had two children, Mary and William. Bridger sent all his children to St. Louis to be educated.

Little Fawn's father, a chief named Washakie, was a powerful man who led the Shoshone in many of their battles. During an 1832 battle against hostile Native Americans, Bridger ended up with two arrows in his back. His friend Tom Fitzpatrick removed one of the arrowheads, but the other stuck fast because it was hooked at the point. It was three years later when Bridger was on his way to Oregon that Dr. Marcus Whitman finally removed the other arrowhead.

Jim Bridger made friends with many Native Americans and learned their customs and languages. Along the way, he also learned French and Spanish. The Crow people adopted him into their tribe and gave Jim Bridger the name of Casapy, "Chief of the Blankets." By 1840, when beaver hats went out of style, Jim Bridger and other mountain men had to retire or turn to new careers. Jim Bridger knew the West and could draw detailed maps of the mountains and their passes. He guided several groups of people into Oregon and California. In 1842, Bridger joined with another trapper, Louis Vasquez, in establishing a trading post along the Oregon Trail on the Black Fork of the Green River.

During the 1850s, Bridger was embroiled in problems with the Mormons who had begun their western migration. Approximately fifteen thousand Mormons were forced to leave the area around Nauvoo, Illinois, and headed toward the Great Basin of Utah. Many reached Fort Bridger in 1847 and 1848. Before long, Bridger and the Mormons had several areas of conflict. The Mormons resented the sale of liquor at the trading post and paying taxes to the government. The Mormon settlements took away some of the Native American trade from Fort Bridger and placed it in the hands of Salt Lake merchants.

The first government to be set up in the area was the Mormon State of Deseret, which was organized in 1849. The Utah Territory was not created until September 1850. Mormon governor Brigham Young was suspicious of Bridger's dealings with the Native Americans and feared he would incite attacks against Mormons. In 1853, Mormon officials ordered Bridger to leave, and when he refused, Young ordered his arrest. Bridger evaded capture and spent the winter with the Shoshones, while Fort Bridger was taken over by the Mormons.

In 1857, President Buchanan, trying to assert the supremacy of the United States over this area, appointed Alfred Cumming to replace Brigham Young as governor of the Utah Territory. Federal troops were sent out. To prevent these troops from getting supplies, the Mormons burned down Fort Bridger. Four years later, General Albert S. Johnston built a military fort on the site and named it Fort Bridger in honor of the mountain man and the earlier trading post.

For a time after this, Bridger ran a ferry west of Fort Laramie on the North Platte River. He hired river men to run his business while he went to Missouri and bought a farm near Westport. Bridger did not settle down on the farm but was away much of the time working as a scout and interpreter for the U.S. Army. Bridger guided Captain Howard Stansbury's group through the Rockies in 1849, finding a new pass in Wyoming that was quicker and easier to cross than South Pass. Bridger's Pass became part of the routes that were established for the Overland Trail, the Pony Express and the Union Pacific Railroad. He served as an interpreter for the Treaty of Fort Laramie in 1851, and he was also hired by General Grenville Dodge to help plot the route of the Union Pacific Railroad. He and Dodge became lifelong friends.

In addition to working for the railroads, the army and guiding migrants, Bridger also worked as a private guide for wealthy hunters. In this capacity, his journeys often brought him into Wyoming and the Colorado Territory. Bridger led Scottish nobleman Sir William Drummond Stewart into areas that later became part of Yellowstone National Park. Around the campfire, Bridger would amuse the nobleman by telling his stories.

Between trips, Bridger returned to his farmland in St. Louis and cleared an area on the crest of a ridge just south of Indian Creek about eight miles from the city's business district. He then moved a two-story house to the site for his family. One of the grandest homes in the area, it had large rooms, a fireplace with double chimney and a porch that extended across the front of the house.

While visiting in St. Louis during the spring of 1854, Bridger met Sir George Gore, who was organizing a party of men to go on a big game safari in the Wild West. Gore promptly hired Bridger, who helped select the rest of the members of the group and equip them for the journey. They all joined up in Fort Laramie. Bridger was the chief guide for the group that included sixty-one-year-old Gore and another forty men, over one hundred horses, twelve yoke of cattle, six wagons and twenty-one carts. The party

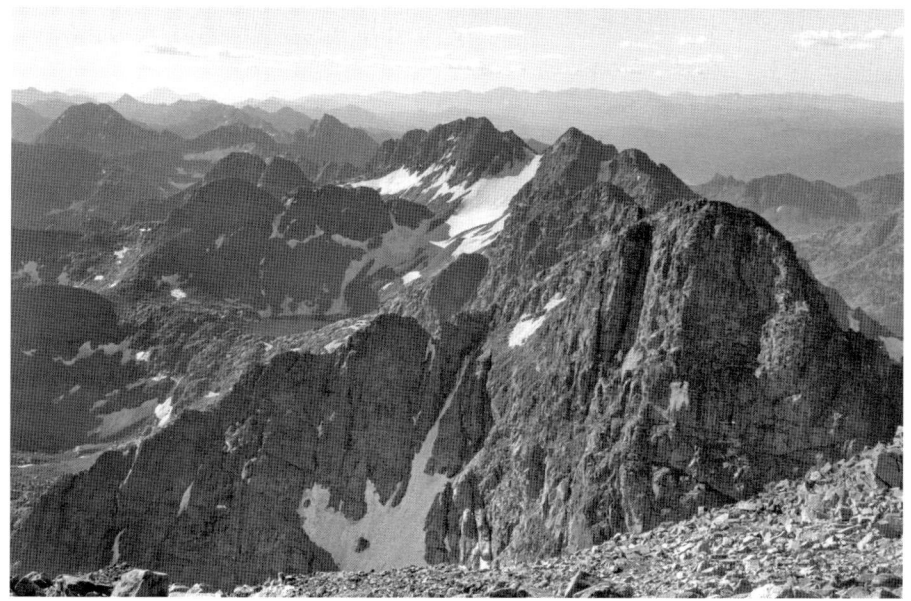

The Gore Range, Colorado. *David L. Perry.*

included stewards, cooks and hunters. In the spring of 1855, Bridger led the group into the Black Hills of Dakota. After being challenged by Dakota Indians, the hunting party journeyed to the lower Powder River where they are reported to have killed 2,500 buffalo, forty grizzly bears and numerous deer, elk and antelope.

According to Bridger, Sir George slept until ten or eleven o'clock in the morning, bathed, had breakfast and set out alone to hunt. He'd come back, boasting of his exploits and ready for a huge dinner. After dinner, Sir George would read aloud, often sharing his evenings with Bridger. Bridger recounted these experience to General Randolph B. Marcy, who included them in his book *Thirty Years of Army Life*. He writes that Bridger told him Gore's "favorite author was Shakespeare, which Bridger 'reckin'd was a leetle too highfalutin for him,' moreover, he remarked that he 'rayther calculated that big Dutchman, Mr. Full-Stuff was a leetle bit too fond of lager beer,' and suggested that probably it might have been better for the old man if he had imbibed the same amount of alcohol in the more condensed medium of good old Bourbon whisky."

Marcy went on to say, "Bridger seemed deeply interested in the Adventures of Baron Munchausen, but Bridger admitted, after the reading was finished that 'he be dogond ef he swallered everything that thar Baren

Mountchawsoen said, and he thout he was a durned liar.' Yet upon further reflection, he acknowledged that some of his own experiences among the Blackfeet would be equally marvelous, 'ef writ down in a book.'"

As western settlement increased, a shorter route was needed through the Colorado mountains. Denver's *Rocky Mountain News* reported that the president of the Central Overland California and Pike's Peak Express Company hired Jim Bridger to assist the company's chief engineer, E.L. Berthoud, in finding a route west of Denver. Bridger arrived in Denver in May 1861. Bridger and Berthoud explored Clear Creek, entered the North Fork and found a pass, now called Berthoud Pass, with an elevation of 11,314 feet.

They continued westward on the Fraser and Colorado Rivers before returning to report their findings. Berthoud, Bridger and their party left again on July 15, 1861, to make a preliminary survey. Crossing the divide from the Colorado River to the Yampa and near the mouth of the Little Snake River, they took a new route over to White River and then west to a Green River crossing. Then Bridger led the Berthoud engineers up the Duchesne and Strawberry down to Provo and north to Salt Lake City.

In 1862, Bridger was employed by the United States mail service as a guard for troops leaving Fort Leavenworth under the command of Colonel William Collins. Collins brought with him his eighteen-year-old son, Caspar, who described their travels in letters to his mother. Caspar Collins gives us a good description of Jim Bridger:

> *These old Mountaineers are curious looking fellows. They nearly all wear big, white hats with beaver around it, a loose white coat of buck or antelope skins, trimmed fantastically with beaver fur; buffalo breeches, with strings hanging for ornaments along the sides; a Mexican saddle, moccasins, and spurs with rowels two inches long, which jingle as they ride. They have bridles with sometimes, ten dollars' worth of silver ornaments on; Indian ponies, a heavy rifle, a Navy revolver, a hatchet and a Bowie knife. They all have a rawhide lasso tied on one side of the saddle, to catch and tie their ponies.*

Caspar Collins wrote to his mother that Bridger "knows more of the Rocky Mountains than any living man…He is totally uneducated, but speaks English, Spanish and French equally well, besides nearly a dozen Indian tongues, such as Snake, Bannock, Flathead, Nez Perce, Pend d'Oreille, Ute and one or two others." In another letter to his mother in August 1862,

Caspar Collins wrote, "It was amusing to see Old Major Bridger cooking his supper. He would take a whole jack rabbit, and a trout about eighteen inches long, and put them on two sticks, and set them up before the fire, and eat them both without a particle of salt; and drink about a quart of strong coffee. He says when he was young, he has often eaten the whole side of ribs of a buffalo."

Bridger worked for the army on a number of assignments after the Civil War began. He always rode in front, on the lookout for an ambush. Bridger guided Colonel Collins again in 1863, and in September of that year guided Lieutenant J. Lee Humfreville with the Ohio Volunteer Cavalry on a scouting expedition to South Park, Colorado. His experience of fighting against the Native Americans saved the detachment when they were attacked by a war party of Arapaho. Bridger advised setting fire to the grass where he knew a large number of Arapaho had hidden and were shooting at them, causing the Native Americans to flee.

Bridger was granted a temporary release from the army in April 1864 to guide migrant miners from Denver to the Montana gold fields. To avoid the hostile Sioux, Bridger led the men on a new, shorter route, south of the Big Horns. This company of about three hundred people and sixty-two wagons went from Denver to Cheyenne and then on to Fort Laramie before heading into Indian country. One of the men on the trip, Reverend E.J. Stanley, kept a journal. He tells of a spot at the Big Horn River when they came upon a large band of Native Americans. Bridger took a small group of unarmed men and approached the band. In turn, the Native Americans sent out a small band to meet them. Stanley writes, "Presently the Indians changed their manner, began to shout 'Bridger! Bridger!' at the top of their voices, and came galloping up to the white men. They were Shoshone or Snake Indians from about old Fort Bridger and recognized our Captain as their old friend." Instead of a battle, there was a feast.

Returning to Fort Laramie, Bridger was reemployed by the army at five dollars a day to assist at an Indian conference. When he was discharged, Bridger spent the winter of 1864–65 at his farm in Missouri. It was there that General Dodge found him and promoted him to chief guide at ten dollars a day to lead the Powder River expedition in July 1865. Under the command of General P. Edward Connor, the group included 480 soldiers, 75 Pawnees, 70 Winnebago and Omaha Indians, six companies of cavalry, 195 teamsters and wagon masters and 185 supply wagons.

General Dodge was concerned about the large number of Native American uprisings and the threat they might pose to the building of the

Pacific Railroad. Bridger convinced him to concede the Indians' rights to the Powder–Big Horn–Yellowstone country and instead to build the new railway across southern Wyoming. Bridger accompanied the Dodge party and showed them the best route to take. General Dodge soon left his command to become chief engineer of the Union Pacific Railroad.

In 1868, Bridger retired to a farm near Kansas City, Missouri. Bridger's wife, Little Fawn, had died many years earlier, and in his old age, Bridger was cared for by his daughter, Virginia Bridger Wachsman. People who met "Old Gabe" during his retirement noticed that he always preferred sitting on a rail fence or squatting on his heels to sitting in a chair. He was proud of his apple orchards and shared the crop with his neighbors. Eventually he lost his eyesight, but he still rode his horse. Occasionally, when Bridger and his horse got lost, his dog, Sultan, would come home and lead the family back to find Bridger.

Jim Bridger died on July 17, 1881, and was buried beside his two sons near his farm. General Dodge did not forget his old friend. On the 100th anniversary of Bridger's birth, General Dodge had the remains of the mountain man moved to Mount Washington Cemetery in Kansas City. Dodge erected there a seven-foot monument chronicling the major achievements in the life of Jim Bridger.

At the dedication of the monument, Dodge said, "No object of interest escaped his scrutiny and when once known, it was ever after remembered…He never lost his bearing. Unquestionably Bridger's claim to remembrance rests upon the extraordinary part he bore in the explorations of the West. As a Guide he was without an equal…He was a born topographer; the whole West was mapped out in his mind…In all my experience, I never saw Bridger…meet an obstacle he could not overcome."

Kit Carson

1809–1868 • Colorado Territory

Crawling on his belly over cactus spines and stones, Kit Carson inched along slowly in the darkness, attempting to sneak undetected through enemy lines. He and two other men were on a desperate mission. They had long since removed clanking canteens from their belts and even taken off their shoes, which they felt made too much noise as they silently threaded their way through dry underbrush beneath their feet. One sound, overheard by the nearby Mexican soldiers, and Carson and his companions knew they were dead men.

It was December 6, 1846. The United States was at war with Mexico, and Kit Carson was in California, a long way from home. He had reached California while serving as a guide into the western mountains and deserts for John C. Frémont, but Carson had been forced to join a small force led by U.S. general Stephen Kearney. He guided them from Socorro, New Mexico, into California, where at San Pasqual they happened upon a camp of Mexican troops led by Andrés Pico. General Kearney's plan for a sneak attack on the enemy encampment failed. An alarm awoke the camp, and the U.S. forces were pinned down by a large group of Mexican soldiers challenging the American occupation of California.

The attack on Kearney's men took place about forty miles north of San Diego. Things were going badly for the Americans. More than two dozen U.S. soldiers from the small band had already been killed, and ammunition and water were scarce. On this third night of the battle, Kit Carson was ordered to take two men and use all his skills as a woodsman to slip stealthily through the enemy lines. Miraculously, the three succeeded and then walked and ran, bootless, all the distance to San Diego to get help for General Kearney and his troops.

The story of how a guide and hunter from the New Mexico and Colorado Territories came to be involved in fighting in California began many years earlier back in Kentucky. Kit Carson's father, Lindsey Carson, who was born about 1755, fought in the American Revolution under General Wade Hampton. He followed Daniel Boone down the Wilderness Trail in Kentucky. Lindsey Carson had five children with his first wife; after she died, he married Rebecca Robinson and had several more.

Christopher Houston Carson, called Kit from an early age, was born on Christmas Eve 1809 near Boonesborough, Kentucky. He was the eleventh of Lindsey Carson's children. Before the boy was two, the Carson family moved from Kentucky to Boone's Lick, Missouri. The tract of land they farmed was at that time part of the Louisiana Territory and had been owned by the sons of Daniel Boone, with whom the Carsons were good friends.

Although several of Kit's brothers were great outdoorsmen and trappers, Kit's father thought Kit should go to school and perhaps become a lawyer. But in 1818, when his father died after a tree fell on him while he was out clearing land, Kit dropped out of school to work on the farm in Boone's Lick. He also hunted, helping to supply food for the family table. At fourteen, Kit Carson left home and was apprenticed to a saddle- and harness-maker in nearby Franklin, Missouri.

At that time, Franklin was on the east end of the newly opened Santa Fe Trail. Carson did not particularly like his work at the saddlery but was fascinated by the trappers and traders with whom he came in contact. As Carson spent time mending harnesses and rigging up freight wagons, he got more and more interested in traveling west himself. The mountain men he met told tales of adventure, and Kit Carson listened and learned. Dreaming of joining them, Carson made himself a "possibles bag" that the mountain men had talked about, which contained a flint, a bit of iron, a needle and thread and a piece of soap in it. Just before his seventeenth birthday, carrying his possibles bag and his father's old gun, Kit Carson slipped away from his work and started out cross-county eighty miles to Osage.

In running off, Kit Carson broke the law that governs apprentices. The saddle maker to whom he was apprenticed, David Workman, was sympathetic to Carson's desire to go west, but as required by law, Workman placed an advertisement in the *Missouri Intelligence* newspaper stating that the boy had run

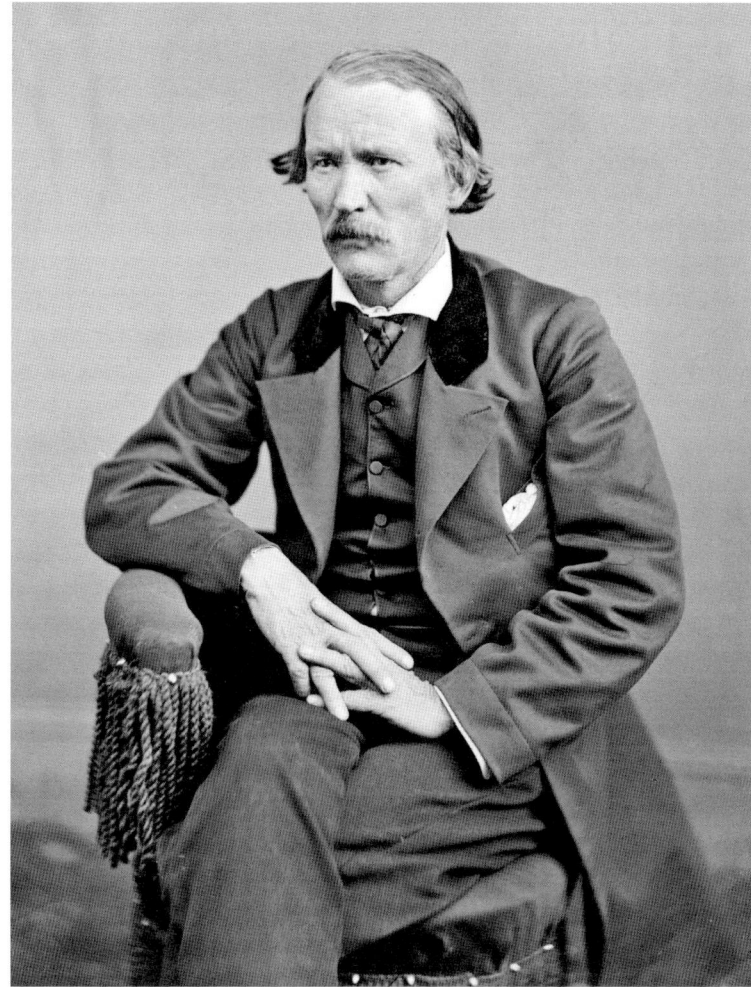

A photo of Christopher (Kit) Carson (between 1860 and 1875) by Matthew Brady/Levin Handy. *Library of Congress.*

away. The notice read: "All persons are notified not to harbor, support, or assist said boy under the penalty of the law." But the ad only offered a one-cent reward to any person who would bring back the said boy. No one ever bothered to report Kit Carson.

Kit Carson, who never grew to be more than five and a half feet tall, was a small but eager teenager who was hired to work on a Santa Fe caravan as a "cavvy boy." His job was to tend to the horses, oxen and donkeys. Carson chose one of the horses to ride and named him Apache.

That first trip through Council Bluffs, along the Arkansas River, past the Sangre de Cristo Mountains and into Santa Fe was a learning experience for Kit Carson. In 1826, he signed on with a second wagon train. During the winter of 1826 and 1827, he stayed with a friend of his father's, Mathew Kinkead, in Taos, New Mexico. Carson took odd jobs, such as repairing harnesses and working as a cook, but he also spent a lot of time with Kinkead learning the skills of trapping. Carson made Taos his home base for trapping from 1828 to 1831.

Skillful and successful, Kit Carson began roaming the country as a fur trapper, gaining expertise in the wilderness of the west. He became familiar with trails, and he learned the languages of several of the western Native American tribes, including Navajo, Apache, Cheyenne, Arapaho, Paiute, Shoshone and Ute.

In 1836, Kit Carson worked for a time as a trapper with the Hudson's Bay Company. When beaver hats suddenly went out of fashion, Carson and others could no longer make a good living as fur trappers. Over the next few years, he turned to being a guide, scout and hunter. During this period of time, Kit Carson married. His first wife, Waanibi (Singing Grass), was Arapaho. She gave Carson two daughters, Adaline, his first child, and another girl about whom little is known. Waanibi died shortly after giving birth to their second daughter. Carson then married a Cheyenne woman whom he thought would care for his children, but she became upset with Carson and moved his things out of her lodge, thereby dissolving the marriage.

In 1840, Carson stayed for a time at Bent's Fort in the Colorado Territory not far from Taos and was chief hunter, supplying the fort with meat. In 1842, Carson took his daughter Adaline to Missouri to live with relatives near Franklin and to attend school. On a Missouri river boat on his return trip to New Mexico, Carson met John C. Frémont, who had just surveyed the Des Moines River area. Carson was thirty-two, and Frémont was twenty-eight. Frémont hired Carson as his guide for an official trip to map western trails to the Pacific Ocean. On Carson's first expedition with Frémont, the two men grew to be good friends as Carson guided twenty-five men for five months to South Pass in what is now Wyoming.

While Frémont hurried back to Washington to report the success of his expedition, Carson remained in New Mexico and married María Josefa Jaramillo, with whom he settled for a short time in Taos. Their first son, named after Charles Bent, died before he was a year old. The Carsons lived in an adobe house at the east end of the plaza, and Carson hoped to farm and raise sheep.

In his reports of his expedition, Frémont highly praised Kit Carson, and as these reports circulated, Carson became famous. A series of popular "dime novels" was released with Kit Carson as the hero guiding people through the wilderness, saving those in danger and killing dangerous savages. The stories had little factual basis, but they increased Carson's fame and popularity.

In 1843, Carson left his family for a time to guide his friend Frémont on a second expedition to explore the latter half of the Oregon Trail. From

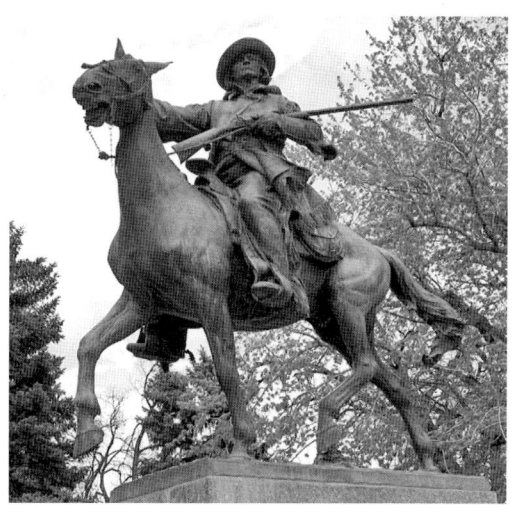

A statue of Kit Carson by Henry Lukeman and Frederick Roth located in Trinidad, Colorado. *David L. Perry.*

South Pass, they went to the Columbia River and into Oregon, crossing into part of California before going on into Nevada and continuing on back to Bent's Fort. Once home again with his family, Carson built a house in Rayado, some fifty miles east of Taos, where he and Josefa planned to farm and raise stock.

Apparently unable to give up exploring, Carson sold his new farm to go on another expedition. On June 1, 1845, Carson joined Frémont and guided him and about sixty men from Bent's Fort along the Arkansas River, across the Continental Divide and to the valley of the Great Salt Lake. From there, they went on to Walker's Lake and then on through the Sierras by way of a pass at the head of the Truckee River. It was December when they turned south and into the Sacramento Valley.

Carson and Frémont stayed briefly at Sutter's Fort to rest and buy supplies. They visited in the San Francisco area and Monterrey. In March, Frémont and his men were camped by the Salinas River when a Mexican officer came and announced that he had orders from the Mexican government to ask the Americans immediately to leave Mexican territory by the quickest route.

Kit Carson led Frémont and his men north into Oregon, where they camped at Klamath Lake. During this trip, they had several skirmishes with Native Americans, both Modocs and Klamaths. During one encounter, Carson and five or six others, including Frémont and a Delaware scout, were charged by a hostile Indian. Carson was in the lead. His gun misfired, and he threw himself on the side of his horse to avoid being hit by arrows. Fremont shot but missed and then drove his horse into the Indian. The Delaware scout, Sagundai, jumped from his horse and killed the attacker with his war club. Carson credited them with saving his life.

Dispatches came, indicating that hostilities were increasing between the United Sates and Mexico. Carson led Frémont and his men back to the Sacramento Valley where Carson became involved in the short-lived Bear Flag Rebellion in 1846. On June 14, 1846, a group of Californians in Sonoma declared independence from Mexico and raised a flag picturing a bear and star. This new Bear Flag Republic named a president and lasted for less than a month when news arrived that a month earlier, on May 13, 1846, war had been declared between the United States and Mexico. Those involved in the Bear Flag Rebellion quickly gave up their idea of an independent republic and joined Frémont in declaring California to be part of the United States. Frémont and his men marched into Monterey and took the town from Mexico without opposition.

Commodore Robert Stockton came into Monterey Harbor, and to further the war effort, he loaded Frémont and his men aboard a ship and took them four hundred miles to San Diego. Carson hated sailing. He referred to this trip in his autobiography by saying, "I was so disgusted that I swore it would be the last time I would ever lose sight of land while I could get a mule to carry me." While on this sea journey, Kit Carson was made a lieutenant. The men arrived in San Diego on Stockton's ship on July 29, 1846, and took the town without a battle. Then, they marched on to Los Angeles and took it, also.

On September 5, Carson was asked to take fifteen men with him and race across the continent from Los Angeles to Washington, D.C., in just sixty days. His task was to personally deliver dispatches to President James Polk informing him that, in a swift series of events, California was now a part of the United States.

While en route to Washington, D.C., Carson met General Kearny at Socorro, New Mexico, leading the Army of the West to do battle in California. Kearney ordered Carson to guide his men to the coast. At first, Carson refused, insisting that they had dispatches to deliver. General Kearny gave the dispatches to another messenger to take to Washington, and Carson, keenly disappointed, suddenly found himself guiding an army general whom he did not respect. It was after Carson had unwillingly joined Kearny and they reached San Pasqual, north of San Diego, that Kearny foolishly engaged the group of Mexican soldiers in battle. When pinned down, Kit Carson and two other men were ordered to slip through enemy lines to bring help to rescue them.

California was not the only spot where the United Sates and Mexico were at war. Back in Taos, during an uprising of Pueblo Indians, Charles Bent had been murdered. Josefa Carson and Charles Bent's wife escaped death by disguising themselves as squaws. The month following, Ceran St. Vrain and a group of volunteers from Bent's Fort defeated the Indian uprising that was being aided by Mexican troops.

After the Mexican-American War, Kit Carson returned to ranching in Taos. In 1851, he made a trip to St. Louis, where he saw his daughter again and brought her back with him to New Mexico. Carson and his wife had a second son, named William, born in 1852.

On one occasion, Carson and his men drove 6,500 sheep all the way to Sacramento. In New Mexico, Carson had bought the sheep for a few cents a head. At gold rush prices in California, he sold them for $5.50 a head.

Returning to Taos from another trip in 1853, Carson learned that he had been appointed the federal Indian agent for Northern New Mexico. Carson tried to do his best for the Native Americans but was handicapped by his illiteracy and inability to keep careful accounts. He hired someone to help him with these tasks. In observing the esteem in which Carson was held by many Native Americans, General Sherman wrote, "Those redskins think Kit twice as big a man as me. Why his integrity is simply perfect. They know it, and they would believe him and trust him any day before me."

Although Carson was not universally loved by all Native Americans, he did take his work seriously and did what he thought was best for them. He tried to keep peace with the various tribes. Carson admitted to fighting Indians when he felt he had to but is quoted by Ellis in his book *Life of Kit Carson* as saying, "I never drew a bead on a squaw or papoose and I despise a man who would."

At the outbreak of the Civil War, Carson was made a colonel in the Union army and helped organize the New Mexico volunteer infantry. After taking part in the Battle of Valverde, Kit Carson was breveted a brigadier general. About that time, the Navajos refused to be confined to government reservations, and beginning in 1863, Carson was put in charge of a campaign to destroy Navajo crops and livestock, trying to force them onto reservations. About eight thousand Native Americans surrendered to him, and Carson and his men led them on what came to be known as the Long Walk. With great hardship, the Native Americans walked three hundred miles from Arizona to Fort Sumner, in New Mexico.

After the Civil War ended, Kit Carson returned to the Colorado Territory to take up a post at Fort Garland, about eighty miles north of Taos. He and his family moved into the commander's quarters. General Carson did the best he could in securing food and supplies for the Utes. In his autobiography, Carson shares his views about the U.S. government's treaties with Native Americans and whether terms would be kept by either side. Carson wrote, "I frequently visit the Indians, speak to them about the advantages of peace, and exert my influence to keep them satisfied."

Carson next sought to retire from the army, to farm and to hold the position of superintendent of Indian affairs in the territory of Colorado. Many influential friends in Washington wrote on his behalf. While waiting to hear if he would get this position, Carson retired and moved to Boggsville, five miles upriver from Fort Lyon. He was mustered out of service on November 22, 1857.

General U.S. Grant commissioned Carson to become superintendent of Indian affairs in January 1868. The Utes had been invited to Washington to discuss grievances and another treaty settlement. Although Carson was in failing health at this time, he agreed to go to promote the welfare of the Utes. A treaty was concluded in March that settled the Utes on a reservation of 15,120,000 acres in western Colorado, but almost immediately white settlers violated the treaty.

Before returning home, Carson consulted some medical specialists in Boston. They gave him little hope of recovery. He rode the Union Pacific Railroad to Cheyenne, Wyoming Territory, and from there went by stage to Denver and then to La Junta. Tired and ill, Carson arrived in time for the birth of another daughter, born on April 13, 1868. Ten days later, when his wife died, Carson, though ill, tried to rally for the sake of his seven children. But as his condition grew steadily worse, Kit Carson was finally moved to be closer to his doctor, the post surgeon at Fort Lyon, Colorado.

When it was clear that the end was near, Kit Carson asked the cook for a good meal, saying he was tired of soft food. He dined on buffalo steak and chili, had coffee to drink, and smoked his favorite pipe given to him by Frémont. Kit Carson died the next afternoon, May 23, 1868, at age fifty-eight, and his remains were taken to be buried with his wife in Taos, New Mexico.

Kit Carson's place in history cannot be confined to a single area or to a single occupation. He was a wide-ranging, multifaceted man who is remembered in many parts of the country as a trapper, guide, hunter, military scout, Indian agent, soldier, rancher and legend.

Richens Lacy "Uncle Dick" Wootton

1816–1893 • Raton Pass

R ichens Wootton was only nineteen years old, a tenderfoot on his first wagon train trip as a muleskinner on the Santa Fe Trail in the summer of 1836. It was his first night to stand guard in the darkness where the wagons had circled and made camp at Little Cow Creek. His instructions were clear: shoot anything that moves. Although nothing had happened so far on the trip to raise any particular anxiety, Wootton was looking sharp because this was Indian territory.

In his own words, Wootton described what happened next:

> *About one or two o'clock at night, I heard a slight noise, and could see something moving about, sixty or seventy-five yards from where I was lying on the ground. I wasn't a coward, if I was a boy, and my hair didn't stand on end, although it may have raised up a little. Of course, the first thing I thought of was Indians, and the more I looked at the dark object creeping along toward the camp, the more it looked to me like a blood-thirsty savage. I didn't get excited although they tried to make me believe I was afterward, but thought the matter over and made up my mind that whatever the thing was, it had no business out there. So I blazed away at it, and down it dropped.*

Of course the shot roused the camp, and men with guns came racing out of their wagons, expecting they were under attack. They saw nothing in the darkness and questioned Wootton, who described what he had seen and done. Several men crept carefully toward the spot where they expected to find a dead Indian lying. Instead they found Jack, one of the lead mules who had gotten loose and strayed.

Although sorry about it, Wootton wasn't overly upset. As he pointed out, "the mule had disobeyed orders, you know, and I wasn't to blame for killing him." This combination of deadly aim, calmness and quick action displayed in his teens were the hallmarks of the long life of Uncle Dick Wootton, a pioneer frontiersman. A jack-of-all-trades, Wootton was a guide, hunter, rancher, store keeper and road builder.

Richens Lacy Wootton, later nicknamed "Uncle Dick," was born on May 6, 1816, in Micklenburg County, Virginia. His great-great-grandfather had come to the United States from Scotland. When he was only seven years old, Wootton moved with his family to Kentucky, where his father ran a tobacco plantation and where Wootton lived until he was seventeen. Then, for two years, he stayed with an uncle on a cotton plantation in Mississippi.

As a nineteen-year-old in 1836, Wootton sought adventure and headed for Independence, Missouri. There he was hired as a muleskinner and joined a Bent, St. Vrain and Company wagon train headed for Bent's Fort on the Arkansas River in Colorado. The small train of wagons to which he was attached quickly joined a larger train of fifty-seven wagons. Because they traveled through dangerous country, there was additional safety in being part of a large group.

As they approached Bent's Fort, Wootton shot his first buffalo. It was the first of hundreds he would kill. Wootton worked as a hunter for William Bent, supplying meat for the fort. Wootton also headed up Bent's supply train, trading with Sioux in what is now northern Colorado, Nebraska and Wyoming. Wootton took along with him blankets, beads, hunting knives, guns, gunpowder, bullets and household supplies such as coffee, sugar and flour. He traded these for buffalo hides, buckskins and ponies. In describing his trading days, Wootton said that he often stayed in various Indian lodges. His host acted as guard to protect the goods. The tribesman doing the guarding was dressed in a military uniform brought along for this purpose and also wore a stovepipe hat with a red feather in it and carried a sword. The guard was rewarded with gifts from the traders.

Wootton also trapped beaver on his own or sometimes with a group of men and found it profitable. After two years at Bent's Fort, in the fall of 1838, Wootton joined eighteen men to go on an expedition to trap beaver in the Rocky Mountains. They trapped in the Wind River Range of Wyoming, near Fort Vancouver in Washington and in Oregon, California, Arizona and New Mexico. While in New Mexico, Wootton rescued an Arapaho woman who had been captured by Utes. By returning her to the tribe, he established a long-term friendship with the Arapahos, who called him Cut Hand because he was missing two fingers of his left hand from an accident with a sharpened axe when he was only six.

Wootton and the other men hoped to make a good profit from their long and dangerous trapping expedition. When fourteen of the original nineteen men returned, five having been killed by Native Americans, they found, to their disappointment, that the price of beaver furs had fallen drastically since silk hats had now come into fashion. Fur trappers had to take up other occupations.

Wootton took a job again as a hunter at Bent's Fort, where he shot mostly buffalo but sometimes bear or deer for a change of meat. Wootton lived in the Taos area.

Buffalo were plentiful at this time, and looking back on those years, Wootton wrote, "There were millions of [buffalo] on the plains at that time…As far as the eye could reach I have seen the plains black with them, and it would actually look as if the prairies themselves were on the move." In 1842, he ran a weekly express using pack mules between Bent's Fort and Fort St. Vrain.

Fortunately, Wootton was away from Taos during the Taos Massacre of January 1847, when the Pueblo Indians rebelled and killed many of the Anglos in town, including Charles Bent. When he learned of it, Wootton and a few other trappers set out cautiously for Taos, wanting to lend support to the Anglos if they could. Colonel Price and a group of men left Santa Fe and marched against the rebels. Other volunteers led by Ceran St. Vrain were picked up along the way. Wootton and his companions joined the volunteer force. They reached Taos on February 3.

The troops engaged the enemy, who were well fortified in and around an old church. Wootton was among thirty-five men who tried to breach the walls of the church with axes. He reported, "It took us but a short time to accomplish what we had started out to do, and when a few shells were thrown through the holes we had made and exploded in the building they created a fearful havoc." The insurgents fled the church and ran in every direction. This ended the Taos rebellion. A detachment of soldiers remained to hunt down and punish those who had stirred up the insurrection.

Soon after this battle, Wootton guided Colonel Doniphan and eight hundred troops to Chihuahua, Mexico, to meet General Wood and his men. Wootton joined the men just south of El Paso. One of the main concerns on such a journey was finding sufficient water in such dry country for the men and horses. Wootton commented, "Something which I can't explain, and which I think must be an instinct, has always enabled me to find water in any country where there was any water to be found." Wootton was not only successful in guiding the army and finding water but also added to their provisions by shooting wild turkeys and rounding up bands of wild cattle.

When they were within thirty miles of Chihuahua, Colonel Doniphan asked Wootton to leave the group and carry dispatches back to Santa Fe. Wootton was offered a small group of men to go with him, but he preferred to go alone, taking two horses and supplies. He made the trip back to Albuquerque in nine days, never daring to light a fire and catching only minutes of sleep at a time on the way through Indian country. He spent one night in Albuquerque for food and rest and the next day rode on to Santa Fe, where he delivered his dispatches.

Having completed his mission, Wootton went to Taos, where he lived for the next several years. He married Dolores Le Fevre in 1848. Far from being grateful for this quiet period, he referred to it as "dull times" on the frontier. In 1852, Wootton sought excitement by making a trip to California, going not to hunt gold but to make a profit from selling meat to the miners. From the area of Watrous, New Mexico, he gathered together nine thousand head of sheep. With a band of twenty-two men and supplies, Wootton started out from Taos for California.

The men followed the Rio Grande del Norte from Taos, turned westward and crossed the Divide. They had several skirmishes with Indians before crossing the Green River, where they turned north, crossed the Wasatch Mountains and went down into the Great Salt Lake Valley. Wootton and his men camped outside of Salt Lake City, where he met Brigham Young. Wootton remained in town for three days while he purchased needed supplies for the last half of the trip. The men and their herd of sheep continued on into the Sacramento Valley. Wootton made the trip in 107 days and succeeded in delivering all but one hundred of the nine thousand sheep he began with. (He explained they had eaten a few on the way.)

Wootton remained in California for the winter, disposing of stock and finishing his business. He visited San Francisco and went by steamer to Los Angeles. There, Wootton purchased pack mules and with three men headed overland back to New Mexico. He carried with him in his saddle bags $14,000 in gold and twice that in bank drafts.

Wootton returned to Taos and his family, and in 1853, he moved to a new settlement at what is now Pueblo, Colorado. Wootton started a ranch near the junction of the Huerfano and Arkansas Rivers about

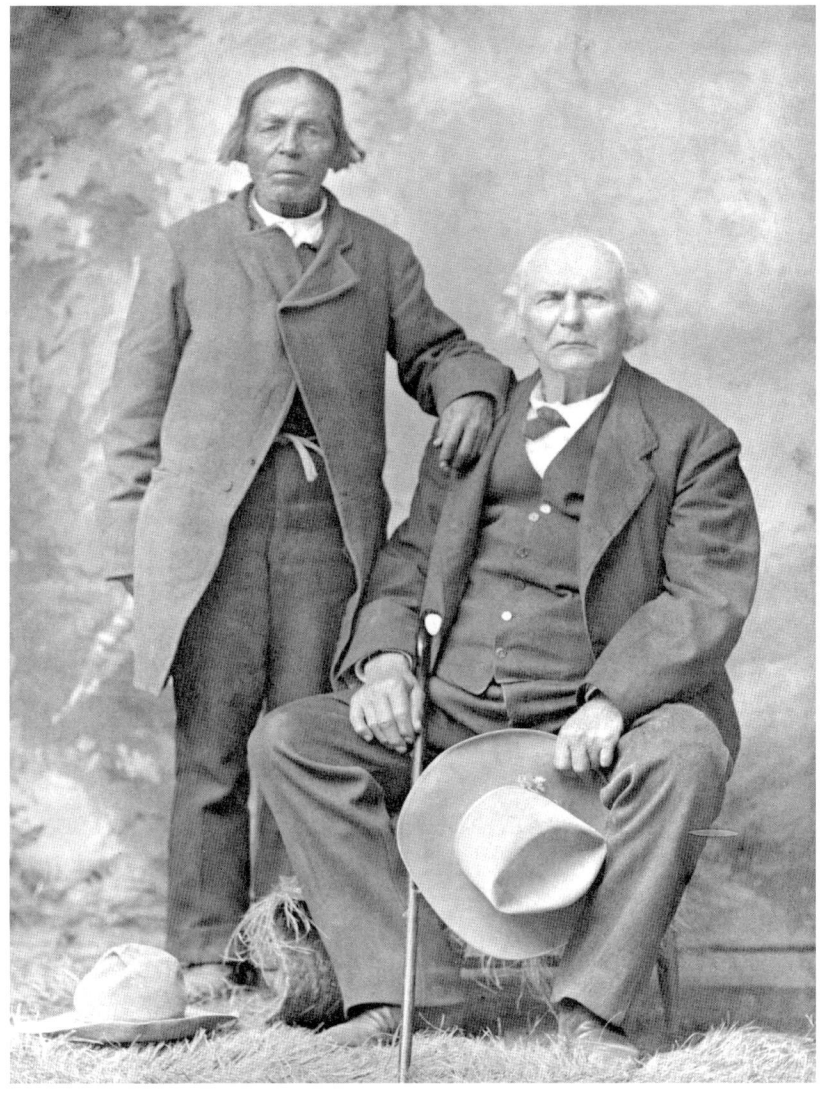

Jesús Silva and "Uncle Dick" Wootton. *Denver Public Library.*

twenty miles from Pueblo. He and his partner, Joseph B. Doyle, built houses only one hundred yards apart. Wootton built a stockade to protect the home he built and within the stockade had a blacksmith shop, wagon shed and a trading room. Once his home was ready, Wootton sent for his family, and they had an escort of soldiers from Fort Garland to their new home on the Arkansas.

Wootton experimented with buffalo farming. He raised cattle and buffalo together in a herd and drove his herd east on the Santa Fe Trail to Kansas City, where he sold them. His ranching was going well when, on Christmas Day 1854, Utes attacked the settlement of Pueblo and killed everyone there. The Utes headed to the Wootton-Doyle Ranch next, but Wootton and his men drove them off and survived the attack. Wootton remained on at his ranch for another year. He did a little farming, ranching and trapping and traded with the Native Americans and emigrants.

Once again, Wootton found the life of farming and ranching too tame and joined his former neighbor Doyle in starting up a freighting business. Doyle supplied the capital, while Wootton ran the wagon trains. Before starting his new line of work, Wootton planned to move his family to Fort Barclay, but his wife, Dolores, died in childbirth, and the infant died, too. Wootton took his remaining four children to his wife's father, Manuel Le Fevre, a Canadian Frenchman who lived in Taos, where the children were cared for by their grandparents until Wootton married again.

Wootton did well serving businesses and the United States government by freighting goods from Kansas City to New Mexico and Fort Union. The average cost of paying his teamsters and providing provisions for a trip came to about $1,000. With these costs, Wootton made about $10,000 profit from each trip. Although freighting was profitable, it was dangerous. Sometimes the wagons were attacked by Native Americans. At other times, teamsters mutinied in the hope of making off with the goods that were being transported. Freighters had to pay for any lost goods.

During this period of his life, Wootton spent little time at home. Some of his trips took him from Atchison, Kansas, to Salt Lake City, Utah, a trail distance of 1,225 miles. Such a trip would take about ninety-seven days. After having been constantly on the road for over seven months, Wootton decided that at forty-two years of age, he'd had enough of freighting. He returned to Bent's Fort and married Mrs. Mary Ann Manning, a widow from Missouri who was with an emigrant train. He left his wife at Fort Barclay and decided to wind up his business in the Rocky Mountains with one last trading expedition before heading back with his new wife and children to visit his relatives in Kentucky.

Wootton loaded up several wagons with goods and headed off in October. He expected to do some trading with Native Americans along the way. Snow fell early that year, and he didn't reach Denver City and Auraria until December 1858. There were only a few hundred people living there at this time and almost no shopkeepers. Wootton found himself surrounded by miners who wanted to buy his goods. Although it would have been more profitable to trade with Native Americans, acquiring furs to sell for a big profit in Kansas City, Wootton sold his goods to the Denverites. At Christmas, to celebrate the holiday, Wootton opened two barrels of Taos Lightning whiskey. This made him very popular and somehow earned him the name of "Uncle Dick."

To encourage settlement, the man who owned most of the land on which Denver was being built offered Wootton 160 acres of land to stay on and open a store. Wootton agreed. He gave up his plans of going to visit his family in Kentucky and instead opened a two-story log building and began merchandising in Denver. His wife joined him but died two years later. Wootton also ran a saloon and a hotel. The hotel failed, partly because he could never turn away a hungry man. The upstairs of Wootton's saloon was the first home of the the the *Rocky Mountain News*.

On April 11, 1859, delegates from local settlements met on the second floor of Wootton's building. They adopted the resolutions calling for a selection of delegates to meet in Denver on May 7 to prepare a state constitution to be submitted to the people in June and to call for an election of state officers and representatives in Congress. Wootton hoped that the new territory would be called "Jefferson" and was disappointed when it ended up being called "Colorado."

Wootton left Denver in 1862. Reflecting back on this decision as an old man, he admitted that from a business standpoint, he might have made a mistake in leaving Denver. If he stayed, he might have become a rich man. But he wanted to head back to country living. He said if he stayed, "I should have been jostled about on the streets instead of having the road all to myself as I do now when I go out for a walk, and should have had the noise and dust of the city instead of the singing of birds and the pure air of the mountains that I have here."

Wootton went back to the Pueblo area and built a home on the east side of Fountain Creek. He married Fanny Brown in 1863 at Doyle's ranch, and his elder children lived with them. Wootton tried ranching again. His new wife died just a year after their marriage, leaving him an infant daughter. Wootton gave up his farm and kept a store for a time. Then his real estate holdings were confiscated when he declared his secessionist sympathies during the Civil War.

Wootton oversaw Doyle's ranch until his death in 1864. Soon after his old partner's death, Wootton was set to marry Doyle's widow, but she mysteriously died the night before the wedding. It was suggested she was poisoned by those who did not want Wootton, a Southern sympathizer, to get control of the Doyle property.

These were uneasy times for settlers and Native Americans on the plains. Comanches joined with Cheyennes, Kiowas and Prairie Apaches to make raids. Many immigrants and farmers were killed. It was during this time that Colonel John M. Chivington led the troops against the Cheyennes at Sand Creek.

Wootton was not attacked by Native Americans, but the terrible flood of 1864 did a lot of damage where he lived. It washed away a neighbor's house, and Wootton's wheat and corn fields were partly destroyed. After cleaning up the debris, Wootton was hopeful that he might save some of his crop when hailstones knocked the heads off the wheat and pounded the corn into the ground.

Now almost fifty years old, Wootton decided to give up on farming and moved the following spring to the Trinidad area with permission from the territorial governors of Colorado and New Mexico to build a toll road over Raton Pass. Road building was hard work, and laborers were scarce. Wootton managed to hire a group of Utes under the orders of Chief Conniache to work for him. He opened his toll road in April 1865. It ran twenty-seven miles from Trinidad, Colorado, to Willow Springs, New Mexico. Of his road, Wootton said, "There were hillsides to cut down, rocks to blast and remove, and bridges to build by the score. But I built a road and made it a good one."

Wootton erected a tollgate right in front of his home. He charged $1.50 for a wagon and $0.25 for a horseman to use the road. He charged $0.05 a head for stock that were driven over the pass. Native Americans and law officers, however, could use the road for free. When stagecoach passengers came by, they usually stopped at Uncle Dick's home and were served hot lunches. He married his fourth wife, Maria Paulina Lujan, on June 17, 1871. She was almost forty years younger than he was, and they had ten children together.

The toll road was in use until the Atchison, Topeka and Santa Fe Railroad bought from him the right of way in 1879. They used it to build the railroad all the way to Santa Fe in 1880. First, they offered Wootton $50,000 for the right of way, but he refused them. Instead, he took $1 and a monthly stipend for grocery money and a free railway pass guaranteed for his wife for the rest of her life. She was thirty-eight at the time and lived for another forty-two years. The railroad company made good on its agreement and also supported Wootton's invalid daughter until her death. In 1879, a monster

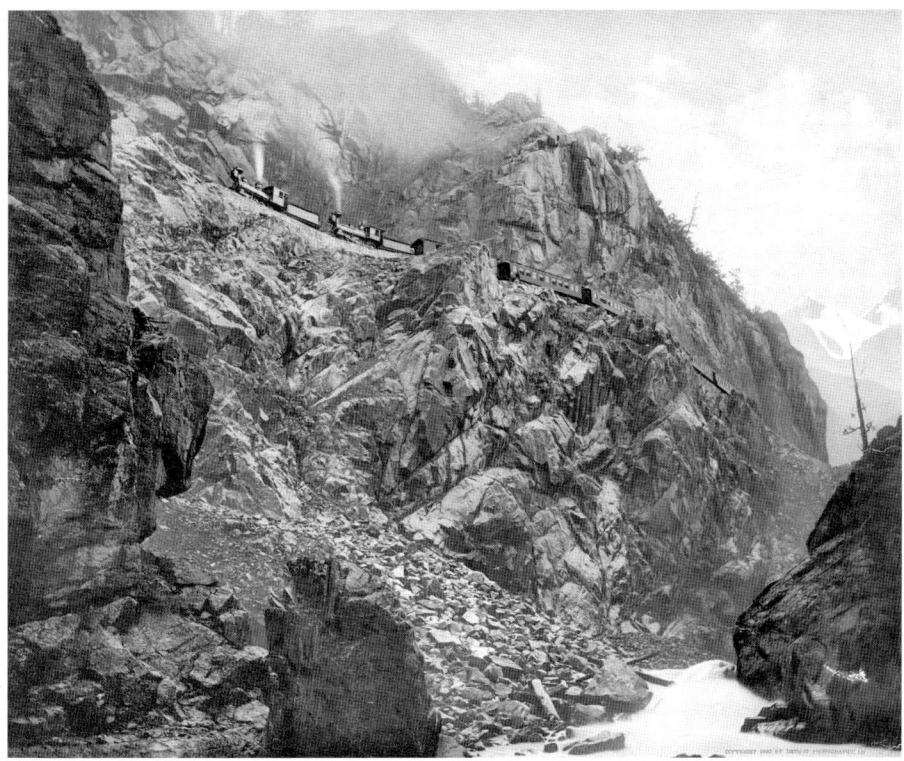

Powerful locomotives like these were needed for Raton Pass. Canyon of the Rio Las Animas, Colorado. *William Henry Jackson, 1843–1942, photographer. Library of Congress.*

locomotive, at the time the largest in the world, pulled cars over heavy grades to the Raton Tunnel. It was named "Uncle Dick."

Although he had trouble with his eyesight, going almost blind before having a successful operation, Wootton was in generally good health and spent the last years of his life in comfort at his home high on Raton Pass. He proudly saw his eldest son elected to the Colorado state legislature. Wootton lived in his mountain home until it burned in 1890 when he moved to Trinidad. Wootton died on August 22, 1893, having lived to the age of seventy-seven. He was buried in Trinidad. On his death, the *Denver Republican* newspaper wrote, "He had trapped beaver where Denver now stands; he owned a buffalo farm on the site of Pueblo, and he fought wild animals and Indians where other prosperous communities now are. The pioneer of Colorado pioneers, [he] has been a maker of history."

John H. Gregory and George A. Jackson

1820–circa 1864 and 1836–1897 •
Clear Creek Canyon

George A. Jackson was out alone prospecting for gold in Clear Creek Canyon in Colorado during the fierce winter of 1858. He spotted a bluish mist rising out of one of the canyons just ahead of him. Campfire smoke? Could he have stumbled upon an encampment of hostile Native Americans? Pushing through snow that was almost waist deep, Jackson slowly climbed to the top of the hill. Cautiously, he peered over the side and looked down.

To his relief and joy, he immediately discovered the origin of the mysterious smoke. It was nothing more than a thick vapor rising in the cold air from a hot spring in the canyon below. Not only were there no hostile Native Americans to threaten him, but Jackson saw the welcoming sight of mountain sheep that had gathered to drink at a nearby cold spring and to graze where the warm vapors had melted the snow off some grasses and shrubs. He had found safety and food.

Jackson had no way of knowing at that time how close he was to the spot where, in a few months, he would make one of the first major gold discoveries in Colorado. Nor did he realize that not far away, separated by a ten-thousand-foot-high ridge, suffering through the same cold winter, was another prospector, John Gregory, who would also soon be credited with a major gold discovery. These two prospectors were among those responsible for beginning the Colorado gold rush.

A decade earlier, forty-niners had participated in the famous California gold rush. Six years before that was the lesser-known Georgia gold rush that reached its peak in 1843. Records show that many of the prospectors involved in the Colorado gold diggings had earlier sought their fortunes in California, and quite a number of them had begun their unending quest for gold in the mines of Georgia.

One of these Georgia miners who finally struck it rich in Clear Creek Canyon was John Hamilton Gregory. Gregory was born on December 27, 1820, to Griffen and Cynthia Gregory in South Carolina. Still a child in the 1830s, Gregory moved with his family to Cherokee County, Georgia. The Gregorys settled near the Wildcat and Sixes Districts of Georgia where many significant gold strikes occurred. This part of Georgia was one of the richest gold mining areas in the United States at that time. Young John Gregory learned the trade of gold mining from his father.

In 1844, Gregory married Christina Payne, whose family lived nearby. They had six children over the next twelve years. By 1850, Gregory owned one thousand acres of land with mineral rights located on the Etowah River. Just as gold was petering out in Georgia, news of gold strikes in California lured Gregory west. Again, he failed to strike it rich. Leaving California, Gregory took a number of odd jobs to survive but didn't give up his dreams of prospecting. He saved up money to equip himself. After wintering at Fort Laramie, which he had reached by driving mule teams for the government, he heard exciting news. William Green Russell, a miner also from Georgia, had found traces of gold in Colorado's foothill streams near Denver. Gregory immediately began prospecting in Colorado.

A Gilpin newspaper editor, Ovando J. Hollister, wrote about Gregory's early prospecting trips.

> *At length he arrived at the Vasquez* [Clear Creek] *Fork of the South Platte which he followed up alone…to prospect thoroughly wherever the creek forked, and to follow the branch which gave most promise…He toiled up the canyon, perhaps the first white man who had ever invaded its solitude, to the main forks of the creek…then up the north branch to the gulch that bears his name…Here he left the creek and took up the gulch. Where the little ravine…comes in, he again prospected, and finding it the richer of the two, he turned aside into it…Gregory now felt certain that he had found the gold. But before he could satisfy himself, a heavy snowstorm occurred…during which he nearly perished.*

When the snowstorm abated, Gregory needed to return to the valley for provisions and leave his promising discovery. By now, he was out of funds and was forced to remain that winter in the Denver area, where he is reported to have talked with the Russell brothers about their diggings at Cherry Creek.

The winter storm that turned John Gregory back from his promising gold find was the same one that George A. Jackson was sloughing his way through when he came upon the plume of mist from the hot spring. George A. Jackson was not a Georgian but a native of Glasgow, Missouri. Born on July 25, 1836, he was a cousin of Kit Carson. Like Gregory, he went to California as a young teenager after he heard about the 1849 gold discovery. He, too, failed to strike it rich there.

Giving up his search for gold in California, Jackson tried a little farming before moving back to Missouri. He married Belle Hendricks, originally from Kentucky. They had one child, a daughter. But Jackson was restless and still had gold fever. Soon, he left again, heading this time to Colorado in the spring of 1858. Older and wiser at this point, Jackson realized that if he couldn't find gold, he might make a living as a hunter and trapper. Jackson arrived at Cherry Creek in Denver and camped at John Smith's trading post. He bought supplies and headed up the Cache la Poudre River, where he joined up with an old trapper called Antoine Janis. Jackson did a little prospecting and trading, founding the trading post of La Porte.

Although a hunter and a gold seeker at heart, Jackson took other jobs when offered. Sometimes he delivered mail from places like Laramie to the men in mining camps. He took the names of all the men in the camp and rode off to collect and deliver the mail, often riding twenty to forty miles a day. Jackson was paid a dollar for a letter and fifty cents for any newspaper that he delivered that wasn't more than a month old.

Jackson continued his life of trapping, hunting and trading with Native Americans and occasionally serving as an army guide, but he also kept prospecting in the area, gradually advancing up the stream. In the fall of 1858, Jackson left an Arapaho village with his companions and decided to winter in what is now the town of Golden. When the winter weather allowed it, Jackson continued prospecting in the mountains, which he reached via Mount Vernon Canyon heading into what is now known as Clear Creek and Bergen Park. He kept a diary, later published, of his hunting and prospecting days.

On December 26, Jackson left camp with two friends and his dog, Drum, to go on a week's elk hunting trip. They followed the old Ute trail, traveling about seven miles southwest through the snow and setting up a camp. He reported killing two elk and then, because of wind and snow, remained in camp the rest of the day. Over the next two days, hunting was good as the men killed and butchered a number of elk.

Such winter hunting trips were difficult. Jackson writes of being tired from traveling through four feet of snow and of building a big campfire to dry out his clothes and blankets by the Idaho Hot Springs. On January 1, 1859, he wrote, "Clear day. My supply of state's grub short, two pound bread, one pound coffee, one-half pound salt. Plenty dried elk for myself and dogs yet…Killed mountain lion today. Made eight miles and camped at Warm Springs near mouth of small creek coming in on south side. Snow all gone around springs. Killed fat sheep and camped under three cottonwood trees. About 1,000 mountain sheep in sight tonight; no scarcity of meat in future for myself and dogs."

Although he was always seeking gold, Jackson hunted and found enough game to continue. Jackson must have been a good shot, and game must have been plentiful in the area because his diary contains entries about killing an antelope, shooting sprigtail grouse and bringing down a fat doe. During the winter months, he reports spending time in "graining skins to make coats and pants" and buying buckskin needles and saddlers' silk.

Jackson, as only a lucky few prospectors ever did, experienced the thrill of a major gold discovery. On January 7, 1859, Jackson wrote, "If I only had a pick and a pan instead of a hunting knife and cup, I could dig out a sack full of the yellow stuff…Panned out eight Treaty cups; found nothing but fine gold. Ninth cup got one nugget of coarse gold. Feel good tonight." Of the next day, he writes:

> *Dug and panned today until my belt knife was worn out; so will have to quit or use my skinning knife. I have about an ounce of gold; so will quit and try to get back in the spring.*
>
> *I jumped up and down and told myself the story I would tell…when I got back to our camp at Table Mountain…My mind ran upon it all night long. I dreamed all sorts of things—about a fine house, good clothes, a carriage, horses, travel, what I would take to the folks down in old Missouri, and everything you can think of—I had struck it rich!*

His diary entry of February 9 reads, "We will bounce out for the head of Vasquez [Clear Creek] in the early spring. Tom [Golden] is the only man who knows I found gold up the creek, and as his mouth is as tight as a No. 4 beaver trap, I am not uneasy."

So both George Jackson and John Gregory had found gold, but the coming of winter forced them to abandon their most promising diggings to await spring. Each prospector spent part of the winter months in the Golden and Denver area. Some historians speculate that they may have even met and talked with each other.

On April 17, Jackson and twenty-two men returned to his claim bringing with them teams, wagons, supplies and tools. Each claim was allowed one hundred feet up or down a stream and a width of fifty feet. Since most of Jackson's companions were from Chicago, they named their spot "Chicago Creek." It was a long journey to the diggings because there were no roads for the wagons. Sometimes the men were forced to unload the wagons, carry them over obstacles and then load up again. It was the first of May before they reached the spot that Jackson had marked.

On arrival, Jackson and his men began mining in earnest. Jackson washed out his first gold with a tin cup. He is reported to have kept the gold from his very first find to make into a ring for his wife. In the first week, the group netted $1,900. This spot is marked by a monument today and is less than half a mile from the Placer Inn in Idaho Springs, an inn named in honor of the placer miners.

That spring, John Gregory also set off to seek his claim. Gregory returned to his mountain diggings on May 6, along with a few other men he had persuaded to pay for needed grub and supplies in exchange for his mining know-how and willingness to lead them to rich diggings. At the original site, which he had been forced to leave in the winter, Gregory scraped up a pan full of dirt, panned it down, and immediately found four dollars' worth of gold. Word leaked out that these major gold strikes were being made in Clear Creek Canyon.

William Byers, editor of the *Rocky Mountain News*, went to Gregory's claim, where he was shown three days' worth of diggings that were worth $1,000. Byers wrote in his paper that Gregory "had ceased operation under the strong apprehension that he would be robbed if it became known that he had a large amount of treasure. In his anxiety, he slept little. There were only 17 men in the gulch. The following day there were at least 150." This was only the beginning of the horde of prospectors that would come rushing in.

News of a gold strike spreads quickly. Covered wagons were soon on the trail carrying men and families through a long and dangerous journey to the gold fields. Some of the wagons were decorated with the slogan "Pikes Peak or Bust."

Gregory's gold strike, in what would later be called Gregory's Gulch, was an outcrop of gold-bearing quartz, feeding the placer below. The outcrop had crumbled, and sometimes the men hammered pieces in order to free the rock. Panning below yielded about $10 a pan. Gregory worked there only a

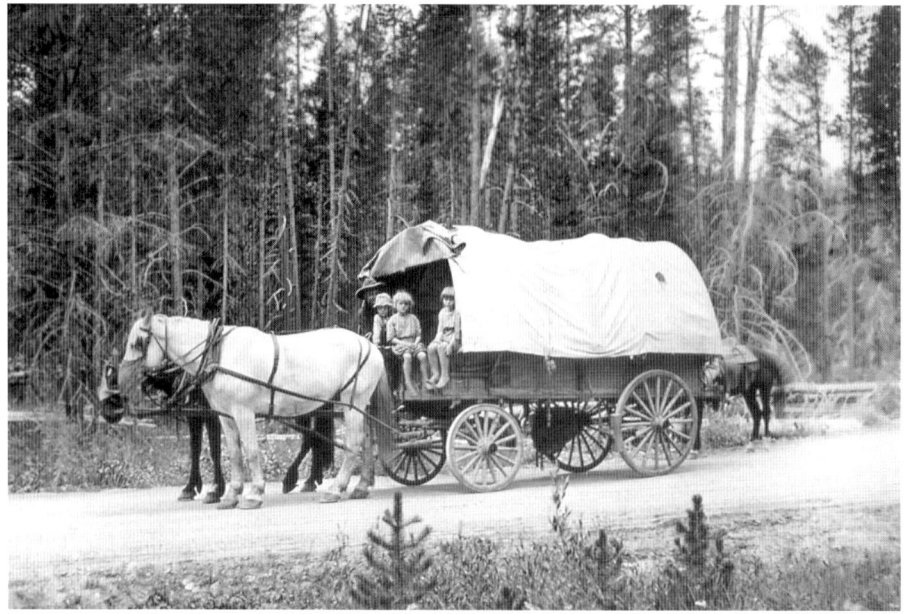

Horse and covered wagon. Historic photo No. 114,049, around 1924. *Yellowstone National Park archive photo.*

short time before selling his two discovery claims for $21,000. He then hired himself out at $200 a day to find sites for others. Many were rich strikes, enhancing his reputation. This "Gregory Diggings" district eventually produced $85 million in gold.

News of the gold strikes spread as headlines all over the country heralded the "Pikes Peak or Bust" slogan. An estimated fifty thousand men rushed in searching for gold in the Idaho Springs area in 1859. For the most part, they lived in tents and wagons and an occasional log cabin. Among the first five thousand seekers, only twelve were women. Supplies were scarce, brought in seven hundred miles from the Missouri River. Purchases were made with gold dust carried in buckskin pouches. Scales were available in businesses, and the dust was weighed and valued at eighteen dollars an ounce.

Some of the gold seekers, or argonauts, were experienced. They knew what was involved. Placer mining is often referred to as "poor man's diggings" because little money is needed to get started in this type of mining. A man would scrape up a pan full of material from a gulch or river bottom and wash it with water in a swirling motion. Being heavy, gold would sink to the bottom of the pan.

Sometimes placer miners used a "rocker" to wash the debris from the gold. A rocker is like a cradle with a coarse iron screen across the bottom. The miner pours water with one hand while rocking the cradle with the other. At other times, a sluice was used. A sluice is a square, wooden box open at the top through which a stream of water is run. Miners shoveled dirt into the sluices, and particles of gold dropped to the bottom. A further step was the introduction of crushing mills used to crush quartz rock to release the gold. In the fall of 1859, five of these crushing mills worked in Idaho Springs.

While experienced miners such as Gregory and Jackson knew what they were doing, many people far from the diggings were ignorant of mining processes. They believed any wild story they heard or read. The following story appeared in an Iowa newspaper: "We learn from a gentleman just returned from the Peak that the gold lies in bands or strata down the slope. The custom of the best miners is to construct a heavy wooden float with iron ribs, similar to a stone boat; this is taken to the top of the Peak where several men get in and guide it down over the gold strata. The gold curls up on the boat like shavings and is gathered in as they progress. This is the usual method of collecting it."

Responsible journalists checked out reports before publication. New York editor Horace Greeley came to visit the Gregory district. Recounting what he found, Greeley wrote, "The entire population of the valley sleeps in tents, or under booths of pine boughs, cooking and eating in the open air. I doubt there is yet a table or a chair in these diggings, eating being done around a cloth spread on the ground, while each one sits or reclines on mother earth."

What happened to a prospector after a gold strike? John Gregory was selected that June to serve as a delegate to the first Constitutional Convention held in Denver and Auraria. He returned to Georgia that September, taking $25,000 with him. In 1860, he came back to Colorado, made several more gold discoveries and ran a quartz mill. He stayed in Colorado for some time and then seemed to disappear. One historian writes that he gambled away his money and died poor in Montana sometime prior to 1865. Today, a historical marker in Clear Creek Canyon marks the site of his find.

George Jackson returned to Missouri after his famous gold strike and joined the Confederate army as a captain of sharpshooters. He moved up the ranks to lieutenant colonel. Some years after the war, he returned to Colorado and settled in Ouray about 1888, building a home for his family five miles below the town.

Jackson took part in 1895 in Denver's historic celebration called Festival of Mountain and Plain. He traveled back to the spot of his original gold

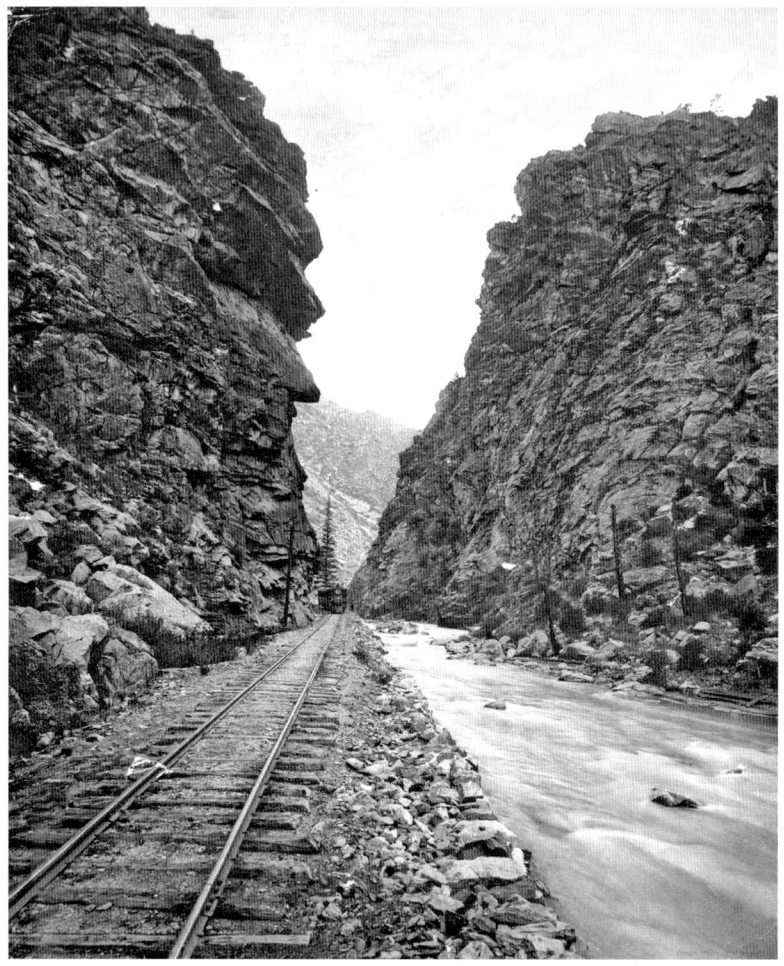

Clear Creek Canyon, Colorado, circa 1899. *William Henry Jackson, 1843–1942, photographer. Library of Congress.*

discovery and pointed it out to visitors. He and his wife later moved to Bonham, Texas, where both of them are buried. A plaque marking the site of his lode gold discovery near Idaho Springs was erected in 1909 on the fiftieth anniversary of his gold strike.

After the exciting discoveries of 1859, placer mining continued for many years in Clear Creek Canyon. Claims that numbered 13,158 were registered from 1859 to 1861. Both George Jackson and John Gregory will be remembered for their fabulous gold strikes that precipitated the Colorado gold rush.

Chief Niwot (Left Hand)

1823–1864 • Boulder County, Sand Creek

The tall, long-haired man stood up in the wagon and whistled for his horse. Handing the wagon reins to his wife, he leapt from the wagon onto the back of his buffalo pony. Giving a wild shout and holding his rifle above his head, he swiftly rode toward the huge herd of buffalo. Fearlessly, and with skill developed over years of experience, the rider picked out a fat cow from the herd and fired his rifle. A second shot brought the buffalo down. The man leaped to the ground, straddled the buffalo and slit its throat. The members of the wagon train at first watched in awe as the hunter began cutting long strips from the hide and lopping off great pieces of meat. Then they rushed over to help. That night everyone enjoyed a feast provided by their Native American guide, Chief Left Hand.

The exact place and date of the birth of Chief Left Hand are not known. It was in a village of the Southern Arapaho people sometime in the early 1820s in what would today be eastern Colorado or Western Kansas, Nebraska, Wyoming or Oklahoma. What is known about Left Hand's childhood is based on what is known about the early years of other boys born in Southern Arapaho tribes. Until he was old enough to walk, Left Hand would have been strapped to his mother's back on a cradle board. Since this little boy reached out with his left hand, he was called Niwot (Left Hand). Niwot was one of three children. He had an older sister, MaHom, and a younger brother, Neva.

Left Hand would have lived with his family in a lodge made from a covering of buffalo skins around poles. His lodge would be part of a small village. Carl

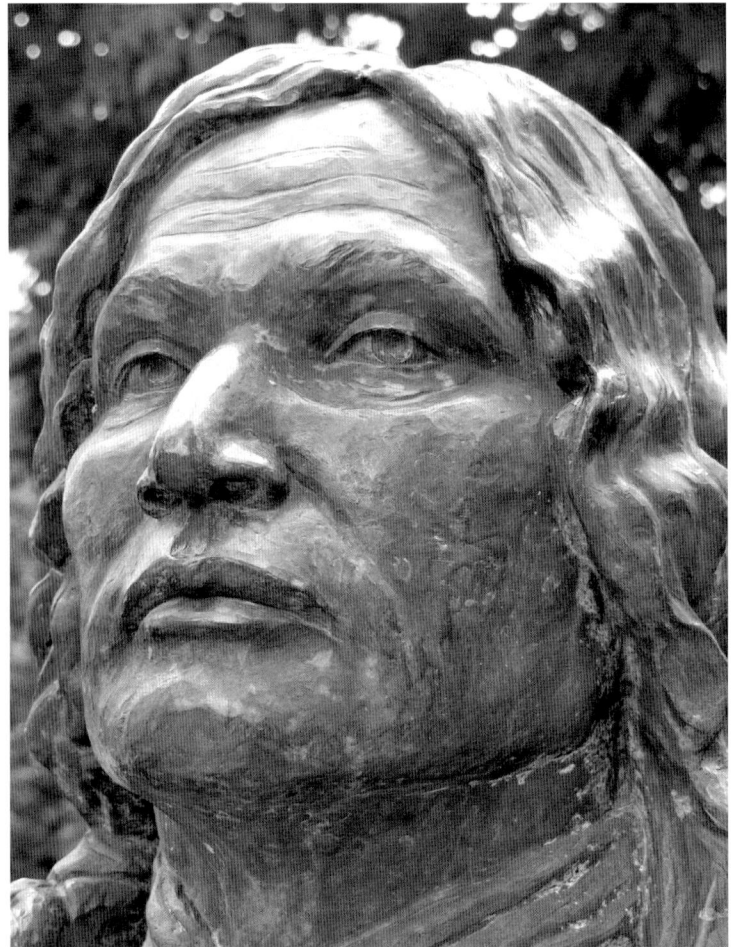

A symbolically rendered statue commemorating Chief Niwot by Steven Weitzman and Tara Brice, located in Boulder, Colorado. *David L. Perry.*

Sweezy, a Southern Arapaho, describes a typical Arapaho village. "Dogs played around the doorways; ponies grazed in the open spaces; children romped with the dogs and climbed on the ponies, women sat on the ground sewing moccasins or beading pouches; men straightened arrowwood or strung bows or combed and dressed their long hair."

When Europeans first arrived in what is now Colorado, the primary tribes of Native Americans along the Front Range were the Arapaho, a name that may have come from the Pawnee and means "traders." Some called them the "Blue Sky People." Others referred to them as "Tattooed

People" since they scratched designs into the skin using yucca leaf needles and then colored the wounds with wood ashes, leaving an indelible tattoo. The Arapaho called themselves "Our People" or "the Bison Path People." They moved their villages across the plains depending on the season of the year, and they shared their lands with the Southern Cheyennes. Many times at encampments, bands of Native Americans came together and traded. Left Hand learned to also speak the languages of the Cheyennes and Sioux.

In 1833, Left Hand's sixteen-year-old sister married a white trader, John Poisal, a twenty-four-year-old Kentuckian, who worked at Bent's Fort. Recognizing Left Hand's gift for languages, Poisal tutored him until he became fluent in understanding and speaking English.

When he was seventeen, Left Hand joined one of the tribe's eight societies, the Fox Men, all young men between seventeen and twenty-five years of age. They were responsible for hunting, guarding the village and fighting enemies. At this time, Left Hand married a seventeen-year-old Southern Arapaho girl. Although there are no known pictures of Left Hand, he was described in the diary of a white immigrant, Julia Lambert, as being "the finest looking Indian I have ever seen. He was over six feet tall, of muscular build…[He was] the only Indian I ever saw who did not braid his hair; it hung loosely over his shoulders."

A great western migration across the plains began as white settlers crossed on their way to Oregon. In 1845 alone, three thousand immigrants came West, passing over the lands of the Southern Arapahos and Cheyennes. As they came, they slaughtered buffalo and spread to the Native Americans diseases, such as cholera. It was during this time, when he was in his early twenties, that the first written account of Left Hand was made. A trader named Alexander Barclay made an entry in his diary on June 10, 1846, mentioning the young warrior as assisting his brother-in-law, Poisal, who was still an active fur trader.

Left Hand's niece, who was the teenaged daughter of trapper John Poisal and Left Hand's sister, MaHom, married fifty-year-old Thomas Fitzpatrick, a respected Indian agent. In 1849, Fitzpatrick was named a United States commissioner with authority to reach various agreements with the Indian tribes.

In looking for a council meeting site, the first choice was Bent's Fort, but before a meeting could be arranged, William Bent, exasperated by his treatment by army officials, blew up the fort, so Fitzpatrick decided to hold the meeting at Fort Laramie on the Platte River. Thousands of Native Americans gathered there on July 25, 1851, and remained for six weeks while messengers were sent out to bring in missing Native American bands.

The tribes represented were the Arapaho, Cheyenne, Sioux, Assinibone, Arikara, Gros Ventre, Crow and Shoshone. Left Hand was among the group of Southern Arapaho that included his brother-in-law, Poisal, and the main Arapaho chief, Little Raven.

The Treaty of Fort Laramie, signed on September 15, 1851, was the first treaty made between the U.S. government and the Plains Indians. It offered $50,000 a year in allotments of supplies and goods for fifty years as compensation for the destruction of buffalo herds and grazing lands. Each tribe was promised the legal right to the area it had traditionally claimed. For the Southern Arapahos and Cheyennes, the boundaries were listed as the land between the Platte and Arkansas Rivers, from central Kansas to the Continental Divide. The chiefs agreed to permit the government to build roads and military posts on their land and to keep the peace among themselves and with the whites.

After the council, Left Hand and his tribe moved downstream toward the buffalo ranges. It looked as if a new era of peace was about to begin, but in the years immediately following the treaty, immigrant trains and troops came in increasingly larger numbers, slaughtering the buffalo herds. Native Americans relied heavily on the government-promised annuities of flour, sugar, coffee and bolts of cloth that were now distributed at Bent's new fort on the north bank of the Arkansas River.

Sometime between 1851 and 1858, Left Hand became a Southern Arapaho chief. As tribal leader, Left Hand now decided when the village would move, when to send out scouts to find the buffalo herds, when to hold raiding parties and when to hold important tribal ceremonies. In addition to Left Hand's band, other bands of Southern Arapaho were led by Little Raven, the principal chief, or by lesser chiefs, including Big Mouth, Storm and Shave Head. These chiefs formed a tribal council, and because of their excellent leadership, the early 1850s were peaceful.

Fitzpatrick died in 1854, and his replacement was John W. Whitfield. Although Cheyenne chiefs had done their best to prevent it, some of their warriors had raided immigrant trains on the Oregon Trail. The new Indian agent, Whitfield, thought a show of force was needed against the Native Americans. Colonel Edwin Sumner led his troops on several attacks against the Cheyennes in what is sometimes referred to as the War of 1857.

Conditions among the Southern Arapahos were desperate. Many died of cholera and smallpox, while others starved due to the lack of buffalo. White settlers suggested that the Indians turn to farming. Left Hand decided to investigate and find out how the white man farmed. In the summer of 1858,

Left Hand, his wife and children set out across the plains in a small wagon pulled by two ponies for Nebraska, Missouri and Iowa. While he was gone, he left his tribe in the care of his brother at Beaver Creek.

While returning to his tribe in September, Left Hand met up with a wagon train and served as their guide. What we know about Left Hand's farming exploration trip comes from the wagon train leader, Marshall Cook of Kansas, who recorded in his diary conversations he had with Left Hand. Left Hand told him that when he reached Council Bluffs, he worked as a farmhand and determined that his people, used to a life of moving about and hunting, would have a very difficult time adjusting to being farmers. He did think, however, the Arapaho might be able to turn to cattle ranching.

Marshall Cook also recorded in his diary several of the events that occurred involving Chief Left Hand, including his killing a buffalo to feed the wagon train. When a group of Sioux appeared and fired at the wagon train, Left Hand rode out to meet them. Using his peacemaking skills, he convinced them to leave the wagon train alone in exchange for two cups of sugar. Cook wrote that Left Hand's reunion with his tribe was joyous. He said they swarmed "from their lodges, like bees from a hive, throwing their hands in the air and whooping at the tops of their voices." All the wagon train members were welcomed and fed.

Left Hand led his people from their camp at Beaver Creek on October 26, 1858, just ahead of a big winter storm. They traveled to their usual wintering grounds in Boulder County. Angry to find white gold seekers there, Chief Left Hand went to their camp, and Thomas Aikens recorded that Niwot said, "Go away; you come to kill our game, to burn our wood, and to destroy our grass." Aikens explained the settlers would stay only through the winter and then move into the mountains, so Left Hand gave them permission to stay in peace.

Settlements popped up everywhere as gold seekers began founding towns. To observe firsthand, and to talk with Little Raven, Left Hand rode to Cherry Creek and saw the latest influx of miners. Left Hand urged the other chiefs to keep their men under control, and he consistently worked to keep the peace. George Jackson, a prospector in the area, wrote in his diary that Left Hand did not take part in the Cherry Creek feasting around New Year's in 1859 because he had fallen ill and returned to his tribe in the Boulder Valley. Jackson wrote, "Niwot is sick. Mountain fever I think."

Chief Left Hand recovered from his illness in the spring only to learn that the gold miners in Boulder were not leaving as they had promised but were building a town. To avoid confrontation, Left Hand moved his tribe up the South Fork of the St. Vrain River.

Meetings were called between Native American chiefs and various white leaders. Editor Horace Greeley was among those who met with Chief Left Hand and touted the advantages of farming. Left Hand explained that he had already investigated this possibility and rejected it. Greeley wrote, "He knew that there is a certain way in which his people have lived from time immemorial, and in which they are content still to live."

Regarding the condition of the Arapaho, William Bent wrote on July 23, 1859, in a letter to the superintendent of Indian affairs that "they were starving." Bent went on to report, "The Southern Arapahos and Cheyenne…are already pressed into a small circle of territory. A desperate war of starvation and extinction is therefore imminent and inevitable, unless prompt measures shall prevent."

Washington was incapable of acting quickly. Many more meetings were held and treaties signed, but each removed land from the Native Americans and legalized the status of the white settlers. In April 1860, while Left Hand and his warriors were out hunting, a group of drunken whites came into his Arapaho village, raping the women and girls. Left Hand did not seek vengeance, leaving it up to authorities, but the whites meted out no punishment. Left Hand and his warriors left the Denver area and moved out onto the plains. Left Hand led his men that May and June in frequent raids against the Utes, reestablishing his reputation as a warrior chief.

In May 1860, Chief Left Hand and his tribe returned to their campgrounds on the South Platte near Denver. Some of Chief Left Hand's warriors stole cattle from the white settlers in direct violation of his orders, so Chief Left Hand moved out of camp. He set down terms for his return, which were met. By July, he was back in the village in authority. After receiving their allotment of government supplies, his people camped on the Arkansas.

A new Fort Wise Treaty was drawn up and signed in 1861 while Chief Left Hand was away. In the months that followed, the Cheyenne frequently raided white settlements, and Denver citizens demanded a territorial army. Governor Gilpin obliged. Fearing his people would be blamed for Cheyenne raids, Left Hand made a trip into Denver and spoke to the editor of the *Rocky Mountain News*, encouraging him to tell all his readers that the Southern Arapahos retained "the usual long-standing friendship for the white."

That summer, the First Colorado regiment was organized, made up not of trained army men but of gold seekers and shopkeepers who were hastily trained. John Chivington, a former minister, rejected an offered position as regimental chaplain to take a fighting position as a major. Three companies were sent in the fall of 1861 to Fort Wise near what is now Lyons, Colorado, and a fourth company, led by Major Chivington, remained at Camp Weld, two miles southwest of Denver.

After receiving their government supplies in October 1861 at Fort Wise, the Southern Arapahos scattered across the plains between Fort Wise and Fort Larned. For the most part, the Southern Arapahos remained peaceful for the final weeks of 1861 and the early weeks of 1862. In May 1862, John Evans arrived in Denver to take on his duties as territorial governor. He went to Fort Wise and met with Chief Left Hand but seemed to not listen to complaints of how the Arapahos were being treated. Although there were some Sioux uprisings, the rest of the Plains Indians remained peaceful during the summer and fall of 1862.

Indian agent Colley, trying to settle land disputes between settlers and Native Americans, decided to take some of the chiefs to Washington to speak with the president. Chief Left Hand was invited, but when he arrived at Fort Wise, he learned that Colley had deliberately left early without him, preferring not to have an adept English-speaking Native American chief in their group. At the Washington meeting, there was talk of peace and conciliation, but no action was taken.

In January 1863, after returning from a successful campaign against Confederate troops in New Mexico, Colonel Chivington became commander of the military district of Colorado. Fearing that the majority of Plains Indians wanted war, Governor Evans and Colonel Chivinton agreed to meet the first sign of hostility with an immediate and harsh response. Despite a few incidents involving Native Americans and whites, for the most part, the winter months of 1863 and 1864 passed quietly. Left Hand kept his people away from troubled spots, staying near the Arkansas River.

The governor, still fearing hostilities, issued a proclamation demanding that all Native Americans move to specified locations. Left Hand brought his tribe to Fort Lyon and put them under Colley's protection. Because Colley had not purchased supplies for the tribe, Left Hand's band was forced to move away in search of game. New proclamations were soon posted everywhere authorizing individuals and groups of citizens to pursue all hostile Native Americans who had not assembled at the designed rendezvous points.

Southern Arapaho and Cheyenne chiefs, including Left Hand, wanted another peace meeting with the whites and sent a letter to Agent Colley and Major Wynkoop. Wynkoop agreed to set up a meeting with Governor Evans at Fort Weld. Left Hand remained with his tribe but sent his brother to this meeting. Also at the meeting was Colonel Chivington, who made it clear that if the Native Americans went peacefully to Major Wynkoop at Fort Lyon, troops would leave them alone.

Wynkoop was watching Native American tribes gather at Fort Lyon when, on October 17, 1864, special orders arrived relieving him of his duties and replacing him with Major Scott Anthony. Anthony immediately made all the men in Left Hand's tribe turn over their weapons. These consisted of three rifles, one pistol and all their bows and arrows. Without these, they could not hunt for game.

Black Kettle, who was at Sand Creek, was told by Major Anthony that there were no supplies for his tribe at Fort Lyon, so they should stay where they were and await further orders from the commanding officer of the district. They were advised they would be under the protection of Fort Lyon while at Sand Creek. Anthony met again with Left Hand and returned his tribe's arms, saying he had no rations for them and they should move where they could hunt and feed themselves. Little Raven did not trust Anthony and moved his people sixty-five miles down the Arkansas, while Chief Left Hand took his tribe to wait with Black Kettle at Sand Creek.

Meanwhile, James M. Cook, a Fort Lyon employee, stopped at Chivington's camp near the Arkansas River. He told him about the small band of Cheyennes and Arapahos led by Black Kettle and Left Hand who were waiting for instructions at Sand Creek. On November 25, Chivington led his troops from Spring Blossom on a three-day march to Fort Lyon. Lieutenant Soule was sent by Anthony to Chivington's camp. Soule told Chivington that the group at Sand Creek presented no danger and were considered prisoners of war.

The next day, Chivington rode into Fort Lyon and told Anthony that he planned to attack at Sand Creek. Although he had given Black Kettle and Left Hand his word that they would be under protection, Anthony did nothing to prevent the attack. Agent Colley and other officers who had served under Wynkoop protested the plan. As protests continued, Chivington shouted that he would arrest any man opposed to going to Sand Creek.

At eight o'clock in the evening on November 28, 1864, Chivington led about one thousand men to Sand Creek. The troops continued without rest for ten hours, reaching their destination at sunrise and finding a quiet, sleeping camp. There were about ninety lodges of Cheyenne and ten lodges of Arapaho, a total of about five hundred persons, of whom two-thirds were women and children. The soldiers bore down on the camp, firing their weapons. Black Kettle, awakened by the noise, ran outside. Seeing what was happening, he quickly raised an American flag and a white flag that had been given to him at the Treaty Council with directions to fly these as a sign of peace and friendliness.

Left Hand's camp, located in the center of the lodges, caught the brunt of the attack. Only moments after the attack began, half of his tribe had been killed. It is thought only four escaped. There are differing accounts as to how Left Hand died, and adding to the confusion of battle is the fact that there was another Native American called Left Hand. This second man was only twenty-four at the time of Sand Creek, and he went on to become a Southern Arapaho chief in 1889. Two men with the same name caused some to believe Chief Left Hand had survived into old age.

In fact, Chief Left Hand was killed at Sand Creek. The victims were so mutilated by soldiers cutting off body parts for souvenirs that identification was difficult and hinges on firsthand accounts. One such account by George Bent states that although he was shot, Left Hand escaped up the creek with a few others to a neighboring Sioux camp where he died of his wounds. Basing his theory on interviews of survivors, historian Jerome C. Smiley says that Left Hand ran toward the troops with the palms of his hands turned outward in the Plains Indian sign of peace and was shot down as he ran. Another account by a Lieutenant Cramer provides a picture of the end of a great chief who strove for peace. He states that Left Hand "stood with his arms folded, saying he would not fight the white man, as they were his friends."

John Long Routt

1826–1907 • Denver

When faced with reports that state lands near Creede, Colorado, had been taken over illegally by silver mining prospectors who would not leave without a fight, advisors at the capital urged Governor John Routt to send in troops. The governor replied, "To hell with the troops; I'll go down myself."

And so it was in the midst of a snowstorm in March 1892 that Governor Routt arrived, tugged off his coat and looked out at a hostile crowd. Standing in front of the angry men, he was greeted with cries of "Lynch him!"

Routt remained cool. In the straightforward manner in which he always addressed people, he assured the crowd that if they hanged him, they would receive warrants charging them with murder. If instead they wanted to receive titles to their mining claim lands, they had best listen to him and bargain. He discussed an arrangement in which the state lands would be sold to the miners at public auction with the money going into the state school fund. Those who had threatened him minutes before now cheered him. Another victory, this one coming fairly late in life, was chalked up to John Routt.

John Long Routt was born on April 25, 1826, in Eddyville, Kentucky, into a family that traced its roots back to Wales. His great-great-grandfather was an early colonist in Virginia. John was his parents' fourth child, and his father died just three years after John's birth. His widowed mother moved the family to Kentucky to live near her father. In 1834, Routt's mother remarried a man named Henry Newton, and they moved to Illinois, where John Routt grew up and went to school.

At age seventeen, Routt took a job in Bloomington at a saw- and gristmill, and within a year, because of his energy and competence, he was in charge of the business. The following year, he married Hester Ann Woodson. With few possessions and only twenty dollars to their name, they began their married life. Routt did not have an extensive education, having attended school for only about three months a year, but he was an avid reader. He learned carpentry and the machinist's trade, studied architecture, made designs and drew up contracts. This allowed him to work successfully in the building trades.

John Routt stood only five-foot-two. At age twenty when Routt was considering a run for sheriff, his opponent erred in saying, "It would be a mistake for little Routt to run." That taunting remark convinced Routt to enter the race, and he won handily, getting his first taste of public office as sheriff of McLean County in Illinois. The Civil War cut short his career in politics. Routt entered the Union army as captain of Company E of the Ninety-fourth Illinois Volunteer Infantry, known as the McLean Regiment. This company saw action at many sites. Although not wounded, Routt left the Battle of Prairie Grove with three bullet holes in his uniform. Promoted to quartermaster officer under General Barron, Routt received excellent reports as to the quality of his service.

In June 1863, Routt's regiment was moved up to serve under General Grant in the Siege of Vicksburg. Grant inspected his troops daily. When he found that the Ninety-fourth regiment was short on ammunition, he ordered that this problem be fixed immediately, even though the only source of ammunition available would mean crossing into dangerous territory.

Not only was the nearest ammunition depot twenty miles away behind enemy lines, but there was also scarcely any means to transport the needed ammunition even if it could be reached. Routt and his men took private mounts and everything nearby that had wheels and left for the ammunition depot. When Grant returned twenty-four hours later, he found, to his satisfaction, that the Ninety-fourth Regiment had the needed supplies. Grant inquired as to who had secured the ammunition and made a note of Routt's name.

Three months later, the Ninety-fourth joined the Army of the Rio Grande near Brownsville, Texas, and Routt was promoted to the rank of colonel. When ordered to erect an embankment along the Brazos River, Routt used his knowledge of construction and completed the task in such a sturdy way that it was used as a roadway until 1881.

Routt was sent to Baton Rouge, Louisiana, in charge of an outfitting depot. He remained there until he was mustered out on September 20, 1865.

Although the Civil War caused enormous damage and took many lives, it allowed Routt to be recognized as a leader and secured him some powerful and valuable friends who had a profound effect on his future.

Upon his return home to Illinois after the war, Routt renewed his affiliation with the Republican Party and slowly climbed the political ladder. First he served two terms as treasurer of McLean County, second in population and importance in the state. Routt demonstrated a remarkable ability for handling public funds. Offered a third term, he chose instead in 1868 to accept a federal appointment as chief clerk to the second assistant postmaster general. While serving in this position, President Grant named Routt to the office of United States marshal of the Southern District of Illinois. One of Routt's main jobs was to direct the ninth census in 1870. In making this appointment, Ulysses S. Grant reportedly said, "I am simply putting you into that job to have my eye and hands on you, my friend."

Indeed, Grant did keep an eye on Routt. In the fall of 1871, when, due to ill-health, General Smith applied for retirement, Grant appointed Routt to be second assistant postmaster general. Routt and his family left Illinois to go to Washington, D.C. In his new position, Routt supervised arrangements for conveying all of the United States mail.

Although his career was thriving, at this time, Routt suffered some severe personal losses. His mother died in 1871, and then his wife died a year later, leaving him with five children, three of whom were under the age of ten. Routt's grown son and wife who had accompanied the Routts to Washington helped with the younger children. Two years later, at age forty-eight, John Routt married Miss Eliza Pickrell. Eliza was thirty-five, unmarried and had lived in the home of her grandfather, who had been a military man and a state legislator. The Routts were popular and successful in the Washington scene, but Routt often stated he preferred frontier conditions to city life and he was interested in heading west.

Since the establishment of the Colorado Territory, created by an act of Congress and signed by President James Buchanan on February 28, 1861, seven different men had been chosen to serve as territorial governor. For one reason or another, none had stayed long, and several had proved completely unsatisfactory. A Civil War veteran appointed by Grant was accused of being inept or corrupt. Some short-term governors took a stand against statehood, which made them unpopular with the territory's citizens. One, who appeared to be doing an excellent job, was kicked out of office by detractors in Washington. All this led to dissatisfaction and feuding within the state Republican Party.

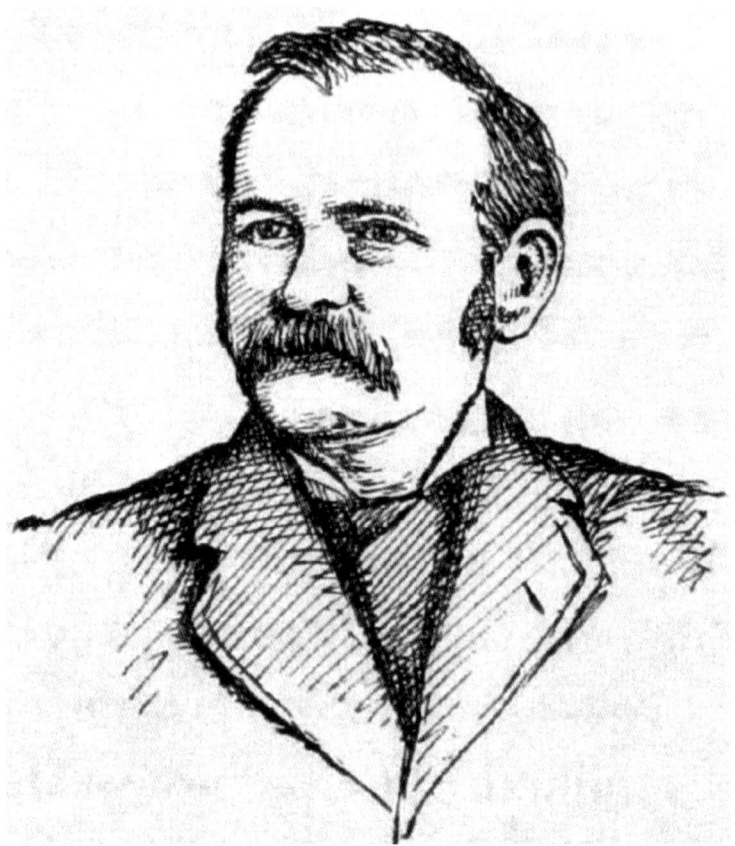

Governor John Routt. *From* Our Great Continent *by Benson J. Lossing.*

Grant decided to appoint a new territorial governor—someone who would be approved by all the powers in the party. John Routt's name was suggested and found to be acceptable because he had made many friends among representatives and senators in Washington while serving in the post office department. On March 29, 1875, President Ulysses S. Grant appointed John Routt as the eighth man to serve as Colorado's territorial governor. Under Routt's strong leadership, much of the opposition that had arisen to the bill granting statehood also dissipated.

When John Routt and his wife, Eliza, arrived in Denver in 1875, Routt was well received. The *Rocky Mountain News* reported, "A very general feeling favorable to the appointment of a man from some other locality, and thus not identified with either of the factions whose warrings have so distracted the Republican party." An article in the *Denver Tribune* that same week pointed out, "No man ever came to Denver or Colorado…with golden opinion so thick upon him as Governor Routt." Other *Rocky Mountain News* articles said, "No man ever accused Routt of taking a dollar that did not belong to him," and "His integrity is perfect." Routt also won over some residents suspicious of an outsider by telling them that even without this appointment, he had been planning to move to the Colorado Territory. Showing his eagerness to please, Routt won more supporters by presiding in April at a spelling bee sponsored by the Ladies' Relief Society of Denver.

Adding to the new governor's popularity was his wife, Eliza Pickerel Routt. A rather proper Victorian lady, she quickly learned to be a woman of the West. In Washington, Eliza had already mastered the art of being a politician's wife. Promptly after their arrival in Denver, Eliza joined the Central Christian Church and met the other leading ladies of the city. Soon she held positions on various boards, including the Women's Home Club and the Colorado Women's College. She was also active in the Denver Orphan's Home Association, no doubt especially involved in this group because she had been orphaned herself shortly after her own birth. Eliza Routt enjoyed her position of prominence and quickly earned the nickname of the "Martha Washington of Colorado." Gracious and effective without being strident in any way, she fully supported her husband.

John Routt spent the majority of his first year in office clearing the way for the territory to become a state. A good many Easterners objected to this idea. One New York publication went so far as to print, "There is something repulsive in the idea that a few handfuls of miners and reckless bushwackers should have the same representation in the Senate as Pennsylvania, Ohio, and New York." A Philadelphia newspaper wrote, "Colorado consists of Denver, the Kansas Pacific Railway, and Scenery."

Forging ahead, Routt called for an election of representatives to attend the constitutional convention, and he examined and helped determine the contents of what would be Colorado's state constitution. He worked with this group of citizens, and their efforts were approved by a popular vote on July 1, 1876. A huge celebration was held on July 4. The official proclamation of statehood, which came on August 1, 1876, in a bill signed by Ulysses S. Grant, was due at least in part to Routt's effective leadership. Colorado had become the thirty-eighth state.

Routt had been popular and effective as territorial governor, but a number of resident candidates were vying for the new position of governor of the State of Colorado. In an effort at party solidarity, the other candidates came to Routt and said they would retire from the race in his favor. Routt faced the Democratic candidate, Bela M. Hughes. Although short and stout, Routt had jet black hair and was a striking figure. Choosing to meet and greet people face to face, rather than making speeches, he successfully campaigned and won the election by about one thousand votes.

As the new governor, Routt faced a number of issues including economic problems created by crop devastations caused by grasshopper infestations in 1874 and 1875. Routt immediately requested funds to try to exterminate the insects. He also called on the federal government to live up to its agreements and treat Native Americans fairly while at the same time pleading for the establishment of well-trained troops that could be called on to handle any uprisings. Routt attempted to have the federal government pay the cost of outfitting and supplying troops.

A cornerstone of the new governor's efforts to establish the state of Colorado was to build a sound financial base. Routt recommended an increase in property evaluation to help provide revenue. He also took a strong interest in educational issues. Citing that 45 percent of children were not in school, Routt sought to bolster public education by increasing the length of the school year. In 1879, he proposed compulsory attendance in schools with the allocation of school funds based on average daily attendance.

Routt faced challenges in many other areas. He dealt with a dispute involving the merger of the Colorado Central and the Kansas Pacific Railroads. He had to face the squatters in Creede who had seized state lands for mining claims, built structures on them and defied anyone to take them. And from the very beginning of his political life, Routt and his wife proved strong supporters of women's suffrage. In 1878, he arranged a speaking tour for Susan B. Anthony and personally escorted her throughout the state. At one point on this tour, when there was no speaker's platform, he climbed on a barrel while Anthony climbed on another to make their case. Colorado became the first state to grant women voting rights through a popular election in 1893, and the first woman to register to vote in the state was Eliza Routt. She was the first woman to serve on the Colorado Board of Agriculture at the State Agricultural College (now Colorado State University) in Fort Collins. While connected with the university, Eliza Routt helped establish the School of Domestic Economy, ensuring a foothold for women in higher education.

Although he had limited means, Routt had invested a number of times in mining properties without success. In 1877, he had been persuaded to take out a personal loan and buy a Leadville silver mine called the Morning Star, which yielded two types of ore: a lead-bearing sand and ore heavy with silver. Because he had little left after his $10,000 investment, Routt had hired only a few men to work at the mine. Busy as governor, Routt decided to sell a part ownership in the mine to George Corning and Jasper Watson. Whenever possible, Routt visited the mine and worked there himself. He took off his suit, put on miner's garb and handled a pick and shovel. Routt slept on the floor of a cabin nearby. At a New Year's reception in 1879, he announced that as soon as he left the governor's office, he would be heading to his mine in Leadville.

True to his word, Routt started working at the mine full-time. Occasionally, a few pockets of low-grade ore would be found. Finally, they uncovered an immense deposit of carbonate ore. Within two weeks, the profits of the mine were sufficient to cover all the invested funds and yield a considerable profit. Routt now had a new name: "Bonanza King." Routt and his partners incorporated as the Leadville National Mining and Milling Company with a capital stock of $1 million. Routt headed the directors of the firm, which had offices in New York and Boston.

In 1881, Routt went to New York and sold his share of the company for half a million dollars. Routt invested in other claims, including buying one-half of the Red Jacket mine, which turned out to be one of the richest silver veins in the district.

Routt also invested far less successfully in cattle, buying a two-thousand-acre ranch near Fort Collins. With his money, Routt installed Eliza and the family in a mansion in Denver at the intersection of Fourteenth and Welton Streets.

In January 1880, Routt was elected to the board of directors of the First National Bank of Denver. He accepted a similar position with the Denver, Utah and Pacific Railroad. Late that year, the Routts had their first and only child together. Lila Elkin Routt was born on November 11, 1880. Lila soon became the center of the Routts' world and shared her mother's interest in music.

John Routt was now a wealthy man and a generous one. He pleased his wife, Eliza, by hiring an American sculptor to make a lovely statue of their daughter, Lila. He hosted a Colorado visit of his old benefactor, Ulysses S. Grant, who not only stayed in Denver but also traveled in the mountains, including up to Leadville. In 1885, when Grant died, having lost most of his money in poor investments, Routt came to his aid one last time by paying Grant's funeral expenses.

Although he had left the governor's office and devoted his time to successful mining ventures, John Routt continued to be interested in politics. Active in the Colorado Republican Party, Routt tried unsuccessfully to secure nomination to the federal cabinet and to make a run for the United States

Senate. Finally, to the surprise of many, he ran for mayor of Denver. He may have run for this office out of party loyalty or perhaps to get in the public spotlight again. Routt served as mayor from 1883 to 1885. He immediately made putting the city on a sound financial foundation his top priority.

After serving his term as mayor, Routt dropped out of the public eye. But once again, the Colorado Republican Party was divided into factions. A Democrat was elected governor in 1882, and party leaders scrambled to find a candidate to run in 1890. They turned to John Routt, who was now sixty-four years old. Routt was nominated by acclimation and won the governorship, even through Democrats took the offices of treasurer, attorney general and superintendent of public instruction.

Splinter groups within the Republican Party made it impossible to pick a Speaker of the House. Arguments were so heated that Routt was asked to send in troops to prevent a riot at the capitol. Routt refrained but did put house soldiers in the State armory in case they were needed. Routt submitted the matter to the Supreme Court to decide which of two men was the legal Speaker of the House. This move earned Routt the nickname of the "Peace Governor."

As soon as the legislature could set to work, Routt tackled finance. The previous state treasurer made himself a wealthy man off state funds, so Routt signed an act prohibiting treasurers from loaning state monies and "making profit for themselves." He also sought legislation limiting the powers of the land commissioners. Routt advocated economy and insisted that the outstanding state indebtedness be paid off. He demanded reforms in the conduct of elections.

After finishing his term as governor, Routt retained only one public office, as a member of the board of capitol managers. Walking about with a stout hickory stick that he preferred to gold-headed canes, he proudly helped oversee the building of the $3.5 million statehouse. In 1897, the legislature repealed the statute providing $2,500 a year for members of the board. In spite of his own personal wealth, Routt resigned. He thought this act was wrong and asked, "What is the state coming to when it expects its officials to work for nothing?" In ill health, he left for Europe with his wife and daughter, Lila. On his return, he and his family lived in Denver. Lila married Edward Collins in 1906, and Eliza Routt died the following year at age sixty-eight. Five months later, John Routt died on August 13, 1907, at the age of eighty-one. Both died in their daughter's home, surrounded by their children.

Routt's service to Colorado was recognized in many ways. Routt County, one of sixty-four counties in the state of Colorado, with its county seat in

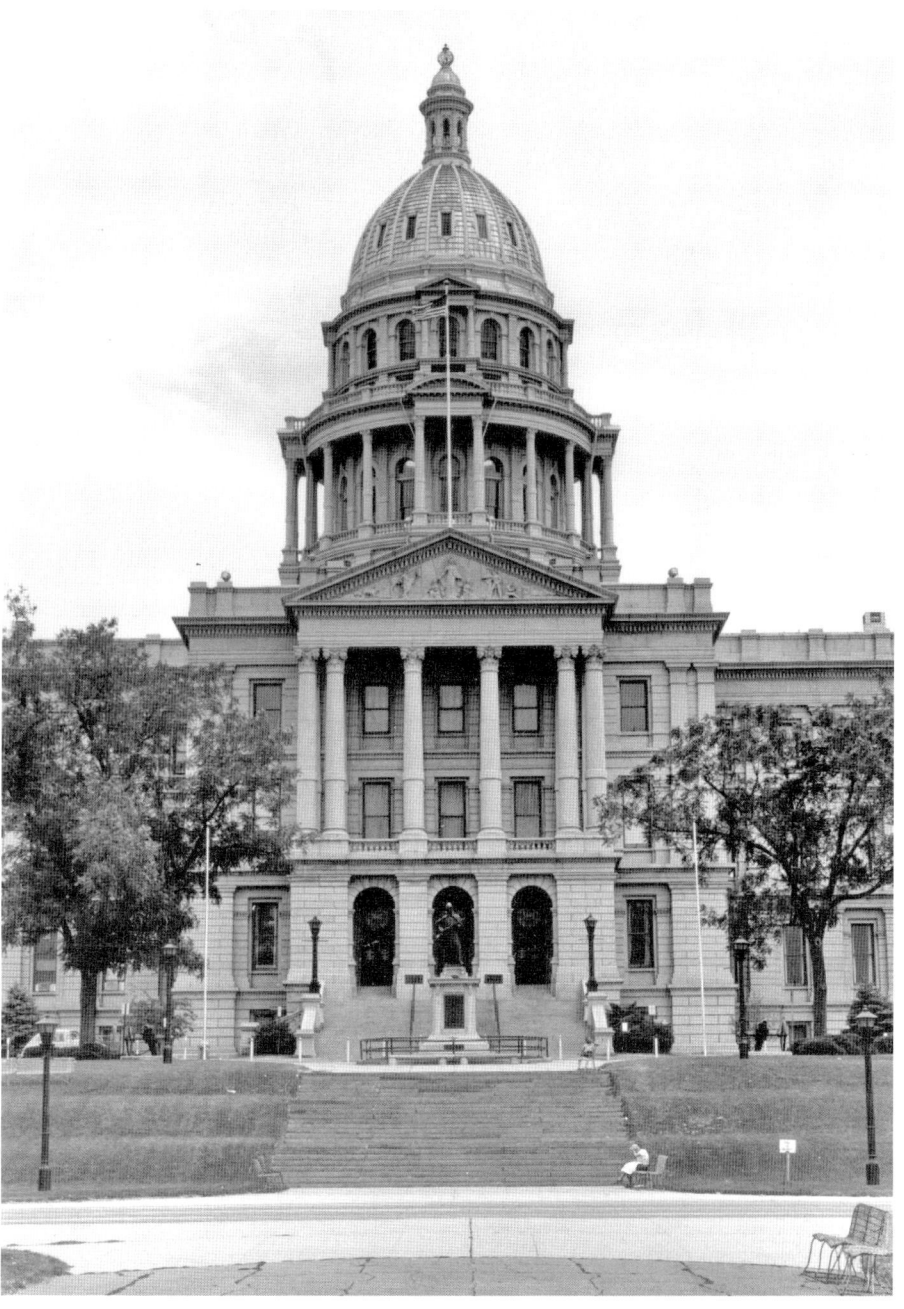

The Colorado State Capitol in Denver. *David L. Perry.*

Steamboat Springs, was created on January 29, 1879, and named after him. Routt National Forest also carries his name. Routt is one of seven men and women honored with a stained glass portrait window in the senate chamber in the state capitol in Denver. At his funeral oration, Routt was described as "sheriff, captain, colonel, federal officer, governor, miner, cattleman, politician, statesman, and good citizen. He served Colorado long and well, and…everyone who spoke of John Long Routt recognized his invincible honesty."

James "Rocky Mountain Jim" Nugent and Lady Isabella Bird

1828?–1874 and 1831–1904 •
Muggins Gulch and Longs Peak

Not for the first time that afternoon, Isabella Bird's long hiking skirt became snagged on one of the countless boulders along the precipitous trail up Longs Peak, rising high in the Rocky Mountains. Barely pausing, Jim Nugent whipped out his hunting knife and cut off the offending piece of cloth that was jammed between the rocks. Putting his knife away, Nugent, ever the gallant gentleman, once again began lifting, pulling and coaxing Bird up to the top of the peak.

Although James Nugent, known best as "Rocky Mountain Jim," was experienced in climbing mountains, surely he had never before guided anyone quite like Lady Isabella Bird. And surely she had never been guided by anyone like Rocky Mountain Jim. In addition to climbing mountains, Nugent was a hunter, trapper, rancher and teller of tall tales. He told so many stories, especially about himself and his youth, that it is next to impossible to determine the truth. Sometimes he said he was the nephew of a southern gentleman. At other times, he was the son of a British army officer stationed in Montreal, Canada. Occasionally he reported that he was a defrocked priest or a former schoolmaster. Frequently he said that he had worked for the Hudson's Bay Company and the American Fur Company. Most historians agree that he had been a trapper for one or both of these companies.

Wherever he came from, in the summer of 1871, James Nugent, riding his big white mule, with his dog trailing behind them, made his way up the Colorado River to Grand Lake. There, Nugent made camp, left his mule and took his knife and revolver to follow the tracks of a deer that he hoped to have for supper. He found the deer, but unfortunately, he also found a large bear, with her two cubs. The bear rushed Nugent, who managed to get out his gun and fire several times. The shots did not stop the bear, which swiftly caught and mauled Rocky Mountain Jim. She bit him in the arm and the scalp, scraped her huge paw across his face and crushed his arm. Nugent lost consciousness.

When he woke, bloodied and battered, Nugent somehow dragged himself back to his camp and managed to climb on his mule. Though his memory of that journey was confused, he remembered falling off his mount several times. Finally, he made it to Grand Lake, where two men found him half dead and called for a doctor from some miles away. Although he had lost a thumb, the sight in one eye and the right side of his face was badly disfigured, Nugent recovered. By August, he was well enough to ride over the mountains to the Estes Park area, where he built himself a cabin in Muggins Gulch and settled down to a solitary life of trapping and raising a few cattle.

Not too far below Nugent's place was that of another settler, Griff Evans, a Welshman, who was living in an old cabin that had belonged to Joel Estes, the very first settler in the area. When Estes and his family left, tired of the hard and cold winters, Griff Evans moved in. At first, Nugent and Evans got along well, except for occasional quarrels when both had been drinking. But their friendship cooled in time and ended tragically.

Instead of continuing with ranching, Griff Evans realized that he could make a much better living by catering to visitors. He and his wife built and ran a guesthouse where people could come to stay, enjoy the scenery, hunt and fish and eat good country food. Evans eventually built a hotel for visitors, and rustic cabins around the small lake he formed by building a low dam on Fish Creek. A tourist paid eight dollars a week for room and board.

An early lodger with Griff Evans was an English woman, Isabella Bird. She was born in 1831 and had grown up in Yorkshire, England. Although sickly at home, she seemed to thrive when traveling. She had already been to Canada, Scotland, Australia and the Sandwich Islands (Hawaii), where she climbed Mona Loa. On her current visit to the United States, when she was forty-two years old, Bird landed in San Francisco and went by train through northern California to Greeley, Colorado. She was in Longmont, waiting to take a train to New York, when she was put in touch with two law school students. They agreed she could ride along with them on horseback as they were about to set out for the Rocky Mountains, which she very much wanted to visit.

Escorted by the two men, Bird rode up St. Vrain Canyon into the Estes Park area. In her writings, she described her first look at the towering

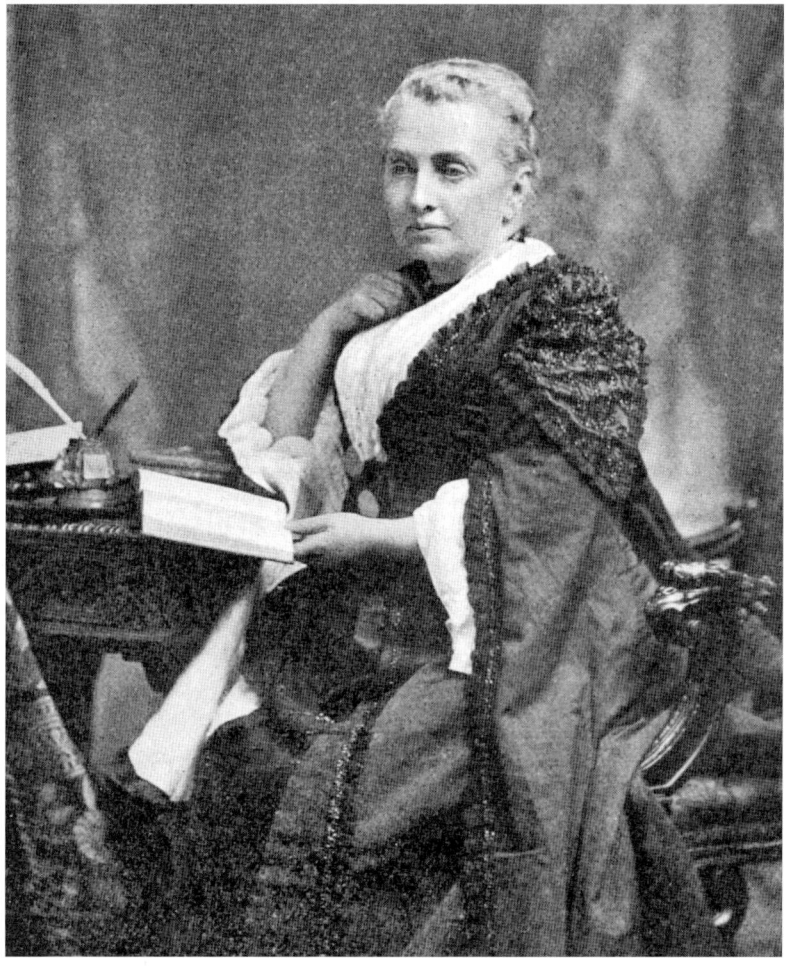

Isabella Bird. *From* The Life of Isabella Bird: (Mrs. Bishop) *by Anna M. Stoddart.*

mountain: "Longs Peak was aflame, the glory of the glowing heaven was given back from the earth." Bird was a colorful sight herself, riding her pony called Birdie and wearing a Hawaiian riding dress, which included a jacket, a skirt reaching to the ankles and full Turkish trousers.

One look at Longs Peak had been enough to convince her that she had to climb it, although only two women so far had achieved this feat, and she was by no means an experienced mountain climber. Everyone she talked with discouraged her from such an undertaking, but they all said if anyone could take her to the top, it was Rocky Mountain Jim Nugent. Bird took lodging with Griff Evans, who, like all the others, told her she certainly could not climb the peak. It was too difficult a climb, and it was too late in the year. But after Evans left on a trip to Denver, Bird went to Nugent's cabin to seek his services as a guide.

In her book, *A Lady's Life in the Rocky Mountains*, which was published in 1879, Isabella Bird described her first look at Nugent's home:

> *Among the scrub, not far from the track, was a rude, black, log cabin...with smoke coming out of the roof and window...it looked like the den of a wild beast. The mud roof was covered with lynx, beaver and other skins laid out to dry, beaver paws were pinned out on the logs, a part of a carcass of a deer hung, at one end of the cabin, a skinned beaver lay in front of a heap of peltry just within the door, and antler of deer and old horseshoes lay about the den.*

In letters to her sister and in the book she later published, Isabella Bird described her first look at James Nugent, concentrating on the unscarred side of his face. She reported that after Nugent's dog began to bark at her approach, Rocky Mountain Jim came to the door of the cabin: "His face was remarkable. He is a man about forty-five, and must have been strikingly handsome. He has large, grey-blue eyes, deeply set, handsome aquiline nose, and a very handsome mouth. His face was smooth shaven except for a dense mustache and imperial. Tawny hair in thin, uncared-for curls, fell from under his hunter's cap and over his collar. Desperado was written in large letters all over him."

Bird convinced Nugent to guide her up Longs Peak. The two law students, Rocky Mountain Jim and Isabella Bird left Muggins Gulch on horseback early one morning in late September and made camp at timberline, just opposite a huge snowbank on the slope of the peak. They spent the evening around the campfire with Nugent telling his spellbinding stories and reading some poetry that he had written. This spot is now called Jim's Grove. In later reports, she and the mountain man were widely rumored to have had a romantic affair. Bird wrote that he was "a man any woman might love but no sane woman would marry."

At sunrise the next morning, they were off again. Nugent and the two men walked, while Bird continued to ride her pony. When it was no longer possible to ride, all four of them went on foot through what is called "the notch." One of the law students described how Nugent got Bird up the mountain, "by alternately pulling and pushing her." At the top, the party split up, going two different routes to get to the famous keyhole rock

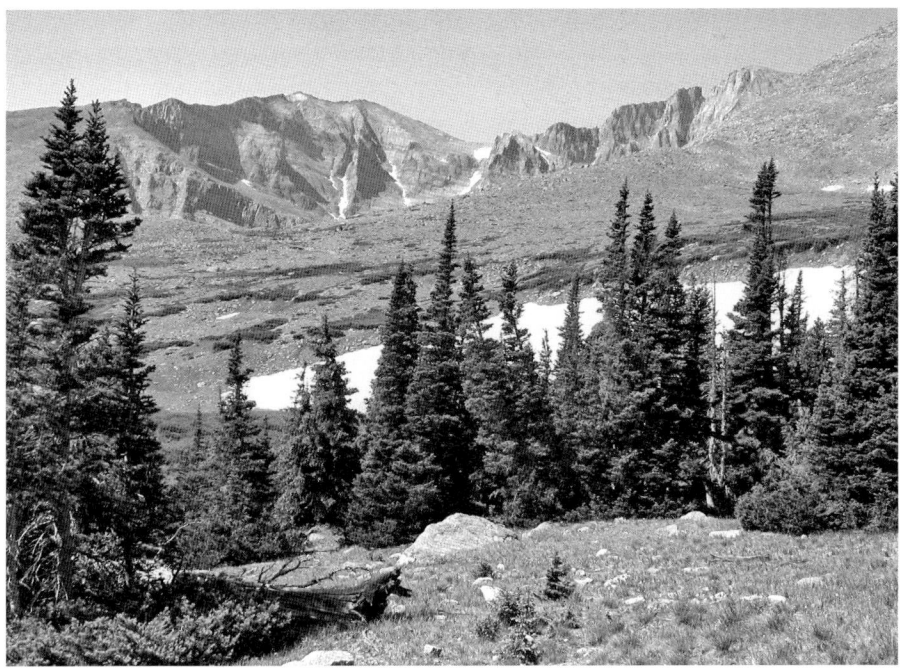

Jim's Grove is a timberline camping site east of Longs Peak in Rocky Mountain National Park. *David L. Perry.*

formation. Bird went with Nugent, and the two men went together. The two men reached the keyhole first and waited for Bird and Nugent. Then all four went to the summit.

Bird was so tired by this point that they stayed only a short time and started down again. When they got back to the spot where Bird's horse had been tethered, Bird was so exhausted she had to be lifted onto the animal. The men walked, and Bird rode back to their camp. There, Bird had to be lifted down from the horse. They spent another night at the campsite so that Bird could recover. The next morning, they returned to Griff Evans's cabin.

Isabella Bird stayed on in the Estes Park area until December and then returned home. Although she corresponded with Rocky Mountain Jim, she never saw him again.

Shortly after Isabella Bird left the area, which is now at the edge of Rocky Mountain National Park, another person was about to cause fatal trouble between Rocky Mountain Jim and Griff Evans. His name was the Right Honorable Windham Thomas Wyndham-Quin, Fourth Earl of Dunraven. The earl had heard of exceptional hunting in the American West. He arrived in Denver in 1872 and made his way to Muggins Gulch. Griff Evans welcomed the earl and his companions.

The earl was delighted with the good hunting, so he returned in 1873 and 1874. He decided to buy the Estes Park area as his own private hunting preserve. Since he was not an American citizen, he could not buy land under the Homestead Act. He hired an agent named Theodore Whyte. Whyte would hire a man for $100 to file a claim under the Homestead Act for 160 acres of land. The man would then turn over the deed to Whyte. Whyte might lay four logs out in a square to show that an attempt was made to construct a cabin, and he might plow an eighth of an acre. This would satisfy the minimum requirements of the Homestead Act. The earl formed the Estes Park Company, Limited, and all the claims Whyte bought were transferred to the company. Soon Dunraven claimed control of 15,000 acres.

News of this obvious land swindle appeared in the newspapers, and there were numerous protests. When legitimate settlers arrived, wanting to homestead this land, they started challenging these titles.

Griff Evans supported Dunraven in his land speculation because it increased the number of visitors for his business. Rocky Mountain Jim Nugent violently opposed Dunraven and refused to let the earl have any access through his property at Muggins Gulch. These disputes with the earl made things unpleasant between Nugent and Griff Evans. Adding to their difference of opinion over the Earl of Dunraven were rumors that in some way Nugent had insulted Griff Evans's daughter. Yet another rumor suggested that Rocky Mountain Jim and the Earl of Dunraven were both interested in a woman who lived in the area.

What is not rumor, but rather fact, is that Nugent and a friend named Brown were coming back from a trip and stopped to water their horses at a little stream near Griff Evans's house. The Earl of Dunraven and Griff Evans were in one of Evans's cabins, drinking. On seeing Nugent, the earl handed Griff Evans a double-barreled shotgun and encouraged him to shoot Nugent. As Nugent passed near, Evans shot twice in rapid succession without warning. The first shot missed, but the second eventually proved fatal. Nugent fell from his horse with buckshot in his body and head. Nugent refused to be carried into Evans's house for treatment, so he was bandaged as best as possible by the creek and taken to his own home. A doctor attended him, and for a time, it appeared Rocky Mountain Jim might survive, but he died several days later.

The matter did not come to trial for some time, and by that date, Brown, who might have been a powerful witness, had disappeared. Some suggested he was paid to leave the area. The earl of Dunraven made it clear that he approved of the shooting and that Rocky Mountain Jim had come to Griff Evans's place intent on causing trouble. At trial, Evans was not convicted of a crime.

The land dispute did not end with the death of Rocky Mountain Jim. Theodore Whyte, who had been hired by the earl to care for his property, found it increasingly difficult to keep settlers off the earl's land. Whyte finally gave up and left in 1896. Faced with squabbles and lawsuits, the earl of Dunraven eventually sold most of his land to Enos Mills, Freelan O. Stanley and J.D. Sanborn of Greeley.

After her remarkable trip to Colorado, Isabella Bird returned home. She had vivid memories of Rocky Mountain Jim and Longs Peak. Bird wrote and published *A Lady's Life in the Rocky Mountains*, which became very popular. It went through seven editions and was one of the first books to publicize the wonders of this area.

Bird eventually married a clergyman and, after his death, traveled alone again as a missionary to India and went down the Yangtze and Han Rivers in China and Korea. She died in 1904 in Edinburgh at age seventy-three and at that time was planning another trip to China. Isabella Bird was elected as the first female member of the National Geographic Society.

Helen Hunt Jackson

1830–1885 • Colorado Springs

The well-dressed woman visiting the silver diggings in Georgetown, Colorado, stepped through a trapdoor to begin her guided trip down into the mine where the men were working. With only candlelight, she climbed into a sort of bucket that carried two people from the surface down to the tunnels where miners were working. Helen Hunt Jackson later wrote about the harrowing descent, reporting that for three minutes in a "swinging, twisting, bumping bucket, I fixed my eyes on that candle-flame as earnestly as if it had been a lighthouse, and I a sailor steering to shore by its guidance."

Helen was exhilarated by her trip deep in the mine, where she caught glimpses of glistening veins of silver and heard the noise of miners picking in the rock. Although it was frightening, on reaching the surface again, she said she would "not have missed it for anything" and quickly offered her guide money for having taken her on this journey. In an essay describing the trip, Helen writes that the guide declined money for himself but suggested she might want to make a donation to a reading room with books and newspapers that the miners were trying to set up.

Helen Hunt Jackson promised to help. In her published essay telling about her visit to the Terrible Mine in Georgetown, she tells of the miners' need for books and gave the guide's address. No doubt, books and papers began to pour in for the reading room because she had a wide audience. Whether it was seeking books for miners toiling in darkness or aid for Native Americans whom she believed were having their lands taken unfairly by the government, Helen wrote eloquently, and she always urged action.

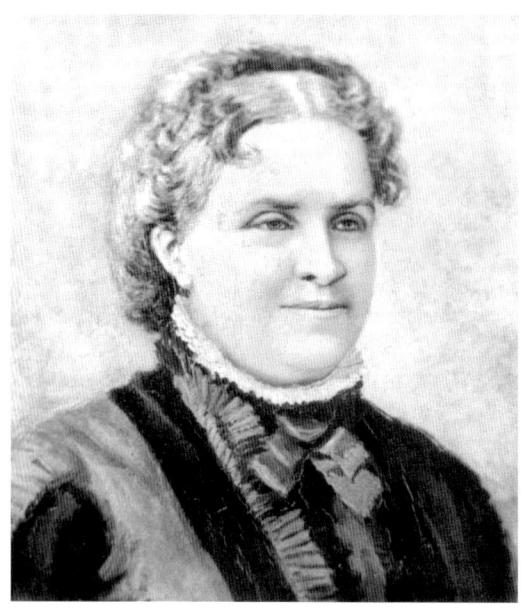

Helen Hunt Jackson. *Library of Congress.*

Helen Maria Fiske was born in Amherst, Massachusetts, in 1830, the older of two daughters. Her father, Nathan Welby Fiske, was a minister trained at Dartmouth and on the faculty of the College of Theology at Amherst College. Helen appeared to be radical and impulsive and often said, "I inherited nothing from either of my parents except my mother's gift for cheer." When Helen was only twelve, her mother died from tuberculosis, and three years later, her father died of the same disease.

After the deaths of her parents, Helen and her sister were separated. Helen lived in boarding schools until she became a teacher at the Abbott Institute, where she had been a student. In 1852, at age twenty-one, Helen married Edward Bissel Hunt, an army officer somewhat older than she, who had graduated second in his class at West Point. Fifteen months later, the couple had a son whom they named Murray. The little boy died of what was diagnosed as "dropsy of the brain" before reaching his first birthday. A second son, Warren Horsford Hunt (called Rennie) was born a year later in 1855.

The family of three lived happily. Helen and her son often followed her husband on his assignments. Considered a promising physicist, he wrote several papers for the *American Journal of Science*. When the Civil War began, Major Hunt was dispatched to Key West to defend Fort Taylor and then to Virginia. Next, in 1863, he was sent to the Brooklyn Naval Yard to test his own invention, a submarine gun, a sort of prototype of the modern torpedo. During testing, he was killed in an accident when he entered a chamber of a watertight hull that was filled with a deadly gas.

Just two years after this tragedy, Helen's son, Rennie, died of diphtheria. Helen's husband and two sons were buried next to each other at West Point. For months afterward, Helen shut herself in. Perhaps as a response to these terrible losses, Helen began to write poetry. She submitted a poem to the

New York Evening Post called "Keys to the Casket," which was published on June 9, 1865. She signed the poem "Marah" referencing "Ma of Rennie Hunt. This was the first of a series of poems. From this point on, Helen became serious about her writing. The best known of her Marah poems, "Lifted Over," sought to bring encouragement to other bereaved mothers.

Helen moved to Newport, Rhode Island, where she spent many hours a day writing poems, articles, reviews and children's stories. As one of her biographers, Antoinette May, notes, "A child of her times, she sensed almost immediately what people wanted to read and soon acquired the skill to give it to them." One of Helen's new friends and sponsors was the influential literary critic Thomas Wentworth Higginson. He called her "the most brilliant, impetuous, and thoroughly individual woman of her time, whose very temperament seemed mingled of sunshine and fire."

Helen quickly established connections with several newspapers and magazines that regularly published her writings. Among these were the *Atlantic Monthly*, *Scribner's Monthly*, the *New York Independent* and the *Nation*. For many of these early works, she used the pseudonym Saxe Holm since, at this time, writing for publication was considered by many to be "unwomanly." It was some years before she admitted to authorship and received credit for her writings, after which Ralph Waldo Emerson acknowledged her work and called her the "greatest American woman poet" and even suggested the word "woman" might well be omitted from that evaluation.

Among her circle of literary friends, Helen included her childhood friend Emily Dickinson, who was only two months younger than Helen and had lived just down the street from her in Massachusetts. She had many famous summer friends in Newport, Rhode Island, such as Henry and William James, Julia Ward Howe, Nathaniel Hawthorne and Horace Greeley. At this time, Newport was reputed to have more resident authors than any other city in the country. Although Helen generally didn't approve of female lecturers, after meeting Anna Leonowens and wanting to share the governess's experiences in Siam, Helen arranged for her to give a lecture at the Newport Opera House. Neither could have imagined that those adventures in Siam would one day result in the successful musical *The King and I*.

As a young widow, Helen enjoyed attending house parties at her friends' homes and going on picnics and sailing parties, but writing remained important to her, and she treated it as a business. Once she began making money from her writing, she gained a reputation with editors for insisting on good payment. She said, "I don't write for money—I write for love—I

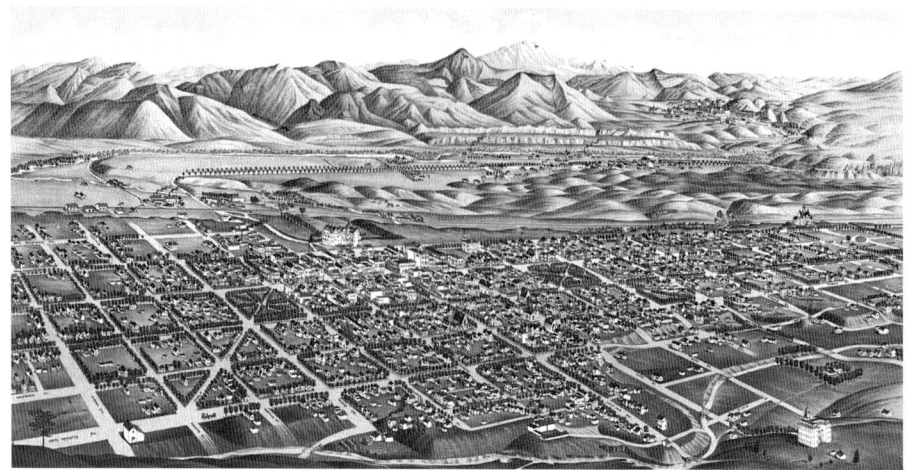

An 1882 map of Colorado Springs, Colorado. *Wikimedia Commons.*

print for money." She insisted that if selling one's writing was an honorable business for men, it ought to be for women, too.

Since both her parents had died of tuberculosis, when Helen developed a constant cough and was diagnosed with consumption, she took seriously her doctor's advice to move to Colorado. Perhaps she and her doctor were aware of the comment made by P.T. Barnum, who once said Colorado people were the most disappointed he ever saw. "Two-thirds of them came here to die, and they can't do it. This wonderful air brings them back from the verge of the tomb."

Helen took a train to Colorado Springs in November 1873, hoping to benefit from its sunshine and dry air. Despite her sadness at leaving her friends in the East, she began writing even as she rode the train. Commonly, Helen took notes in pencil on a yellow pad because she said "a pen slows me down," referring to the necessity at that time of stopping and dipping the pen into ink while writing. In no way did she want to slow the flow of her thoughts.

Helen's first impressions of Colorado Springs appeared in an essay on August 13, 1874, published in the *Independent*. She wrote, "I shall never forget my sudden sense of hopeless disappointment at the moment when I first looked on the town. It was a gray day in November, I had crossed the continent, ill, disheartened, to find a climate that would not kill. There stretched before me, to the east, a bleak, bare, unrelieved desolate plain. There rose behind me, to the west, a dark range of mountains, snow-topped, rocky-walled, stern, cruel, relentless. Between lay the town—small, straight, new, treeless."

Looking about her, a disheartened Helen wrote: "One might die of such a place alone." Her spirits were not raised when she moved into her new residence only to learn that locally it was called "Deadman's Row" in reference to the many tuberculosis patients who had died on that street. When a vacancy occurred in the Colorado Springs Hotel, Helen was quick to move there. This beautiful hotel had been built by General William Palmer, who had founded Colorado Springs, and it boasted of many well-known visitors over the years.

Another hotel guest whom Helen met at dinner was a bachelor, six years younger than she, named William Sharpless Jackson. Jackson had worked for the Superior and Mississippi Railroad, a company that built railroad cars. He worked his way up to company treasurer and came west to be secretary-treasurer of the Denver and Rio Grande Railroad, owned by General Palmer. Eventually, he became vice-president of that railroad and then became president of a bank in Colorado Springs.

When she next described Colorado in the *Independent*, Helen wrote, "That plain and those mountains are to me well-nigh the fairest spot on earth." She did not mingle much with other people in the town, several of whom thought her very standoffish. To the annoyance of the locals, she also did not attend church, and she offended others by admitting in print that she "worshiped God best in nature."

On many of her trips to see the Colorado countryside, Helen either rode a burro or took a private coach. She explains this preference in one of her essays on Georgetown. "The public coaches are here, as everywhere, uncomfortable, overloaded, inexorable. I know of no surer way to rob a journey of all its finest pleasures than to commit one's self to one of these vehicles. It means being obliged to get up at hours you abhor, to sit close to people you dislike, to eat when you are not hungry, to go slowest when there is nothing to see and fastest when you would gladly linger for hours, to be drenched with rain, choked with dust, and never have a chance to pick a flower. It means misery."

William Jackson soon asked Helen to marry him, but she put him off, saying she needed time to think. Apparently she worried about the age difference between them and thought their separate careers might cause conflict. Helen spent the summer traveling throughout Colorado, gathering material for her essays, and then went east to see her literary friends. While she was away, Jackson bought a house in Colorado Springs and, upon her return, convinced Helen to agree to marry him in the following fall of 1875.

Both agreed that they would each continue with their careers after marriage, although this meant that they sometimes lived apart or traveled alone.

Helen had decided opinions about her new house, pointing out that the best views were from the kitchen, where she did not expect to spend much of her time. So she made major alterations, moving the entrance from Weber Street to East Kiowa and changing the back porch and kitchen into a living room with views of Cheyenne Mountain and Pikes Peak. Under her directions, the gingerbread Gothic house was changed into a showcase, with alcoves, fireplaces and floor-to-ceiling shelves for books. When the remodel was finished, the couple moved in and often entertained eastern friends. Helen continued to write and make trips back to New England.

As she approached fifty, Helen Hunt Jackson seemed happy and content. Then her husband horrified her by announcing that he would run for state senator from Colorado Springs. She seldom went with him to political rallies and said, "To see my husband in that crew of liars and psychopaths will almost kill me." She was greatly relieved when he did not win.

Helen Hunt Jackson continued to pursue her writing. When she had first come to Colorado in 1873, even before the state had been admitted to the Union, she had planned only a short visit, a time to recover from illness. But she had remained and remarried, and it was in Colorado where she wrote fifteen of her seventeen books. Many of these are for children, such as *Nelly's Silver Mine*, but she also wrote poetry and travel articles for adults, some of which included vivid descriptions of historic Colorado places and detailing the living conditions of early settlers.

During late summer in 1879, Helen was invited to Boston to join a celebration honoring Oliver Wendell Holmes's seventieth birthday. One of her poems would be read during the festivities. During her trip, Helen suddenly found a new cause and a new purpose in life. Everyone she met was attending and talking about lectures being given by a group of Plains Indians, the Poncas, in which they described the terrible treatment they had received from the U.S. government. Helen went to one of these lectures given by Chief Standing Bear and his interpreter Bright Eyes and became so interested that, on that very night, she sat down and wrote an article for the *Independent*. It was the beginning of her dedicated efforts at Indian reforms. She did much of her research for her writing in New York City's Astor Library.

On May 21, 1880, Helen signed a contract with Harper & Brothers to publish a book, which she titled *A Century of Dishonor*. This time, her own name, rather than a pseudonym, appeared on the front cover of the book. Citing public documents, Helen showed how poorly the government had treated Native Americans. The book devoted a chapter apiece to the Delawares, the Cheyennes, the Nez Perces, the Sioux, the Poncas, the Winnebagoes and the Cherokees and describes three massacres of Indians by whites, including Colorado's notorious Sand Creek Massacre. The chapters are written in great detail, and the information in the book is supported by fifteen appendices. In her conclusion, Helen wrote, "It makes little difference where one opens the record of the history of the Indians; every page and every year has its dark stain…Colorado is as greedy and unjust in 1880 as was Georgia in 1830, and Ohio in 1795; and the United States Government breaks promises now as deftly as then, and with an added ingenuity from long practice."

Antoinette May, one of Hunt's biographers, writes, "In 1881, Helen Hunt Jackson declared war on the U.S. government with the publication of *A Century of Dishonor*, a scathing indictment of federal Indian policy." In that report, Helen told how the United States government had treated its native people from 1776 to the 1880s. Upon publication of *A Century of Dishonor*, Helen Hunt Jackson sent a copy to each congressman at her own expense. One result was that in March 1881, Congress passed a bill allowing individual Poncas to choose a piece of land and to receive reimbursement for their losses. It also sparked a paper duel with Secretary of the Interior Carl Schurz. The result of Helen's barrage of petitions, tracts and newspaper articles finally led to her appointment by President Chester Arthur as special commissioner to study the condition of the Indians in California.

This was the first time that a woman had been given such an important assignment, and Helen took her appointment seriously, journeying through the Santa Barbara, Los Angeles and San Diego areas. On one occasion, she wore a hat that included the entire head of a gray owl; upon realizing it frightened Native American children, who thought of it as a death symbol, she quickly removed it. She wrote and submitted her report on the California Mission Indians. Seeing that her report was largely ignored, Helen decided to take another approach. *Uncle Tom's Cabin* had had enormous influence as a popular piece of fiction exposing the plight of slaves in this country. Helen thought perhaps a fictionalized account of Native Americans might have a similar impact.

Determined to produce a strong national reaction, with her published novel, Helen returned to New York in the fall of 1883, staying in the Berkeley Hotel. There she began her novel, *Ramona*, incorporating what she had learned in California. The story centers on the life of Ramona Ortega, the daughter of an Indian woman and a Scotch seaman. Ramona is raised by Señora Gonzaga Moreno, who runs a sheep ranch and dotes on her son, Felipe. Ramona falls in love with an Indian sheepherder, Alessandro, and they elope. They suffer many hardships and are run off their land by Americans. Alessandro, almost out of his mind, rides off on an American's horse and is shot. In the meantime, Señora Moreno has died. Before the book ends, Felipe finds Ramona and marries her, and they return to Mexico.

Helen finished the book on March 8, 1884. In addition to a love story, *Ramona* is a piece of propaganda. It was serialized in the *Christian Union* and became very popular as a piece of fiction, eventually going through three hundred printings. It was also made into a pageant, a popular play and a motion picture.

On completing the book, Helen Hunt Jackson was exhausted and returned to Colorado to rest. Shortly thereafter, she took a fall down the stairs and suffered a compound fracture. When she also came down with a lingering cold and cough, Helen returned to California hoping that the warmer climate would improve her health. It did not, and she was soon confined to bed, where she kept up a letter writing campaign on behalf of Indian causes, especially those relating to citizenship and land rights. She had never loved San Francisco and did not want to die there. She was planning a trip into the mountains in hopes of a cure when she collapsed and subsequently died on August 8, 1885, at the age of fifty-four. Shortly before her death, Helen Hunt Jackson wrote to a friend, "A Century of Dishonor and Ramona are the only things I have done of which I am glad…They will live and they will bear fruit."

Often she had pleaded eloquently for those being oppressed. She was particularly forceful in advocating justice for Native Americans through *A Century of Dishonor* and *Ramona*. It was another two years after her death before the federal Dawes Act was drawn up, bringing about many of the reforms for which Jackson had worked, addressing allotting lands to the Native Americans, granting citizenship and doing away with the requirement of treating each tribe as a separate nation requiring separate treaties. Her persistence had brought about changes in national policy.

Upon the death of her friend Helen Hunt Jackson, Emily Dickinson sent a note of sympathy to William Jackson. Dickinson wrote, "Helen of Troy will die, Helen of Colorado, never. 'Dear friend, can you walk?' were the last words I wrote to her—'Dear friend, I can fly.' her immortal reply."

The Tabors

Horace Tabor 1830–1899 • Augusta Tabor 1833–1895 • Elizabeth McCourt (Baby Doe) Tabor 1854–1935 • Leadville and Denver

All eyes were on the radiant, beautiful, blond bride. She wore around her neck a rope of pearls rumored to have been the very ones used by Queen Isabella of Spain to finance the first voyage of Columbus to the New World. The site of the wedding ceremony and reception held on March 1, 1878, and presided over by a Catholic priest was the Willard Hotel in Washington, D.C. Among the distinguished guests was the president of the United States, Chester Alan Arthur. The proud, mustachioed bridegroom, a member of the U.S. Senate, was known to all as the Silver King.

The fairy tale elements of the lavish Washington wedding masked some strange truths. Horace Tabor, the bridegroom, served as a senator for only thirty days. And in spite of the Catholic ceremony, not only had the bride and groom both been married before, they had also secretly married each other several months before. It did not take long after the wedding for these facts to come out in endless gossip and newspaper articles, marking another bizarre episode in the lives of the Tabors: Horace, Augusta and Baby Doe.

In 1830, Horace Austin Warner Tabor was born in Holland, Vermont, a small farming village about three miles from the Quebec border. In his teens, Horace became apprenticed to a stonecutter. He followed this trade for eight years, working in quarries in Vermont, Massachusetts and Maine. In Maine, Tabor worked for a man named William Pierce. Pierce had always made a good living as a stonemason, hired a number of men and kept his family in comparative comfort. His daughter, Augusta, grew up in the Universalist-Unitarian Church, with the rather modern notion that women were the

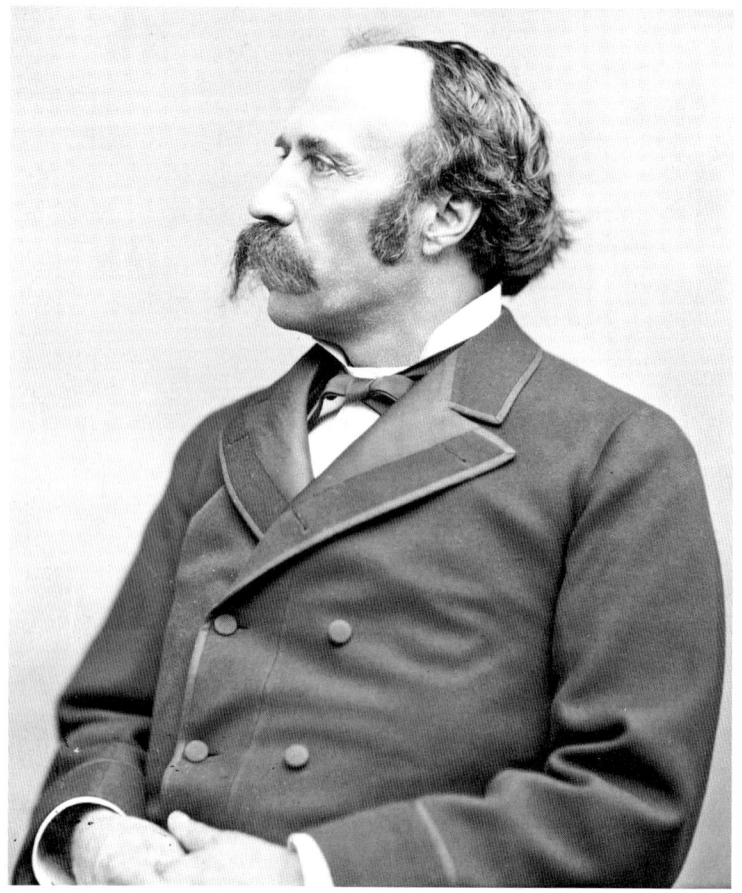

A photographic portrait of Horace Austin Warren Tabor by Matthew Brady/Levin Handy. *Wikimedia Commons.*

equals of men. Tabor met and fell in love with the boss's daughter, and he and Augusta became engaged.

Not wanting to remain a stonecutter, in 1855, Tabor decided to try farming and moved to the Kansas Territory with the New England Emigrant Aid Company to help populate the territory with antislavery settlers. Tabor chose 470 acres of farmland in the central valley of the Kansas River just below its junction with the Big Blue River.

In 1857, Tabor briefly returned to Maine to marry Augusta Pierce. After a month, the couple returned to Kansas. In *Tales of the Colorado Pioneers* by Alice Pelk Hill, Augusta is reported as recording her thoughts on first seeing the small cabin that was to be her new home. "I sat down upon the trunk and cried; I had not been deceived in coming to this place…But I was homesick and could not conceal it from those around me."

After that brief moment of despair, Augusta drew on her strong spirit and set right to work. She cared for the house, helped in the field, sold butter and eggs and cooked for some of the nearby bachelors. In October 1857, Augusta and Horace had a son. Horace happened to be away when the baby was born, and one of their boarders either delivered the baby or took Augusta to the doctor. In gratitude, the Tabors named their son Nathaniel Maxcy Tabor after him.

Although the Tabors had a good harvest in 1858, market prices for crops were low. The family survived, but life was hard. Horace Tabor decided to rent his farm and move his family west to Denver, then part of the Kansas Territory, along with the great surge of fifty-niners. At that time, Denver was a small, rough town, containing only eleven pioneer women. After staying a week, to recover from their journey, the Tabors moved as far as Golden, where Horace left Augusta and the baby temporarily while he searched out a place to settle.

Tabor chose Payne's Bar (now Idaho Springs) and moved his family to that mining camp. While Tabor prospected with pick and shovel, Augusta again helped out, tending to the home and selling baked goods to hungry miners. They survived their first Colorado winter and even paid off the debt on their farm in Kansas. The next year, Tabor found what he thought was a profitable claim and worked it until he moved Augusta and baby Maxcy to Denver for the winter months. When he returned, Tabor found that his claim had been "jumped" while he was away, based on an "abandoned" claim law, and that he could do nothing to reverse it.

In the months that followed, Augusta and Maxcy stayed in Denver and took in boarders while Horace remained in the mountains seeking gold and silver. Their next move was to Colorado City, where the Tabors were given a lot, since Augusta was the only woman in town. When Tabor decided his fortune was not to be made in Colorado City, they traveled for a month going over Ute Pass through South Park, arriving in California Gulch in May 1860. Again, Augusta found herself to be the first woman to arrive in town. In fact, in her honor, the men of the camp built her a log cabin in just two days.

Tabor again set to work, washing sand and gravel, swirling the mixture in a pan and collecting the heavier gold that sank to the bottom. He gleaned about $6,000 worth of gold that summer. Prospectors poured in, and the spot grew to be known as Oro City. Augusta boarded some miners, took in laundry and made friendships with the few other women who moved there. She also served as postmistress, and Horace used gold scales and weighed gold for the miners.

That winter, Augusta and Maxcy went back to Maine. Horace followed later. On their return trip to Colorado, they bought flour and other supplies for a store. In the spring, while Horace mined, Augusta opened and managed their store. Horace found a rich deposit in April, but it turned out to be only a small pocket. Again Tabor decided it was time to move on to richer diggings.

For the next seven years, the Tabors lived in Colorado in an area on the other side of the Mosquito Range known as Buckskin Joe. In 1863, Tabor was appointed postmaster of the little town, which boasted a newspaper and theater and served as the county seat until Fairplay grew in population and took away that honor. Although Tabor had no more success here than he had in Oro, the Tabors' store, which was in front of the cabin that served as their home, did well. They sold groceries and mining equipment. Augusta put in a garden and raised vegetables. She also sewed clothes for her son and husband. People gave Augusta most of the credit for their flourishing family, because Horace often took time off to fish or play cards.

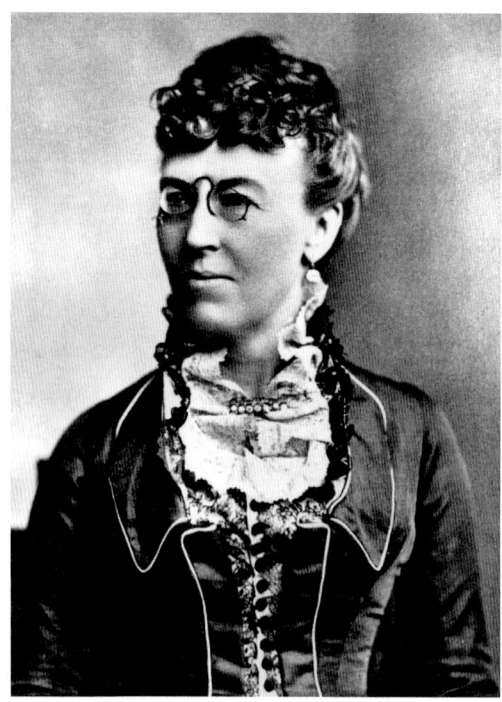

Augusta Tabor. *National Mining Hall of Fame and Museum.*

In time, Buckskin Joe's mines began to play out, and in the late spring of 1868, the Tabors moved back to Oro City and built a four-room cabin. By June, they were well reestablished. Horace became postmaster again, they opened another store and Augusta took in boarders. Horace Tabor began to take more of an interest in politics in Lake County. He got himself elected county treasurer, serving from 1876 to 1880, and appointed his son, Maxcy, deputy treasurer to do most of the work.

When a second rush to California Gulch began, the Tabors moved their store a mile farther down, on the south side of Chestnut Street and by July 1877 had settled into the town, which came to be called Leadville. A year later, on January 26, 1878, Horace Tabor was elected as the town's first mayor. Business was good. Tabor advertised, "If you want anything from a small size needle to a large sized elephant, come and see me, for I positively declare I will not be undersold." The Tabors did well over the next ten years, becoming the richest residents in town.

This was a time when it was common for storekeepers to "grubstake" other miners. This meant they supplied food and equipment for prospectors with the understanding that if gold or silver was discovered, the "grubstaker" would be entitled to a portion of the claim. Tabor had often grubstaked miners, but never with great success. Finally, he hit it lucky. In April 1878, Tabor grubstaked two German miners, August Rische and George Hook. For a third of whatever they found, Tabor supplied them with seventeen dollars' worth of food and supplies. The miners went to Fryer Hill and staked a claim. A few days later, they came back for shovels, a hand drill and blasting powder to sink a shaft. This cost Tabor another forty dollars. The miners dug about twenty-seven feet and hit a vein of rich silver. They sunk a shaft on May 1, having discovered what was called the Little Pittsburg vein, a discovery that set off the Colorado silver boom.

The Little Pittsburg netted Tabor $500,000 in the next fifteen months. Tabor and his partners applied for a federal mining patent and ended up in court defending their claim. A compromise resulted in the Little Pittsburg Consolidated Mining Company. Tabor held a large percentage of the stock and invested in other holdings including the Chrysolite, the Little Eva, the Eaton, the Belle of Colorado, the Lime Mine and the Dolly Varden.

With his money, Tabor established a newspaper, a bank and an opera house in Leadville, and he built the Grand Opera House in Denver. He invested in real estate such as the Tabor Block in Denver and became known as Silver Dollar Tabor. Now a rich man, he began spending evenings in variety halls in the company of a number of different women.

In September 1879, Tabor sold his interest in the Little Pittsburg for $1 million. He bought the Matchless Mine for $117,000, and it proved to be a bonanza. Tabor bought over eight hundred shares of stock of the First National Bank in Denver and took Augusta on a trip East for six weeks. When they returned, Augusta remained in Denver, while Horace Tabor spent most of his time in a bachelor suite in Leadville. A successful businessman, Tabor no longer relied heavily on Augusta to help manage their affairs and keep the family financially afloat. The two often quarreled.

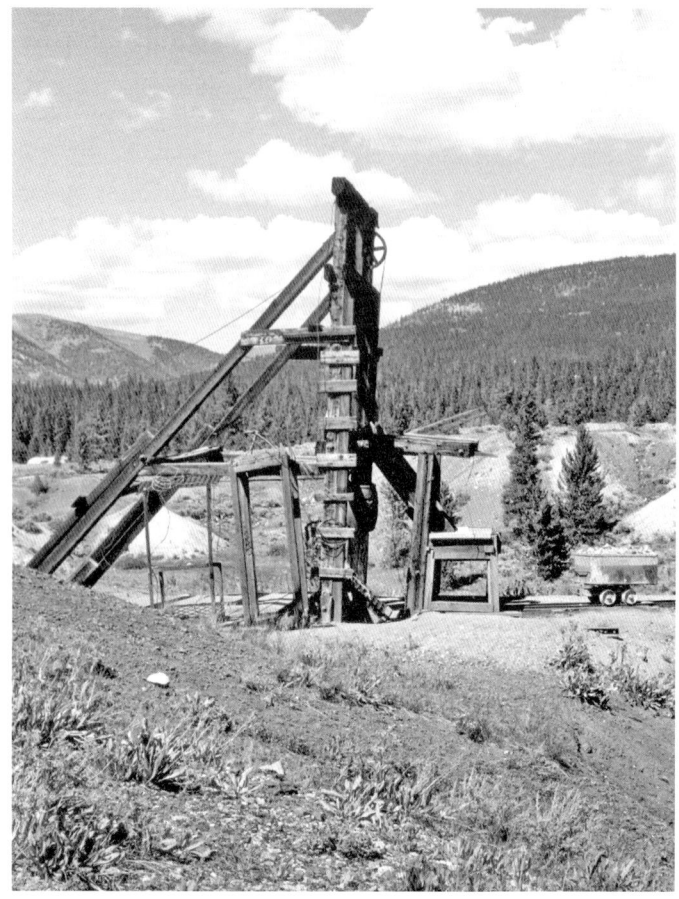

The hoist at the Matchless Mine near Leadville, Colorado. *David L. Perry.*

Tabor now turned his attention to state politics. Many people of his day said that Tabor's riches were simply the result of luck. And he was lucky, but as Eliot Lord observed in commenting on Tabor, "Fortune sometimes favors fools, but never long, and men who fail to use opportunities aright soon have no opportunities to misuse." Tabor was not one to misuse his opportunities. He prospected himself, grubstaked others and worked hard before getting rich. Once he had money, he invested wisely and made influential friends. Tabor used his connections and political savvy in 1878 to take part as a delegate from Lake County to the Republican State Central Committee meeting in Denver. The word began spreading that Tabor would make a great candidate for lieutenant governor.

Tabor secured the nomination and found himself in a mud slinging campaign with personal smears and attacks against him, some involving affairs with women. For a time, Tabor simply denied what was being said about him, but finally he brought a libel suit against William Loveland, director of the Union Pacific Railroad and the Democratic candidate for governor. He demanded an apology and $30,000. Months after the Republican victory, Tabor finally received his apology and dropped the suit. Tabor served as lieutenant governor of Colorado from 1879 to 1883.

Tabor moved to Denver to take up his governmental duties, using a private suite of rooms in the Evans block. His political office took only part of his time, so he occupied himself in other ways. He bought the Henry C. Brown home on Broadway, furnished it lavishly and brought Augusta to Denver, introducing her into its social whirl. Although Augusta presided pleasantly enough at grand receptions in their new home, she clearly did not like extravagance. Augusta had exchanged housework and gardening for a life of affluence and was not happy with the trade. She began to drift away from her husband, and in January 1881, Tabor gave her $100,000 and moved out of their house.

Tabor began living in a suite at the Windsor Hotel, of which he was part owner, and divided his time and interests between Denver and Leadville. He maintained an apartment and office in Leadville, and largely through his efforts, Leadville gained improved gas and waterworks, paved streets, fire protection and a national guard unit. He contributed to churches and charities and built the three-story Tabor Opera House in Denver, which opened in 1881.

Augusta took a trip to Europe in April 1881 and, on her return to Colorado, wrote her husband a letter apologizing for anything she might have said or done to offend him and asking for forgiveness. She begged that he take her to the grand opening of the Tabor Opera House and stop the gossip about their being separated. Augusta concluded by writing, "Pity, I beseech you and forgive me and let us bury the past and commence anew and my life shall be devoted to you forever."

Tabor refused her request. After its opening, headlines proclaimed that the new opera house was "perfection," but people also observed that the Tabor box, while garlanded with flowers, stood empty on opening night. In truth, far from wanting to reconcile with Augusta, Tabor now wanted a divorce, so he would be free to remarry, but was quiet and careful in how he pursued it.

After having served as lieutenant governor, Tabor was eyeing the position of senator. The likely candidate for this position was Henry Teller. But on the death of President Garfield, Chester Arthur offered Teller a cabinet position as secretary of the interior. Since the state legislature was in recess, this meant that Colorado governor Pitkin would appoint someone to fill Teller's vacancy briefly until the legislature met and appointed someone for the unexpired term. Although Leadville Republicans pushed the name of Tabor, Governor Pitkin chose to name George Chillcott from Pueblo.

Once Tabor decided to actively pursue the Senate position, he did not publically pursue a divorce from Augusta, knowing it would hurt him politically. He sent a business friend, however, to try to quietly work out divorce details with Augusta. He arranged to hold the divorce proceedings in a Durango court, as far from Denver as possible, and without Augusta ever appearing in court. Their divorce was granted by proxy.

Although the Durango divorce degree was signed by a judge, Augusta was not only absent from the courtroom but swore under oath that she had never received a copy of the complaint, and she appealed to the Colorado courts. Since it was unclear whether or not the divorce was legal, and to avoid further bad publicity, Tabor managed to convince Augusta to file her own petition for divorce, suing him on the grounds of desertion and nonsupport. This petition was granted in January 1883. Augusta received about $300,000 worth of property. Not long after the decree, Augusta Tabor sold her house and moved into an apartment in the Brown Palace Hotel. Then later, in failing health, Augusta went to California for the winter.

After his divorce, Horace Tabor was ready to begin a new life. He suffered from the unfavorable publicity that was the fallout of the divorce proceedings, so it wasn't surprising that the Republican nomination for the next senator went to Thomas Bowen. But as a sort of consolation prize in recognition of heavy monetary contributions to the party, Tabor was appointed by the legislature to serve as senator for the final thirty days of Teller's unexpired term.

Tabor was sworn in as a U.S. senator on February 2, 1883, and he worked very hard at his new job. He had an excellent attendance record and filled in vacancies on two important committees. But Tabor also used this one-month term as senator to give the new woman in his life a dream wedding. To the amazement of many, Tabor announced that he would marry Elizabeth McCourt Doe. At this time, Tabor was fifty-two, while his bride-to-be was only twenty-eight.

Elizabeth McCourt was born on May 5, 1854, and grew up in Oshkosh, Wisconsin. Acclaimed for her beauty and often called the "Belle of Oshkosh," Lizzie dreamed of a career as an actress in the local opera house. A fire in Oshkosh burned her family home and ruined her father's business. Greatly reduced in social circles, Lizzie sought marriage as a way out. She settled on Harvey Doe.

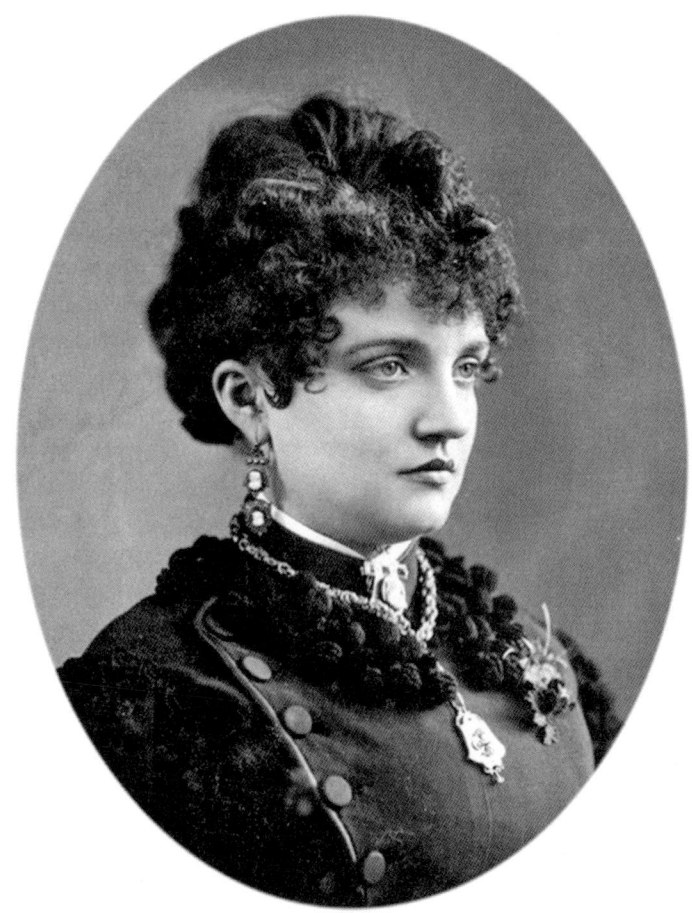

Baby Doe Tabor, 1883. *Wikimedia Commons.*

Lizzie and her new husband, William Harvey Doe, left Oshkosh by train for Colorado on their wedding night. They arrived in Denver in June 1877. After two weeks, they moved on to Central City, where Harvey Doe was to manage one of his father's gold mines. The mine played out, and Harvey was quickly reduced to working as an ordinary miner. Lizzie stirred up scandal by spending a lot of time with a handsome shop owner. The two often went out dancing, and Lizzie's nightlife earned her the nickname of "Baby Doe" and a reputation as a party girl.

In July 1879, Baby Doe gave birth to a stillborn son. After this, she and her husband grew apart, and in March 1880, Baby Doe divorced her husband after just three years of marriage on what most thought was a trumped-up grounds of adultery. It is not clear exactly when Baby Doe met Horace Tabor, but when she did, he was smitten with her beauty. Not long after meeting Baby Doe, Horace Tabor began plans to seek a divorce rather than just maintain a separation from Augusta.

Although Tabor finally managed to divorce Augusta, serve briefly as a senator and marry Baby Doe in a gala wedding, his future in politics was over. The press was relentless with its questions. How could a Catholic priest have married them? Did they both lie about being previously married? Was the Durango divorce legal? Was Tabor actually divorced when he married Baby Doe in St. Louis on September 30 in a private ceremony?

Horace Tabor was never elected to a position of note after his marriage to Baby Doe, but he remained active in the Republican Party. He helped in local elections and defrayed expenses of delegates to national conventions. But all the people who thought Baby Doe would quickly tire of Horace and leave him were proved wrong.

Although Denver's social elite turned their backs on Baby Doe, Horace and his bride were happy. The two of them often enjoyed their box at the Tabor Grand Opera. Before long, the couple had children: Elizabeth Bondeul Lily, born in 1884; a son who died the day he was born in 1888; and another daughter, Rose Mary Echo Silver Dollar, born in 1889. Horace Tabor appeared to be a happy man who doted on his wife and daughters.

Augusta Tabor remained far away from the happy couple. She had been given enough property and money to live well, and she did, managing her fortune carefully. When she died in Pasadena, California, in 1895, Augusta left an estate of $1.5 million.

Once divorced, Horace didn't seem to waste another thought on Augusta. He was busy enjoying his new life. He and Baby Doe and their daughters enjoyed everything they wanted. Tabor romped with his children, whom he called Cupid and Honeymaid; played poker with his friends; and was generous to his relatives and many charities.

But financial difficulties finally hit Horace Tabor. Numerous lawsuits had cost him a great deal of money, and in the 1880s and 1900s, he dabbled unsuccessfully in railroads and engaged in land speculation. Several times, Tabor was forced to use the Matchless Mine for security deposits, but he always redeemed it. In 1887, trying to save his heavily mortgaged empire, Tabor went to Arizona and bought a gold mine, the Vulture. The mine was in poor repair, and British investors hired a mining engineer to look after their interests. When it did not immediately make a profit, the engineer shut it down.

Finding himself deep in debt, Tabor did what he could. He tried to sell the Tabor Block in Denver, but the deal fell through. Desperate, in 1892, Tabor bought a mine in Mexico. In the silver panic of 1893, silver mines were hit hard. In Colorado alone, 485 mines closed. Tabor's mine in Mexico was failing because Tabor had no more money to invest in it. When Tabor failed to get another large loan, he lost everything.

Horace, Baby Doe and their two daughters had moved out of their beautiful home by Christmas 1896. In addition to his home, Tabor had lost all of his mines. Tabor dealt with his losses as best as he could, finally buying a house for $10 near Ward, in Boulder County. One of his friends gave him a $15,000 loan, and Tabor turned to mining again. But it was not like the old days. Tabor was now sixty-seven years old with a wife and two young daughters.

Much as he had in his early years, Tabor was talking about pulling up stakes and moving to some place more promising, perhaps the Alaskan gold fields, when he got some good news that changed his plans. In a generous act, Senator Edward O. Wolcott nominated Tabor to become postmaster of Denver in January 1898, and President McKinley approved it. The once fabulously wealthy Tabor family happily moved back to Denver with a $3,700 a year salary.

With a small but regular income, Tabor reinvested in a few mines. He sought additional funds by letting his name and picture be used by a cigar company and even endorsed Paine's Celery Compound to restore health and strength. But it was simply too late to strike it rich again.

In April 1899, Horace Tabor went out to vote in a city election and came home complaining that he did not feel well. The next day, he remained in bed, and the doctor was called. Tabor was diagnosed with appendicitis, and because of age and his weakened condition, a decision was made not to operate. On Sunday, Tabor was baptized into the Catholic Church, something he had planned to do later that month, and the next day, on April 10, 1899, he died.

Baby Doe returned to Leadville. After her daughters left, an almost destitute Baby Doe lived for thirty-five years in a dilapidated cabin at the old Matchless Mine. To keep her feet warmer, she stuffed newspapers in her old boots. Baby Doe was found on March 7, 1935, frozen to death in her cabin. She and Horace Tabor were buried next to each other at Mount Olivet Cemetery in Denver.

The Tabor story was made famous when, in 1956, Douglas Stuart Moore wrote an opera, *The Ballad of Baby Doe*, which premiered at the Central City Opera House and later opened in New York.

Chief Ouray and Chipeta

1833–1880 and 1843–1924 •
Los Pinos Indian Agency

Chief Ouray stepped through the door into the blacksmith shop at the Los Pinos Indian Agency as he did almost every morning. But this day was different. The moment he entered, from out of the darkness, a man lunged at him with an axe, missing Ouray's head by only inches. Ouray instinctively sidestepped, putting a post between him and his attacker. A second swing of the axe struck the post. Ouray leaped forward, grabbing the man by the throat and pinning him to the ground. As Ouray reached for his knife to kill his attacker, he heard the scuffle of other men in the shadows as they fearfully ran away. Ouray stared down to discover that the man on the ground in front of him was Sapovanero, his wife's brother. Ouray realized then how deeply opposed some of those closest to him were to the government treaties he was making to try to save the Utes.

The life of this great Native American peacemaker began in Taos, New Mexico, in 1833. His mother was a Ute, and his father was an Apache. When Ouray's parents moved to Colorado Territory, they left their son with a Spanish couple near Taos to live on their ranch. He worked there as a sheepherder into his teens. So although Ouray was a Native American, he was raised in a Catholic, Spanish-speaking community and learned to speak English, Spanish, Ute, Apache and sign language.

Seventeen-year-old Ouray and his brother left Taos in 1850 and went to join his father, who, even though he was born an Apache, had become a Ute leader. The Tabeguaches were the largest of seven bands of Utes living in Colorado and New Mexico. Ouray joined in the Ute culture and traditions.

He became recognized as a good hunter. Shortly after Ouray joined the Ute band, his father died.

In 1850, Ouray married a young woman of the tribe named Black Mare. A daughter was born to them, but she lived only a short time. Then, around 1857, a son was born, whom Ouray called Parone, meaning "apple." Shortly after the birth of his son, Ouray's wife died. Two years later, Ouray took a second wife, Chipeta, who had been born about 1843. There are several different stories about Chipeta's ancestry, but the most likely is that she was a Kiowa-Apache girl who had been raised by the Utes after her family was killed in a raid by an enemy tribe. Her name, Chipeta, is translated as "White Singing Bird." She was raised in the Tabeguache band of Utes and was married to Ouray when she was about sixteen years old.

Chipeta and Ouray were well suited to each other. Unlike most Utes, Ouray had few close male friends and seemed to prefer the company of Chipeta. Both wanted to make peace with the white men and hoped to save what they could of Ute culture. Ouray and Chipeta took on typical roles of the tribe where men were hunters, fishermen, protectors and tool makers, while women sewed, gathered and preserved fruits and vegetables and cared for the home and children.

As the year passed, Ouray took on more responsibilities. He was involved in five skirmishes with other Native American tribes between 1856 and 1860 and distinguished himself in all of these. By 1860, at age twenty-seven, Ouray was a sub-chief. Many tribal leaders did not agree with his views on how to survive in an increasingly white-dominated world. They were not interested in making treaties, believing that this land rightly belonged to the Utes and not to white settlers.

When Kit Carson became the Indian agent in New Mexico and needed to talk with the chiefs of neighboring tribes, he often called on Ouray, who became his friend. The two of them conversed in Spanish, a language in which each was fluent. By 1862, Ouray was the chief negotiator for the Tabeguache, although other Ute tribes did not officially have him speak for them. Kit Carson was aware of the desperate situation that many Utes faced. In his annual report on the Indian agency, Carson wrote, "The hunting ground of the Tabeguache being in the section of the country where the whites are in search of gold, their game is becoming scarce; much of it having been killed by the settlers, and a great deal of it driven from the country. Hence it will be absolutely necessary to feed them during the approaching winter months."

In 1860, Ouray made a trip to California Gulch (Leadville, Colorado), where he saw men scrambling over the mountains and looking in streams for gold. Ouray feared the loss of his Native American hunting grounds and asked Chief Nevava to make a treaty to protect them. When the chief would not listen, Ouray attended the tribal council, insisting on a treaty. The majority agreed with Ouray and sent him back to Kit Carson, who helped Ouray draw up a treaty of friendship between the government and the Colorado Utes. Such a treaty would guarantee that the Utes could have the western half of Colorado land forever.

In the summer of 1861, many Utes traveled east over the mountains to hunt buffalo near Denver. While the men were hunting and the women were busy skinning the buffalo, somehow Ouray's young sister, Tsashin (Susan), disappeared. Although a search was made, she could not be found. Arapaho scouts had captured her. Devastated by the event, Ouray and Chipeta returned home without her.

In 1861, Colorado became a territory of the United States. In 1862, Ouray's Tabeguache Utes offered a treaty of friendship to territorial governor John Evans. Ouray served as translator at the treaty conference. The following year, Ouray joined the Ute delegation that traveled to Washington to meet President Abraham Lincoln. Chipeta sewed fancy clothes for Ouray to wear for this occasion. Although the Indian agent purchased Ouray a suit of "white man's clothes" in St. Joseph, Missouri, Ouray wore his Native American dress when he went to meet the president.

Shortly after the Washington meetings, treaties were signed that guaranteed the Utes most of Colorado west of the Continental Divide. In the Treaty of 1863, the Tabeguache Utes promised to give up their land east of the Continental Divide and agreed not to deter the building of roads and military forts. In return, the government promised the Utes $10,000 worth of household goods and provisions for the next ten years and a number of cattle and sheep to encourage them to take up farming.

The treaty did not prove to be worth much, since the government reneged on its promises of livestock and other benefits. Utes and the government alike paid little attention to the treaty. It was a peaceful time, however, and one that brought happiness to Ouray and Chipeta when Ouray's sister, who had been missing for two years, was found in an Arapaho camp by a small group of cavalry. The army men rescued her, only to have her run away from them in fear. While she tried to find her way home, she was discovered wandering in the mountains by Utes, who returned her to Ouray's tribe.

This joyous return of a sister was followed by a tragedy around June 1863. Ouray and some of his Tabeguache band went to join in a buffalo hunt near Fort Lupton, bringing them close to the camps of other Plains

Indians. There are several versions of what happened, but the upshot was that Sioux warriors attacked and took Ouray's son, Parone. Later, the boy was captured or traded to the Arapahos. Ouray and the Utes hunted unsuccessfully for the missing boy for two weeks.

Ouray and Chipeta resumed their normal life while still grieving the loss of Parone. Skirmishes continued to occur between whites and other Plains Indians. In December 1864, Ouray and Chipeta learned of the Sand Creek Massacre and were outraged to find that it was John Chivington, a soldier they had met at an earlier treaty council with the governor, who had led the soldiers in the massacre.

By the spring of 1865, the promised government supplies still had not arrived and game was scarce, so the Utes migrated to their hunting grounds on the forbidden east side of the Rockies. Ouray and Chipeta camped at Fountain Creek near Colorado City. It was during this time that Ouray learned, to his sorrow, that Abraham Lincoln, the president he had met and admired, had been killed.

Leadership was changing not only for the country but also in the Colorado Territory. Governor Evans has been asked to resign because of his role in the Sand Creek Massacre. Trouble broke out with the Native Americans again. Incidents involving stolen horses became common. The new governor, Alexander Cummings, met with the Tabeguache chiefs, including Ouray, and finally delivered to them the government goods they had been promised. With that show of good faith, the chiefs reaffirmed their 1863 treaty and agreed to stay on the west side of the mountains.

The year 1866 started out quietly. Chipeta and Ouray moved to Mosca Pass and set up camp. But in the fall, a messenger arrived with troubling news. A chief called Kaniache and his band of Utes had gone to the east side of the mountains near Trinidad and had stolen horses, corn and livestock and taken prisoners. The cavalry was in pursuit. Fearing his tribe might be drawn into a fight with the soldiers, Ouray left camp and rode forty miles to Fort Garland to talk with Kit Carson. Carson advised Ouray to bring his people to the camp. By October 9, Ouray and his tribe were camped near Fort Garland in some cottonwood trees along the Rio Sangre de Cristo.

Kit Carson and his wife were very kind to Ouray and Chipeta. During this time, Chipeta and Ouray, who had no children of their own, took in four children, two girls and two boys, and adopted them. In an effort to make peace, Ouray sent word to Kaniache, who came to Fort Garland and released the white prisoners he had taken earlier.

During this relatively peaceful period, the U.S. government made attempts to get a new treaty in which the Utes would give up still more land. Ouray would not agree. The U.S. government was already significantly behind in its promised payments. In the Annual Report of the Commissioner of Indian Affairs, Ouray was quoted as saying, "Long time ago, Utes always had plenty. On the prairie, antelope and buffalo, so many Ouray couldn't count. In the mountains, deer and bear everywhere. In the streams, trout, duck, beaver, everything…White man came, and now Utes grow hungry a heap…White man grow a heap, red man no grow—soon die all."

The winter of 1867 was hard. Because Ouray's band had signed a treaty, they received government provisions and were better off than most. Others who had not signed the treaty were in dire straits. It was clear that another treaty conference was needed. Five Ute chiefs, including Ouray, were invited to Washington, D.C. In this 1868 treaty, the Utes sacrificed more land but still kept roughly the western third of the Colorado Territory. Ouray hoped that soldiers would actually protect the land to which the Utes now held title "for as long as grass grows and water runs."

This treaty set up an agency at White River and one at Rio de los Pinos, near present-day Montrose, Colorado, to hear any complaints from the Native Americans. Each agency included a warehouse, schoolhouse, blacksmith shop and sawmill. Ouray was off hunting when a group of men arrived to construct the sawmill at the Los Pinos Agency. These workers relied on the power of Ouray for safety. One wrote, "These Southern Utes ain't going to make trouble. Ouray'll keep 'em quiet. [He is] the big peace-chief of the whole Ute nation. He's not here: he's off somewhere's else just now, but he's an Indian with brains."

In June 1868, Ouray and Chipeta got the sad news that both Kit Carson and his wife, Josefa, had died. They realized they had lost good supporters. Still, in a series of council meetings, forty-seven Ute chiefs signed the Treaty of 1868. When the Los Pinos Indian Agency was completed, Otto Mears of Saguache was made the official Ute trader for the agency. Mears, known as the pathfinder of Colorado, soon built a road from Saguache to the Los Pinos Agency. He and Ouray became friends.

The discovery of rich silver deposits in 1872 in the San Juan Mountains spurred the government to agitate for another reduction of the Ute property to allow prospectors to move in. That summer, a few Ute chiefs agreed to meet with the governor and other officials to discuss terms of a new treaty. The Ute delegation waited for seven days until the government officials finally arrived. Ouray argued that a good treaty was already in place and he

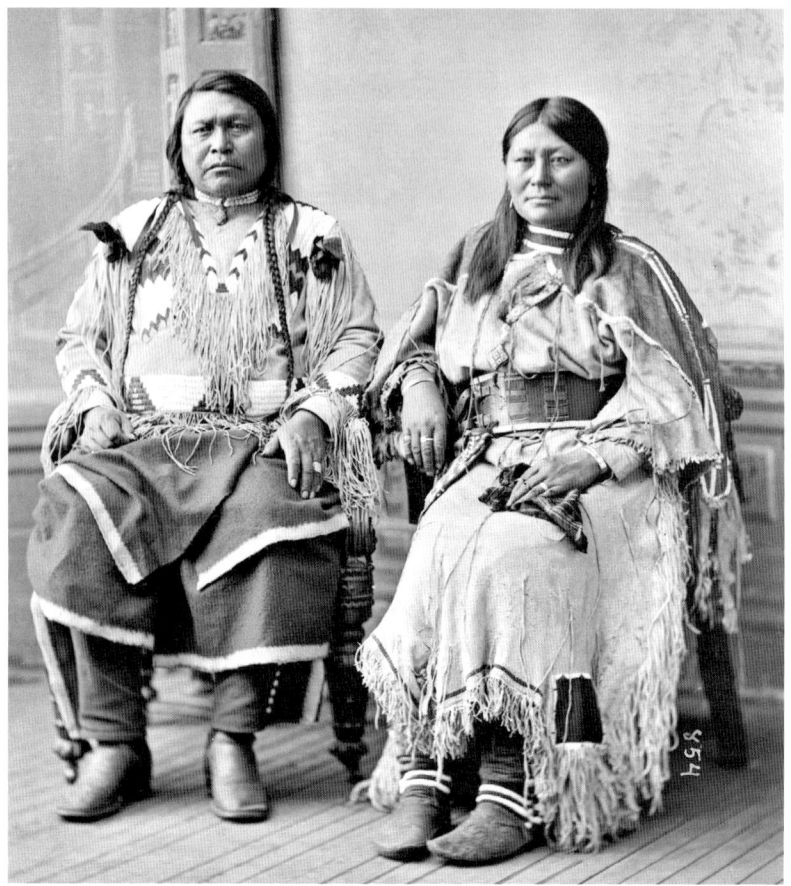

Chief Ouray and his wife, Chipeta, by Matthew Brady/Levin Handy. *Library of Congress.*

expected it to be enforced. According to the Board of Indian Affairs report, Ouray said, "We do not want to sell a foot of our land—that is the opinion of all." Nonetheless, another round of talks was scheduled for Washington.

Ouray and Chipeta attended the next Washington meeting along with others selected by Ouray, including Otto Mears. They left the Indian Agency and traveled in covered wagons to what is now Colorado Springs, where they caught the train to Washington. There they met President and Mrs. Grant, attended a circus and visited a zoo, where they were especially fascinated with monkeys.

Little was being accomplished on the treaty, so a secret meeting was held with Ouray. In exchange for his approval of a new treaty, he was told the government might find his long lost son. A meeting was set for August in Los Pinos at which time Ouray's son, Parone, was to be returned. Although the agent did his best, he did not produce Ouray's son, who was believed to be hidden by the Arapahos.

The meeting moved forward nonetheless, with the Utes agreeing that miners could have the "tops of the mountains" but not the valleys below. When government officials said they didn't think they could confine the miners just to the mountain tops, Ouray asked, "Why cannot you stop them: is not the government strong enough to keep its agreements with us?"

Mears suggested the government agree to pay Ouray $1,000 salary a year for ten years and promise to continue looking for his son. Ouray and seven other chiefs signed the treaty. In October 1872, a seventeen-year-old-boy named Friday was brought by the Arapahos to Washington to meet Ouray. The boy who came did not recognize Ouray, and he did not understand the Ute language. The place from which this boy had been stolen did not match the details of Parone's capture. The boy did not want to go with Ouray, and Ouray concluded it was not his son. The boy returned to live with the Arapahos.

The Senate ratified the latest agreement, called the 1873 Brunot Treaty, in which the Utes gave up some of the San Juan lands for considerations that included the distribution of annuity goods to them. The first of these distributions was set for 1874. The Los Pinos Indian Agency was moved to the Uncompahgre Valley, where Ouray was given land and a house to live in. This angered some Utes, who thought Ouray was becoming a white man. Several attacks were made on Ouray's life, including the one by his brother-in-law. With Chipeta's urging, her husband and brother eventually patched up their differences and became trusted friends.

The winter of 1877 was severe, and the promised government goods once again were not delivered to the White River band of Utes. Ouray began to get complaints about the new Indian agent at White River, Nathan Meeker, who insisted Utes become Christians and attend the school taught by his daughter, cutting the rations of those who refused his orders. More bad news arrived. Whites killed a Ute in Middle Park, and in return, Utes shot a white settler and stole his ponies. The Utes who did the killing fled, and the ponies were rounded up and returned.

This latest outbreak of violence on the part of Native Americans led to still more meetings trying to negotiate an agreement to force the Utes to leave the area. Although Ouray opposed it, in 1879, several Ute chiefs capitulated to the sale of more Ute land. Meantime, at the White River Agency in northwest Colorado, Agent Nathan Meeker continued to stir up the Utes.

On September 30, a number of Utes attacked the agency and killed Meeker and eleven others. Three women and two children were captured and held for ransom. The captives were held for twenty-three days, until a Ute agent, Charles Adams, along with Ouray, secured their release. At the White River Agency, Ouray convinced the Utes to accept a cease-fire, while Adams persuaded General Merritt to remove his troops. William Pollock, an Indian Bureau inspector on the scene at the time said, "Saint Peter could not save this country, but for the council of Ouray."

As a result of the Meeker Massacre, the government decided to force the White River and Uncompahgre Utes to a desolate reservation in northeastern Utah and to a small reservation in southwestern Colorado near Mesa Verde, where two Ute bands were already located. Ouray traveled to Washington and argued that although the Utes were wrong to have killed Meeker and the others, they had been provoked. Ouray said the individuals to blame should be punished, not the whole population of Utes. This time, Ouray's arguments did not prevail, and the Utes were exiled from most of Colorado.

In poor health, Ouray returned to Colorado and died on August 24, 1880, at the Southern Ute agency near Ignacio, where he was buried. When he died, Ouray was only forty-seven years old. A year after his death, most of the Utes had left Colorado. Chipeta joined the remaining 1,458 Tabeguache Utes in moving to the reservation in Utah on August 27, 1881. Although she was not allowed to receive her husband's annuity and was impoverished, she did not complain but said, "I am as well provided as the other members of my tribe…I am not better than they and what is good enough for them is good enough for me." Chipeta made a trip back to Grand Junction, Colorado, in 1909 to greet President Taft and even into her old age was consulted as a wise woman of her tribe. She lived to be eighty-one years old and died in 1924.

An estimated five thousand people attended Chipeta's funeral, at which several dignitaries spoke. A memorial to Chief Ouray and Chipeta was erected at the Ute Indian Museum and Ouray Memorial Park in Montrose, Colorado. Chief Ouray is also portrayed in the rotunda of the state of Colorado Capitol Building in one of sixteen stained-glass portraits. He is the only one of the sixteen to have been selected for this honor by a unanimous vote.

Ouray is often criticized for being far too accommodating to the government. In spite of abundant evidence that treaties would not be honored, he kept making them, believing the alternative might have been complete annihilation. To his credit, much of the Ute culture has survived. In an ironic turn of events, much of the desolate land the Utes were given turned out to have natural gas reserves, and money from this provides economic support for the tribe.

William Jackson Palmer

1836–1909 • Colorado Springs

Spy! That word kept echoing in his brain as William Jackson Palmer tried to remain calm. It was 1862, early in the Civil War, and Palmer, a captain in the Union army in the Fifteenth Volunteer Cavalry, was now cut off behind enemy lines. He knew that when spies were caught, they might be shot, and the truth was he had been spying. He'd come across the Potomac River in Virginia to scout out troop information for General George McClellan. He had found his way in the darkness to the cabin of a miller who was known to be sympathetic to the North. Before he could learn what he needed and return to his men, enemy troops were everywhere.

Palmer thought quickly. If arrested in uniform, he might be sent to prison and avoid being shot as a spy. But he was unwilling to let the people who had taken him in be punished for housing a Yankee soldier. So he quickly changed into some clothing belonging to the homeowner and tried to concoct a good story. When troops came to search the house and he was interrogated, Palmer tried to pass himself off as W.J. Peters, an engineer on his way to inspect mines in Cumberland, Maryland.

The Rebels were suspicious of Palmer, and he was taken to headquarters, where he was detained and finally sent to Richmond, Virginia. There he was imprisoned as a civilian at the notorious Castle Thunder prison. Four miserable months later, still known only as W.J. Peters, Captain Palmer was part of a prisoner exchange. Within two weeks, he was back in service and rejoined his cavalry unit in February 1863. He and his men gained considerable fame for their valor, and because they moved about so often under cover of night, his group became known as "Palmer's Owls."

Palmer and his men saw plenty of action. Chief among Palmer's activities was the pursuit of Confederate general John B. Hood after the Battle of Nashville in 1864. On January 14, 1865, at Red Hill, Alabama, Palmer and his men defeated a much larger force and took two hundred prisoners, without losing any of their own men. For this, Palmer was awarded the Medal of Honor and at war's end retired as a brevet brigadier general.

The Civil War was a long interruption in the life of William Jackson Palmer, who was born on September 18, 1836, in the town of Leipsic in central Delaware.

When he was only five, Palmer's family had moved from Delaware to Philadelphia, where he and his three siblings were enrolled in a Quaker School. Palmer was fascinated with trains and particularly with steam locomotives. His greatest interest was in learning about the DeWitt Clinton locomotive, which at that time ran an amazing fifteen miles an hour.

In 1853, when he was just seventeen, Palmer began working for a railroad building company in Washington, Pennsylvania. At that time, there were only eleven small railways in America. His interest and ability in this field were so strong that with money borrowed from his uncle and the help of the president of the railroad company, Palmer went off to Europe to learn more about railroading. He visited railroad shops, foundries and steelworks and even went down into coal mines.

On his return from England, Palmer came back to work as the private secretary to John Edgar Thomson, president of the Pennsylvania Railway. Palmer suggested that instead of burning wood in their locomotives, they should burn coal. Thomson welcomed this idea because his company was currently burning about twenty thousand cords of lumber a year and had stripped all the trees along their railroad right of way. So the Pennsylvania Railway became the first company in the United States to switch from burning wood to coal in their engines. Trains could now travel thirty miles an hour. Efficiency in combustion was Palmer's main interest at this time.

With the outbreak of the war in 1861, Palmer, twenty-five years old, felt he had no choice but to become active. As a Quaker, he was opposed to war, but even more, he was opposed to slavery. He became part of an elite group of scouts known as the Anderson Troop. This group so impressed Major General Buell that Palmer was asked to create a larger scouting regiment and helped found the Fifteenth Pennsylvania Volunteer Cavalry. He enjoyed a distinguished career in the army. Both before and after being captured, Palmer served bravely, the youngest general in the Union army.

Once the war was over, Palmer headed west. A survey was being planned to find a route for a railroad all the way to California, and in 1867, Palmer took charge of this expedition and set out to map a western route for the Kansas Pacific Railroad. He and his men took the supplies they needed for this exploration trip as far as the end of the railway track in Salina, Kansas. After loading their supplies onto twenty wagons, they set off across the plains.

This expedition braved attacks by Native Americans as they went to Fort Wallace in western Kansas and on to Bent's Fort in Colorado. At Santa Fe, the survey group split into three groups. Under Palmer's leadership, they mapped routes through New Mexico and Arizona to San Francisco, where the groups met up again. With his assignment completed, Palmer covered most of California on horseback before taking a stagecoach through Salt Lake City and Cheyenne back to Kansas City.

As his own fortune grew, Palmer always kept in mind the needs of those less fortunate. Remembering his reason for getting involved in the Civil War, Palmer gave substantial sums of money to Hampton University, a college for black students, near Fort Monroe at Hampton, Virginia. This would be the first of many generous gifts to schools in his lifetime.

While Palmer had been scouting a route to the Pacific coast, the Kansas Railway had been extended on across Kansas Territory and was at a point where the railway had to decide which route to follow to reach the mountains. Palmer went about the country, riding on top of a stagecoach along the Arkansas River. He pulled into the settlement of Colorado City at the foot of Pikes Peak and found it to be a beautiful area. Trains were soon running from Kansas all the way to Denver and Cheyenne.

Appropriately enough, it was while riding on a train that Palmer met his future wife, Mary "Queen" Mellen, who was traveling with her father, William Proctor Mellen. Palmer was married on November 8, 1870, in New York, and he and his young bride honeymooned in Great Britain. Even while honeymooning, Palmer managed to find time to study the narrow gauge, three-foot wide tracks, common on the railroads there, and to think about how these might be used back in the United States to negotiate the sharper curves and steeper grades of the western mountains.

In 1871, Palmer purchased ten thousand acres of land just east of Colorado City. On this land he established the city of Colorado Springs. Within two years, it quickly grew to a population of 1,500. His wife, Queen, at age twenty, opened the first public school in Colorado Springs in November

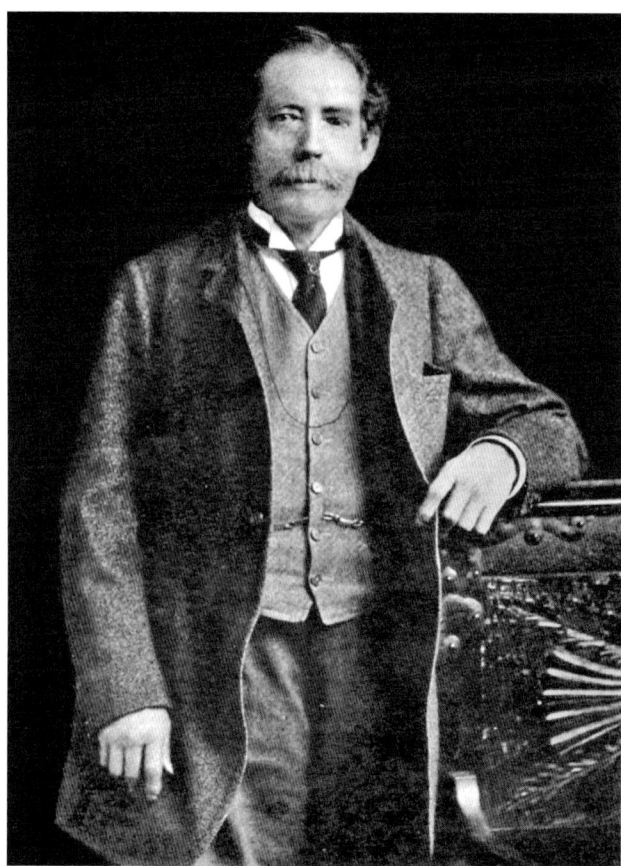

Left: William Jackson Palmer, 1870. *From* The World's Work *by Walter Hines Page and Arthur Wilson Page.*

Below: Woodburytype of 1871 (per pencil notation on original book) photograph of Denver and Rio Grande Montezuma 2-4-0. This is the first locomotive built for the Denver and Rio Grande Railroad. Located outside the Baldwin Locomotive Works in Philadelphia, Pennsylvania, by John Carbutt (1832–1905), uncredited; American Photo-Relief Printing Co., Philadelphia. *David A. Hanson Collection of the History of Photomechanical Reproduction.*

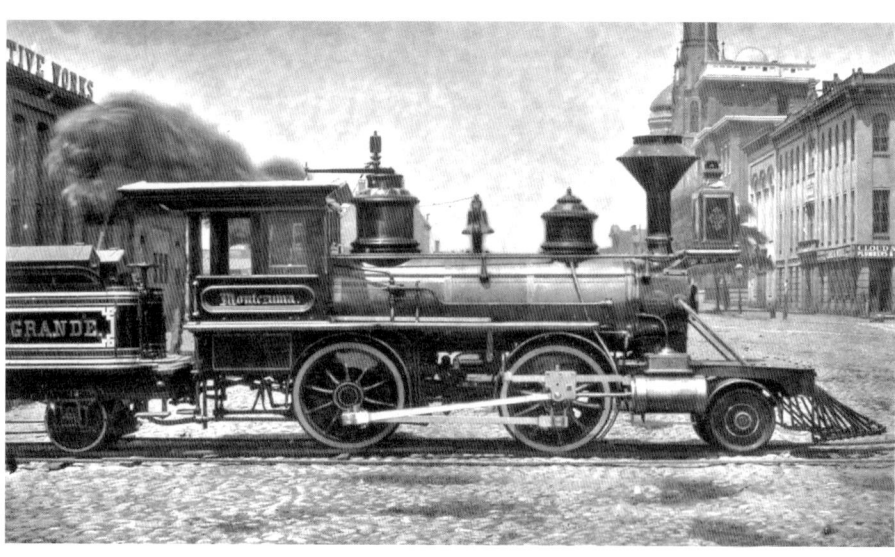

1871. Palmer set about building a dream house for his wife. He called it Glen Eyrie (Eagle's Nest) and located it near the current city of Colorado Springs in the foothills northwest of the Garden of the Gods. First he built a large carriage house where they lived. Then he built a twenty-two-room frame house, which he later remodeled to include a tower and more rooms. The Palmers had three daughters: Elsie, Dorothy and Marjory.

Drawing on his railway experience and business know-how, Palmer founded and was president of his own company, the Denver and Rio Grande Railroad, which eventually operated the largest network of narrow-gauge railroads in the United States. While most people were focused on establishing a transcontinental railroad, Palmer dreamed of a north–south line that would go from Denver to El Paso, Texas, with links on to Mexico City.

Palmer's Denver and Rio Grande railroad reached as far south as Pueblo in 1872. A national depression in 1873 forced a four-year delay before Palmer had enough money to continue construction at El Moro near Trinidad. During this delay, the Atchison, Topeka and Santa Fe Railroad constructed a line up the Arkansas River to Pueblo in 1876.

When the depression was over and businesses were recovering, a rivalry sprang up. The two companies took part in what might be best described as a railroad war over the next four years. The Santa Fe challenged Palmer's plan to build from Pueblo up the Arkansas River to Leadville and from Pueblo south over Raton Pass to New Mexico. The Santa Fe won this battle because their men reached Raton Pass one day ahead of the Rio Grande engineers. Palmer knew that the law would support allowing the company that first started building a railroad to finish the line. He chose to move his operations rather than fight a losing battle in court.

Palmer sent his men to the other branch of his railroad at Cañon City with the plan of building a scenic rail route where the Arkansas River had cut a deep gorge through the mountains. When the Santa Fe Railroad men learned of Palmer's new plan, they rushed their own crews to the Royal Gorge to begin digging on the opposite side of the canyon so that they might again claim the right of way. This time, Palmer did not give up, insisting instead that he had the right to build. The Santa Fe men also refused to leave. Men on both sides built forts. Fist fights were frequent. At night, men from each side did as much damage as they could to any work the other side had completed during the day.

Palmer was forced by a court ruling to lease the Rio Grande tracks to the Santa Fe Railroad from October 1878 to June 1879. He appealed, and the U.S. Supreme Court eventually gave Palmer priority on building in the gorge. Palmer claimed that the Santa Fe had violated the terms of its lease, and he seized the line at gunpoint on June 11, forcing the Santa Fe employees to leave.

Although Palmer now had the right to build, constructing this piece of train track through the Royal Gorge was a huge challenge. A hanging bridge had to be suspended from rock walls to hold the rails above the river. The track curved and twisted over Marshall Pass into the valley of the Gunnison. It went through Montrose and Delta to Grand Junction. Another branch went through northern New Mexico and southern Colorado, to Durango and Silverton, and a third branch went from La Veta Pass to Alamosa, Monte Vista, Del Norte and on to Creed. These small railroads brought food and supplies to miners and carried new gold seekers, too. The railroad

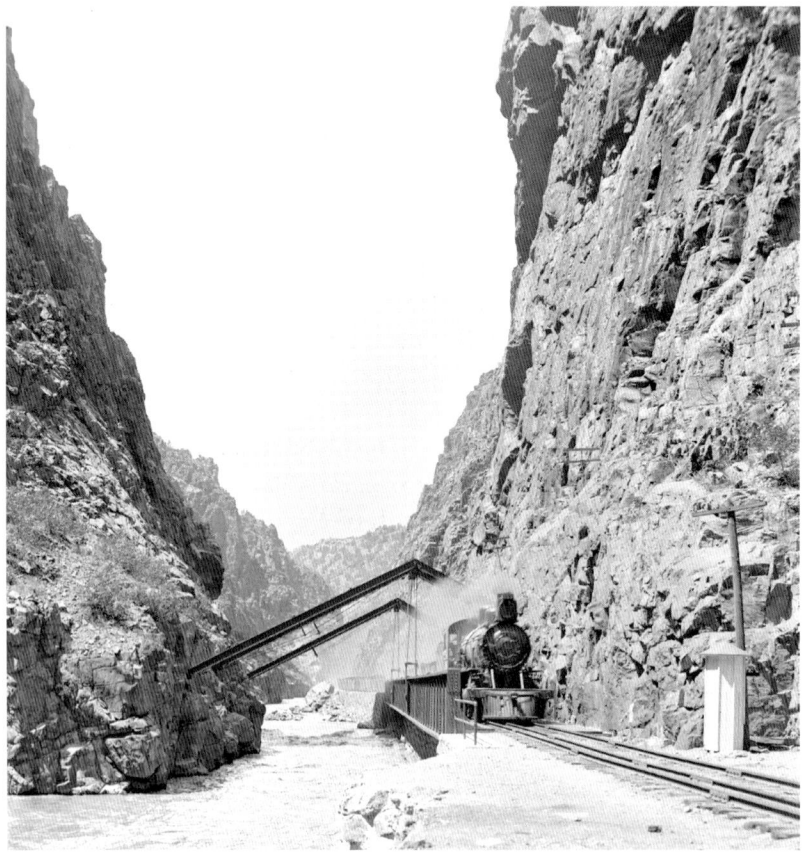

In the Royal Gorge, Rio Grande Southern Railway. *William Henry Jackson, 1843–1942, photographer. Library of Congress.*

grew, reaching almost every mining camp in Colorado and in parts of New Mexico and Utah.

Keeping the Royal Gorge railroad tracks open in winter was difficult. Each engine carried a load of dynamite to blast drifts and heavy snow slides from the tracks. When snows melted and waters reached flood stage, water covered the tracks. The road master had to wade ahead and test the depth with a pole before taking the train through.

A sort of peace treaty in the railroad wars came in 1880, when, through court action, the Rio Grande secured the territory north of the thirty-sixth parallel and west of its present tracks, while the Santa Fe received the region east and south. This decision made Palmer's railroad primarily a Colorado railroad.

Although his grand scheme of a railroad to Mexico City did not work out, Palmer was successful in building a network of tracks totaling close to 1,500 miles and reaching many mountain mining camps. Despite receiving no federal land grants, Palmer and his associates purchased real estate along the right of way at low prices and cashed in later when they began developing the land.

Known throughout the state as one of its most influential businessmen, Palmer's successful life was disrupted in 1880 after the birth of his second daughter, when his wife became very ill. Her doctors suggested that she leave Colorado and go to live at a lower elevation. Palmer moved his wife to England and arranged for a home and tutors for the children. He visited as often as he could get away from his businesses, but Palmer's blissful period of life at Glen Eyrie had ended.

In addition to railroads, Palmer was involved in a number of rail-related industries. Because of the demand for steel rails, he constructed the Colorado Coal and Iron Company steel mill south of Pueblo hoping to establish it as the "Pittsburg of the West." In 1892, CC&I merged with the Colorado Fuel Company to become Colorado Fuel and Iron, which for decades dominated the industry and was the largest employer in the state of Colorado.

In 1883, Palmer resigned as president of the Denver and Rio Grande and took on the leadership of the Rio Grande Western that connected Colorado to Salt Lake City. In 1901, he sold that line to the Denver and Rio Grande. After his wife's death at age forty-four in 1906, Palmer brought his daughters back to Colorado Springs.

Palmer never missed a yearly reunion of his old Pennsylvania Cavalry unit, but a fall in 1906 left him partially paralyzed and unable to travel far. He was determined not to miss seeing his friends, so Palmer invited the entire group to hold their reunion at his home, Glen Eyrie. More than two hundred men came.

Palmer died three years later at age seventy-two. He left a strong mark on Colorado Springs. Among his many charitable acts, he gave land and funds to establish Colorado College, he built the Colorado School for the Deaf and Blind and he opened Cragmor Tuberculosis Sanatorium.

Through his railroading and rail-related industries, Palmer also left a lasting impression on the state of Colorado. Several geographic features in the state bear his name: Palmer Divide, Palmer Lake and Palmer Park. People today can still experience the railroad legacy of William Palmer because a forty-five-mile section of the Durango and Silverton Narrow Gauge Railroad remains in service as a tourist line, as does a sixty-four-mile stretch between Antonito, Colorado, and Chama, New Mexico. Both lines are in the National Register of Historic Places.

David H. Moffat

1839–1911 • Moffat Road

The long-awaited decision was finally announced. The Transcontinental Railroad across the United States would go through Cheyenne, not Denver. The Union Pacific chose to use the lower passes and valleys of Wyoming rather than try to construct a railroad over or through the mountains west of Denver. The vice-president of the Union Pacific recognized this grave blow to Denver's hopes of being a railroad hub by stating that Denver was now "too dead to bury." Colorado territorial governor Evans agreed with this assessment, saying, "Colorado without railroads is comparatively worthless."

David Moffat, one of those who heard the news in dismay, didn't give up on the idea of an east–west railroad. Moffat was not one of those young men during the middle of the nineteenth century who sought his fortune as an explorer, trapper/trader or prospector. He was a banker and a financier with a passion for mining and railroading. In a career spanning about half a century, Moffat's biggest contribution to the state of Colorado was never giving up on his dream of a railroad going west from Denver.

David Halladay Moffat Jr. was born in Washingtonville, New York, on July 23, 1839, the youngest of eight children in a middle-class family with a Scotch-Irish background. His grandfather Samuel took part in the American Revolution and afterward founded the town of Washingtonville. Moffat's father owned a gristmill and a general mercantile store. Young David Moffat left Washingtonville when he was twelve to work as a messenger for the New York National Exchange Bank in New York City. In 1855, at age sixteen, he became an assistant teller. Moffat followed his brother to Des Moines,

Iowa, to work as a bank clerk for A.J. Stevens and Company. This company extended credit to settlers who were starting farms, loaning money for liens on spring crops. This was the beginning of Moffat's long career based on optimism, speculation and risk.

Moffat made friends in financial circles and was hired as cashier and general manager of the newly opened Bank of Nebraska in Omaha. This successful bank profited from a real estate boom. Hoping to make his fortune, Moffat bought land in Omaha intending to sell it at a good profit to the Pacific Railroad. When unexpected delays slowed the startup of the railroad, Moffat lost his investment.

The financial panic of 1857, combined with the tensions between the North and South leading to the Civil War, caused the Bank of Nebraska to fail in 1858. Even in these adverse conditions, Moffat proved himself an able businessman. He distributed a profit to the stockholders and paid off most of the creditors by liquidating the bank's assets. Moffat returned to Des Moines without a fortune but with his good reputation intact.

While in Omaha, Moffat met the Woolworth brothers, who operated a successful chain of stores in Omaha, Leavenworth and St. Joseph. They needed someone to handle their frontier business. Reports flooded in of a boom in Colorado where gold was discovered and where the settlement of Denver was expected to grow into a big city. So Moffat became a junior partner and went to Denver, where he opened a store in March 1860, selling books, stationery and eastern newspapers.

Moffat also ran an insurance company and held an interest in a freighting company and a telegraph agency, becoming the first representative for Western Union in Colorado. Moffat was appointed a brigadier general in the Colorado militia by territorial governor John Evans. In that position, Moffat straightened out problems in procuring militia supplies and began a long association with Evans.

In November 1861, Moffat returned to New York to marry his childhood sweetheart, Frances A. (Fanny) Buckout. The ceremony took place in Saratoga, New York, on December 11, 1861. The young couple took a train and then stagecoach to Denver. Moffat and his eighteen-year-old bride moved into a house on Twelfth Street near Larimer Street. Their only child, Marcia, was born in October of the following year. In 1863, the Moffats moved across Cherry Creek to a two-story house, which they shared with George Kassler, an old Omaha friend, and his wife.

After a fire in 1863 burned a large portion of Denver's business district, Moffat and Kassler formed the Denver Agency of the Home Insurance

Company of New Haven, Connecticut, operating out of Moffat's store. It was the first property insurance office in the area. Moffat eventually left merchandizing to devote himself full time to mining and banking, but the Moffat and Kassler Agency continued into the 1890s, when Kassler retired.

Moffat joined in successfully petitioning to charter the First National Bank of Colorado. In May 1865, he joined the board of directors, and the following year, when the original cashier resigned, Moffat was appointed to fill his position. (At that time, the position of "cashier" was equivalent to "bank manager.") The bank prospered, and many of its resources were invested in projects such as railroads that were dear to Moffat's heart. The bank was a center of political power in Colorado with Republicans such as John L. Routt, the last territorial governor and first state governor, among the bank's leadership. Moffat avoided political positions, remaining a power behind the scenes.

Those who expected that Denver would become a railroad hub had forgotten that the same men who owned the eastern factories also controlled the railways. To prevent competition from Denver, these eastern railroad men fixed rates for transporting goods on trains to benefit themselves. They charged more to take goods from Denver to the West Coast than from New England to the West Coast.

Moffat knew the importance of transportation. Bankers could help keep mines open by building narrow-gauge railroads, which could squeeze through canyons and carry ore up the steep walls of mountains. Moffat financed dozens of investments and served on the board of directors of several railroads, including the Boulder Valley; the Denver, South Park and Pacific; and the Denver, Utah and Pacific.

When the Union Pacific announced that the transcontinental railroad would go through Cheyenne rather than Denver, Governor Evans called a group of influential men together to discuss the railroad problem. In the summer of 1867, they tried unsuccessfully to get the Union Pacific to build a branch line between Denver and Cheyenne. Seeing little promise from the eastern industrial giants, Moffat announced he would build a steam railroad. In November 1867, he, Evans and others incorporated the Denver Pacific Railway and Telegraph Company to build a railroad to connect Denver with the Union Pacific in Cheyenne, Wyoming. Moffat was treasurer, and John Evans became president.

Groundbreaking occurred on May 18, 1868. The Union Pacific, however, was not very interested in a branch line and failed to supply promised help with building the road. Evans sought assistance from the Kansas Pacific, promising right-of-way land grants to the Kansas Pacific. Track laying on the Denver Pacific began in Cheyenne in September and was finished on June 23, 1870, when the locomotive David H. Moffat pulled the first train into Denver. Within a few days, regular train runs were being made between Denver and Cheyenne. Just two months later, the Kansas-Pacific reached Denver from the east providing a railroad connection to St. Louis.

Beginning in the 1860s and continuing into the 1870s, Moffat turned his attention to mining. He grubstaked a miner in Central City and put money into the Boulder Country mines at Caribou. Moffat also sought out investors, including Dutch investors, who spent $3 million in the Caribou mines. Unfortunately for these investors, all the easily mined ore was gone. Failing to make a quick profit, the Dutch sold off their investment at a sheriff's sale. Moffat, with his partner Chaffee, bought the mines for $70,000, a price just a fraction of their worth and, by waiting patiently, began seeing high dividends in two years. Moffat, Chaffee and Horace Tabor went on to create the Little Pittsburg Consolidated, controlling 73 percent of the Leadville mining company. They sold shares of stock, always keeping a majority interest. After taking out high profits, they sold their shares as the rich ores began to decline.

In the midst of business, Moffat took time for pleasure. In 1871, he went to Europe with Governor Evans and his family. Moffat's wife, Fanny, was afraid of water and stayed at home with nine-year-old Marcia. It was rumored that the valuable pieces of jewelry Moffat brought home from foreign trips and lavished on Fanny were to make up for his indiscretions. Fanny never wore these but kept them in her safe.

In 1874, Moffat moved his family into an elegant home at Fourteenth and Curtis Streets. He bought a handsome carriage and a few years later installed one of the first telephones in the state of Colorado. Fanny held a respected place in society and joined other socialites in shunning the notorious Baby Doe Tabor. David Moffat, however, remained a steadfast friend to his old mining partner, Horace Tabor.

Moffat continued infusing capital in mines, gaining a reputation as a man who invested, made mines profitable and sold them when they started to decline. By 1880, Moffat was president of the National Bank of Denver, and in that same year, Leadville mining millionaire Horace Tabor was elected to the board of directors. When hard times hit in 1884, Moffat bought out Tabor's shares of bank stock. With the mining industry in a slump in the 1880s, Moffat turned to his other major interest: railroads.

The Denver and Rio Grande had a network of narrow-gauge railways in Colorado. In 1884, Moffat was appointed to the board of directors of the

Denver and Rio Grande. Later, he became president of the company but maintained his offices in Denver while the board sat in New York. During his presidency, the board usually approved the funds that Moffat requested for rail improvements, but when members became more and more reluctant to do so, wanting to take quick profits, Moffat resigned.

At about that same time, Moffat's daughter, Marcia, now twenty-eight, married James McClurg, an artist. The couple moved into their own house. Fanny Moffat, however, continued to control her daughter, insisting on Sunday dinners, carriage rides and generally interfering in their household. Within a year, the McClurgs had a baby girl, named Frances but called "Cubby." Moffat doted on the little girl.

By 1900, Moffat was the richest man in Colorado. He owned or was a part owner of more than one hundred mines and nine railroads, but Moffat wasn't interested in taking things easy and enjoying his wealth. When someone suggested retirement to him, he said, "I am not satisfied to do nothing. I want to be doing something new—building or developing. That is the way I get my pleasure out of life."

Although generous, Moffat didn't devote a lot of time to philanthropic projects. He gave an organ to the church back in Washingtonville, New York, where he had gone to Sunday school, and he also gave that little community a library. With his friend Evans he helped establish the Colorado Seminary, which eventually grew into Denver University. Moffat served as its first treasurer and was a big fundraiser in the community, but he did not see philanthropy as a substitute for a career.

Even when busy with mining interests, Moffat never gave up the idea that Colorado needed a railway to the west of Denver. He believed a superior railroad route could be made by cutting through some spot on the Front Range with a tunnel. In March 1902, Moffat announced that he would build a steam-operated, standard-gauge railroad west. Surveyors mapped a route from Denver via Coal Creek Canyon to Southern Boulder Canyon through Rollinsville, over Rollins Pass to the Fraser River and on to Hot Sulphur Springs. The Denver, Northwestern and Pacific Road was incorporated, and Moffat actively sought eastern investors. The leadership of the Union Pacific and Denver and Rio Grande was not enthusiastic about another competing railroad.

Even though many obstacles were placed in his way, Moffat, now sixty-three, held on to his vision. When denied access to Denver's Union Station, which was controlled by the Union Pacific and the Denver and Rio Grande, Moffat built his own terminal. He also ran a successful campaign for Denver

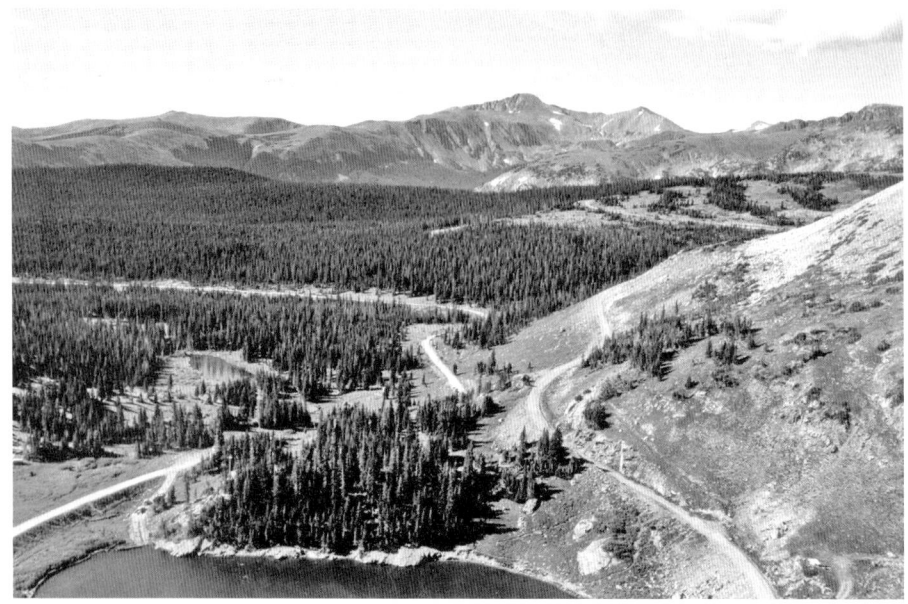

The roadbed of the "Moffat Road" railroad circles Yankee Doodle Lake as it climbs westward toward Rollins Pass. *David L. Perry.*

voters to approve new tracks in the city. Soon Moffat was dipping into his own pocket to pay for construction costs.

Moffat appointed H.A. Sumner as chief engineer and instructed him to find a route from Denver over Rollins Pass and on to Hot Sulphur Springs. Steam shovels could not reach the area where tunnels were needed. Hand drilling holes into hard granite for powder was the method used for blasting and clearing. In February 1903, 187 men were drilling tunnels in South Boulder Canyon. Later that year, 3,800 men were at work on the railroad.

On cold, frosty mornings, railroad crews started work. On some days, by noon, they were shirtless in the heat of the summer sun of Colorado. One day they were laying rails near the entrance of Tunnel 22, nicknamed the "Needle's Eye," and the men could look from their precarious perch on the mountain ridge down the treacherous slope to Yankee Doodle Lake far below.

"Watch your step!" a foreman shouted.

At that instant, one of the workers lost his balance and rolled and slid seven hundred feet down the hill. As the crew watched in horror, the man tumbled to the bottom. But then, slowly, he climbed to his feet, dusted himself off and started the long climb back up to work. He showed the

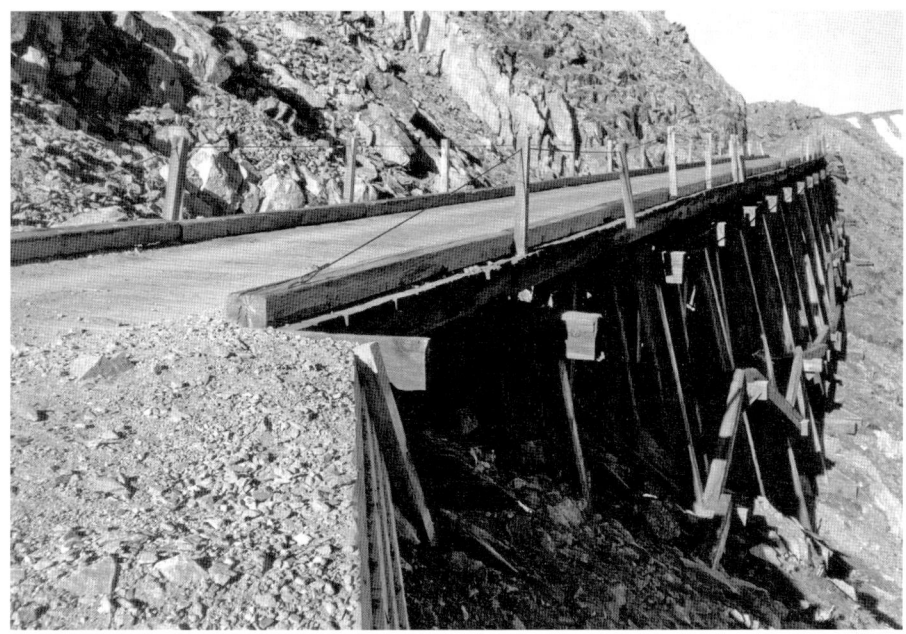

A trestle that carried Moffat's railroad toward the Continental Divide. *David L. Perry.*

same dogged determination to complete a task as David Moffat did in his insistence at building a railroad west.

As track was laid, construction trains carried in steel for trestles. At one point, the men built twenty-seven tunnels in twenty-four miles. This was expensive work, and construction was often halted by snow. On the Rollins Pass line, men were working at 11,660 feet. Wages for these men were increased from the normal $2.00 to $3.43 a day. By the time the railroad reached Rollinsville, Moffat had spent $2.5 million of his own money.

Moffat found it increasingly difficult to get financing, although he tried to stir up interest by talking about the rich coal fields that his railroad would reach. The railway pushed on west to Kremmling and then to Yarmony, west of Gore Canyon. At the close of 1907, Moffat had spent $9 million.

The financial panic of 1907 hit all railroads hard. The small amount of investor money that Moffat had coming in stopped. In January 1908, a fund drive headed up by Colonel David Dodge yielded $1.5 million. With this money, the rail line was pushed on to Steamboat Springs. By this point, the railroad had cost $14 million. In 1909, Moffat secured a loan from a New York financial house, which allowed the railroad to buy twenty new engines.

Buoyed from even a small infusion of investment money, Moffat envisioned a bright future ahead for himself and for Colorado. He began building a palatial mansion for his family at Eighth and Grant Streets. It was built of white brick and had gorgeously decorated interiors with tapestry-covered walls. The windows were made of Tiffany stained glass. With all the markings of a very successful man, Moffat surged onward.

Moffat's granddaughter, Cubby, was back from being educated in Europe. She was a high-spirited girl, often in conflict with her grandmother Fanny. It is reported that when Fanny objected to women smoking, Cubby pointed out that the queen of England smoked, to which Fanny replied, "Then the queen of England is no lady." When Moffat gave a coming-out party for Cubby in 1910, Fanny refused to come because of the unladylike dresses and activities planned for the evening. Cubby's father died later that year, and she and her mother left the United States and went to live in Paris.

In 1910 and 1911, Moffat again went to New York, hoping to raise money for his railroad, which had not yet returned a profit. Freight travel had increased, but accidents were common, and snow blockades proved troublesome. Notes on loans were coming due. Several old business associates and supporters had died. Moffat, now seventy-one, was also somewhat frail. He is described at this time as having silver hair but with eyes that were still "blue and brilliant."

Moffat remained optimistic. His niece, Olive Watson, reported that Moffat told her, "If I can live only two more years, I will build a vast fortune out of this, not only the railroad itself but valuable mining land that is along either side." Seven days later, on March 18, 1911, David Moffat died in the Hotel Belmont in New York City. There are conflicting reports as to whether he died of pneumonia or a heart attack or possible suicide. News of his death was withheld to avoid a run at the First National Bank.

Moffat's body lay in state at the Colorado capitol before his flag-draped casket was taken to the Moffat mansion for services. Hundreds gathered and formed the cortege to Fairmount Cemetery. Many people thought that Moffat would leave a fortune, but all he had left was 7,260 shares of First National Bank Stock and a few shares in the Chesapeake Railway. After Moffat's death, Fanny paid off creditors and had about $100,000 left to support herself for the rest of her life. She moved back to the old house at Seventeenth and Lincoln.

Moffat's death was a severe blow to the Denver, Northwestern and Pacific, but it was not the end of his dream. William Evans led the railroad through these hard times. The Moffat road reached one of its main objectives—the coal fields of Routt County—and a new turn of events provided hope. A state representative introduced a bill to construct a tunnel through the base of James Peak with $4 million in bonds to finance the tunnel. The railroad agreed to lease the tunnel for fifty years. The bill passed, and with this good news, an extension was given on the due date of the earlier loan.

While plans for new construction went forward, the finished section of railroad was used by tourists. Some went to Steamboat Springs to celebrate the Fourth of July. A "fisherman's special" left Denver on Saturday mornings for Steamboat Springs and returned on Monday mornings. Another source of income appeared just after Christmas 1911, when winter sports, especially skiing, became popular. Even so, all of this was not sufficient to save the railroad.

On May 1, 1912, without money to pay off the loans, the Denver, Northwestern and Pacific went into receivership but kept operating. Even though the tunnel-project legislation was defeated by a vote of the people, the railroad was still extended from Steamboat Springs to Craig before it finally died in 1913, only to rise again as the newly formed Denver Salt Lake Railroad.

The idea of a railroad tunnel had been almost abandoned when, in 1921, nature stepped in. A spring flood swept away a good portion of Pueblo. Some legislators from southern Colorado wanted the state to provide flood-control work. In addition to still seeking a railway tunnel, Denver legislators were arguing the need for a better water supply and sought state funding for a water tunnel. The Denver representatives agreed to support the flood-control legislation in exchange for votes to build a water tunnel as well as the long-awaited railway tunnel. The Moffat Tunnel Bill passed.

On February 26, 1928, the first train passed through the Moffat Tunnel. Fanny Moffat was not among the dignitaries at the ceremonies that marked this event. She had died on October 24, 1926, leaving her money and jewels to Cubby. She was buried beside David Moffat in the Fairmount Cemetery. Unfortunately, the marker on their graves is not the one originally proposed, "a rough-hewn block of granite from the heart of the Moffat Tunnel."

Casimiro Barela

1847–1920 • Trinidad

It was Halloween in 1896. Casimiro Barela stood speaking to an attentive crowd in Hoehne, Colorado. He was trying to persuade voters to reelect him to the Colorado state senate. Like any good politician, he had already told them what he thought he had accomplished so far as a senator and now was describing his plans for the future. Barela was experienced, well prepared and came across as a sincere and effective speaker.

Suddenly a shot rang out. Then another, followed by three more. After a moment of shocked silence, this quiet, ordinary meeting suddenly erupted into wild confusion. Barela fell to the ground and touched his cheek, which was stinging. He stared down in astonishment to find his hand wet with blood. A bullet had grazed his face.

The would-be murderers had shot from the window of the second story of an adjacent building. Several audience members, realizing that they had just witnessed an assassination attempt, rushed after the shooters. A posse was quickly organized to chase down the two men seen running away down a dusty alley.

Everyone in the crowd milled about, talking loudly, telling their version of what they had seen, all still very confused. Gradually, people came to understand what had occurred. Two unhappy citizens had attempted to make a deadly political statement of their own against the incumbent Colorado senator.

Most people were both astonished and furious over the shooting. Several of the crowd suggested that as soon as the gunmen were caught, they should be hanged on the spot. There was a lot of support for this idea, and indeed, emotions were so high this might have happened, except for Barela. Composed and calm, he said, "Violence is not the answer. Let the law take its course." The gunmen were eventually caught, jailed, tried and punished under the law, while Barela went on to win his reelection bid and serve again in the state senate.

The history of this man, who became such a strong voice for otherwise disenfranchised members of the communities in the southern half of Colorado, is an interesting one. Casimiro Barela's ancestor Casimiro Varella headed a colony of eighty emigrants from Spain who landed in San Jose, California, on February 25, 1777. Varella and his descendants gradually made their way east to New Mexico, where they settled in the little town of Embudo. It was here that Casimiro Barela was born on March 4, 1847. Casimiro's birth came right in the middle of the U.S.-Mexico War, which lasted from 1846 to 1848. At the end of the war, Embudo became part of the United States in New Mexico Territory.

Although he did his share of work on the family farm, young Barela received extensive schooling from Bishop J.B. Salpointe at Mora, New Mexico. Barela was a good student and showed leadership abilities early on. When he was seventeen years old, he was invited to go on a business trip with some of the padres to Colorado Territory. This small group made the hard journey over Raton Pass. Although he loved what he saw in Colorado, Barela returned home to New Mexico Territory in time to help with the fall harvest on his father's farm.

Three years later, in 1867, when Casimiro Barela was twenty years old, he and his family decided to moved to Colorado Territory. In the 1860s, traders from New Mexico brought supplies over Raton Pass to feed the growing city of Denver. Gold miners also passed this way. Situated at 6,025 feet in the foothills just east of the Sangre de Cristo Mountains, it was great farming country. Instead of passing through as traders and gold seekers, twelve families from Mora decided to settle here, and they established the little town of Trinidad.

When they arrived in Colorado, searching for a place to farm, Barela and his family were also impressed with the fertile valley of the Purgatory River. They began farming about twenty miles from Trinidad. The little town was only six years old when Barela and his relatives staked out sections of land under the Homestead Act.

Barela and his family immediately settled into the small community. They planted grain and raised cattle, sheep and Thoroughbred horses. He and his family members worked hard and were successful. Barela went back very briefly to New Mexico to marry Josefita Ortiz in the chapel of El Sepello. He and his bride immediately returned to became actively involved in the life of Trinidad.

Casimiro proved himself to be a businessman as well as a farmer and rancher. He took his extra produce in wagons to sell at Fort Union and other settlements along the old Santa Fe Trail. Over the years, as railroads moved into the area to carry both produce and coal, the Colorado and Southern Railroad established a small station at Casimiro's land and named it Barela, Colorado. Casimiro Barela and his family were now "on the map."

At age twenty-two, Casimiro Barela was elected justice of the peace in Trinidad. In 1870, he became the county assessor. Within five years, Barela had become successful and well known. Using his money wisely, he invested in a large sheep ranch; continued his interest in cattle, Thoroughbred horses and farming; and was soon investing in railroads, banks and real estate. He became an officer in the incorporation of the San Luis Valley Railroad and was a director of the American Savings Bank of Trinidad.

Barela erected a building at 234 North Commercial just left of the United Presbyterian Church. Dr. Michael Beshnar, the first medical doctor in southern Colorado, established his practice there and later bought the building, which later housed the first daily newspaper in Trinidad. Barela also owned a blacksmith shop and a dry goods store, and he was named postmaster for the little town of Barela.

Family was very important to Casimiro Barela. He and his wife had nine children, although only three daughters survived early childhood. For his wife and children, he built a mansion called "El Porvenir" at the base of a mountain. It was a very elaborate home and included gardens, pools, a drawbridge and turrets so that the whole estate resembled a castle.

Casimro Barela and the territory of Colorado were both growing and thriving, and somehow Barela managed to make time not only for family and business but also for an increasingly active role in government. He became the county sheriff in 1871. And it was no surprise that when a group was organized to govern the growing territory and do the initial work of proposing statehood, Barela was elected to the Colorado Territorial Assembly in both 1871 and 1873.

When Casimiro Barela went to Denver as a territorial representative from the newly formed Las Animas County, he joined four other Spanish-speaking legislators at their first session. These four represented many people in the Colorado Territory who spoke Spanish and could not read or speak English. Barela had the advantage of being fluent in both languages and an eloquent speaker.

In 1875, Barela was chosen to be one of the forty-nine people to write a constitution for the new state of Colorado. Knowing that many people in the

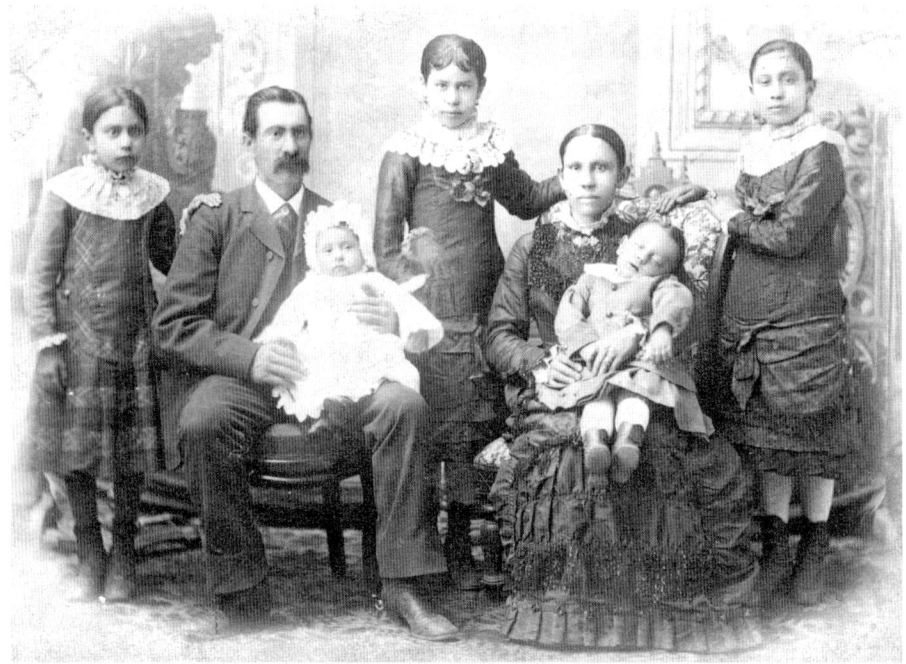

Casimiro Barela and family. *Courtesy of Cheryl Olsen.*

southern part of the state did not speak English, Barela worked hard to have the new constitution written in Spanish and German as well as English, so that everyone would be able to read and understand it. This was not an easy task to accomplish. Other committee members wanted the constitution to be written only in English. Barela held firm until a compromise was reached. The Colorado constitution was written in English, but it was agreed that it would also be printed in Spanish and German for thirty years.

When Colorado became a state in 1876, Barela was elected as a state senator from Las Animas County. For his service, like other senators of his day, he received four dollars a day and fifteen cents a mile when he traveled to take part in the workings of the senate.

After his first wife died, Barela married again in 1884. His second wife was a very wealthy woman from New Mexico named Damiana Rivera. With their combined assets, Barela and his wife were the wealthiest Hispanics in southern Colorado. In fact, by the mid-1880s, Barela was considered one of the three richest men in the entire state.

Barela continued to run for office and to be reelected for term after term. His tenure lasted forty years, until 1916, making him one of the longest-serving state senators in the history of the United States. In Colorado, Barela earned the name of "the perpetual senator."

Barela was a successful politician partly because he kept in touch with the times. In his early political career, Barela was a Democrat. But in 1904, when Teddy Roosevelt ran for president on the Republican ticket and on an enormously popular reform movement, Barela switched parties. He became a Republican.

Barela was active at the state level in spearheading reforms and in the progressive movement. He also attended the national Republican convention as a delegate and assisted in the nomination of William Howard Taft for president in 1908. Whichever party he joined, Barela continued to work for causes that were important to him.

Barela could always be counted on to be supportive of the interests of cattlemen and sheep men. Ranching had been an important way of life for him and his family. All his life, he understood and championed their causes. In addition, he was an ardent supporter of the silver mining interests.

Barela also tried to maintain good relations between the United States and Mexico. He delivered a memorable speech on the floor of the senate, asking that the state return several battle flags that were captured during the Mexican war. He stated that such a gesture would "touch the hearts of that people and stimulate them to closer ties with ours."

Any minority group might find an advocate in Casimiro Barela. He was a strong voice in support of women's rights, and he helped Colorado become the first state in the Union to approve women's suffrage in a popular election. This was achieved through a constitutional amendment passed in a general election on November 7, 1893.

In 1900, there were only thirteen Italian residents in Las Animas County. By 1910, Italian immigrants numbered well over three thousand. Barela immediately took note of this new growing minority group. Barela sponsored a Columbus Day Bill, creating a holiday for these immigrants. This bill became law in the state of Colorado in 1907.

While Barela championed all minorities, Hispanic causes were of special concern to him. Barela represented Hispanic interests not only in Colorado but was also a strong advocate for statehood for the Territory of New Mexico. Due in part to his help, this was finally achieved in 1912. To reach many Hispanics with his political messages, Barela founded two printing businesses. Las Dos Repúblicas was located in Denver, where large numbers of Hispanics were congregating, and El Progresso was located in Trinidad. With these resources, Barela provided free leaflets and articles in Spanish. He reached out to new Hispanic immigrants as they made their transition to

American culture. He also served as the Denver consul for the Republics of Mexico and Costa Rica.

Toward the turn of the century, coal deposits in southern Colorado brought in many newcomers. As more and more Anglos poured in to what had been a largely Hispanic farming area, many of the newcomers challenged the various land grants that old Hispanic families had held for many years. Some of these grants dated back to the Republic of Mexico before the American annexation of this area in 1848.

In one notable case, two Hispanic cattle ranchers felt that their land holdings were being threatened by the powerful Colorado Fuel and Iron Company. When these ranchers refused to sell their land to CF&I, the large coal company tried to take the land anyway by maintaining the cattlemen's claims to the land were fraudulent.

Barela immediately took on the ranchers' cause and referred the matter to the state land board for investigation. The appraisers for the board resolved the matter within a week and decided that the cattlemen rightfully owned the land. Barela had again stood up for Hispanics and ranching interests, and in so doing, he had made enemies.

Things were clearly changing in southern Colorado politics in the early 1900s.

Opposition increased to Hispanic interests and to Senator Barela, who represented them. Barela won reelection by a slim margin in 1900. The election was so close that a recount was needed. Barela was declared the winner and was returned to the senate.

After winning reelection in 1902 as a Republican, Barela knew that to remain in power, he had to balance his efforts to fight for Hispanic rights with cool political sense. Barela had to depend more and more on Anglo votes if he wanted to remain in office.

In spite of his best efforts to keep changing with the times, Barela's long tenure in the senate came to an end in 1916, when he was defeated by Wesley De Busk. Casimiro Barela then retired to Rivera, where he spent the last few years of his life. He died on December 18, 1920.

The old town of Barela, Colorado, is no longer on the map. But the legacy of Casimiro Barela remains. Many years later, another prominent Hispanic politician, Federico Peña, in an upset victory, became mayor of Denver. To be elected, like Barela before him, Pena had to bridge the gap between ethnic groups.

Casimiro Barela is one of sixteen important figures in Colorado history to be honored with stained-glass windows in the rotunda of the state capitol building.

Adolph Coors

1847–1929 • Golden

It was Memorial Day 1894. A flash flood came rushing down Clear Creek Canyon into Golden, Colorado. Townspeople gathered what possessions they could and fled the onslaught of water. Everywhere were dead sheep, flattened trees and the ruined bits and pieces of buildings that had already washed away. How much of the town was going to be lost? Amid this devastation, Adolph Coors stood his ground between the raging waters of Clear Creek and his brewery. Determined not to leave, Coors watched as the waters sheared off an expensive new addition to his business. The man-made ice ponds where his workers cut ice blocks in winter went under, and the waters kept rising, inch by inch, up the slope.

What happened next was described in Golden's newspaper, the *Colorado Transcript*: "When Mr. Coors found the raging torrent encroaching on his grounds, with his accustomed energy, he purchased several lots on the opposite side of the creek and put an army of men to work tearing down the houses on them and cutting away the ground in an endeavor to turn the channel away from his premises."

This desperate plan, quickly acted on, worked. Despite having to abandon his residence for a time because it was surrounded with water, Coors was able to save it, as well as the main brewery, which was located on slightly higher ground. Even though his losses amounted to $10,000, the brewery survived, and so did Adolph Coors, who went on to build his fortune and to lead the Coors brewery for thirty more years.

Adolph Herman Kohrs was born on February 4, 1847, in Barmen, a Prussian city located in the hill country. It was about forty miles from the Rhine River and would later be known as the German city of Wuppertal. When Adolph was only thirteen, he went to work for two years at the book and stationery store of Andrea and Company in the nearby town of Ruhrort to help support his family.

Adolph's family moved to the larger town of Dortmund, Westphalia, early in 1862. Soon after that, his mother died. Three months later, Kohrs was apprenticed for a period of three years to a brewery owned by Henry Wenker. In November, Kohrs's father died, leaving Adolph an orphan at age fifteen. To pay for the privilege of learning the brewer's trade in his apprenticeship, Kohrs worked as a bookkeeper for the company and, after completing his training, continued to work at the Wenker Brewery as a paid employee until May 1867. Later, Kohrs worked in breweries in Kassel, Berlin and Uelzen in Germany.

At this time, Prussia was seething with unrest. William I, king of Prussia since 1861, sought to become emperor of a united Germany, and many men were being taken into the army to fight the king's wars. Kohrs faced the choice of joining the army or leaving the country. He chose to emigrate, becoming one of the half million Germans who came to the United States between 1866 and 1870. In 1868, Kohrs made his way to Hamburg and then stowed away on a ship sailing to Baltimore. Discovered before the ship docked, he was permitted to pay for his passage with money he earned later in Baltimore.

Once in the United States, he changed his surname name from Kohrs to Coors. Adolph Coors was twenty-one years old, almost penniless and spoke little English. Like many immigrants, he took whatever jobs he could get. In the spring, he was a laborer; in summer, he worked in a brewery, and in the fall and winter he worked as a fireman loading coal into the firebox of a steam engine in the Baltimore area. For a time, he also worked as a bricklayer and a stone cutter. Paying his fare by working in various positions, Coors had made his way to Chicago by May 1868.

Throughout his many odd jobs, Coors never lost sight of his dream of being a great brewer of beer. In the summer of 1869, Coors took a job as foreman of John Stenger's brewery in Naperville, Illinois, just thirty-five miles from Chicago. Learning more about his trade and saving money, Coors was soon ready to make his next move. He resigned from his job in January 1872 and, with his savings, headed west, paying his way to Denver, Colorado, by working at various railway jobs.

Arriving in Denver, Coors did not spend his savings but immediately took work for a month as a gardener while he looked for business opportunities. Then, in May 1872, Coors purchased a partnership in the bottling company of John Staderman. Later that year, he was in a position to buy and take control of the entire business. His company bottled beer, ale, porter, cider, wines and seltzer water and was located in Denver between what are now Fourteenth and Fifteenth Streets on Market Street. He became friends with Jacob Schueler, a confectioner, on Larimer Street.

Although a successful businessman, Coors had not abandoned his dream of owning his own brewery. He was constantly on the lookout for just the right place that would have remarkably good water. Brewing was a good business to enter after the Civil War. During the Civil War, brewers had formed themselves into the United States Brewing Association and helped the federal government by collecting the first tax on beer as a way to help finance the war. Mergers of these companies meant that most beer was now produced in large plants.

Fifteen miles from Denver was the city of Golden. For a short time, Golden had competed with Denver to be the head of the Colorado Territory. In fact, when the U.S. Congress established the Colorado Territory in 1861, Golden did its best to become the capital of the new territory by offering legislators "board and room for $6.00 a week, wood, light, and hall free." With this incentive, the legislature approved Golden as territorial capital in August 1862, and it remained the capital until a decision was made to move it to Denver in 1867.

Golden was making a name for itself as a thriving and enterprising city. One businessman took advantage of the natural clay in the area to build a brick works and pottery plant in 1872. By that time, there was also a smelting works and several flour mills, as well as many new homes and businesses. But eventually it was Denver, not Golden, that got the railroad connections to the East and West Coasts, guaranteeing its place as the major city in the territory.

One Sunday, while out walking near Golden, Coors traveled up Clear Creek Valley east of town. The area reminded him of his home in Germany. When he saw crystal-clear water bubbling up from the ground, he knew he had finally found what he had been searching for. Almost immediately, Coors sold his bottling company, and a few months later, with his own money and monies invested by his confectioner friend Jacob Schueler, Coors bought the abandoned Golden City tannery on the banks of the river at the base of Table Mountain.

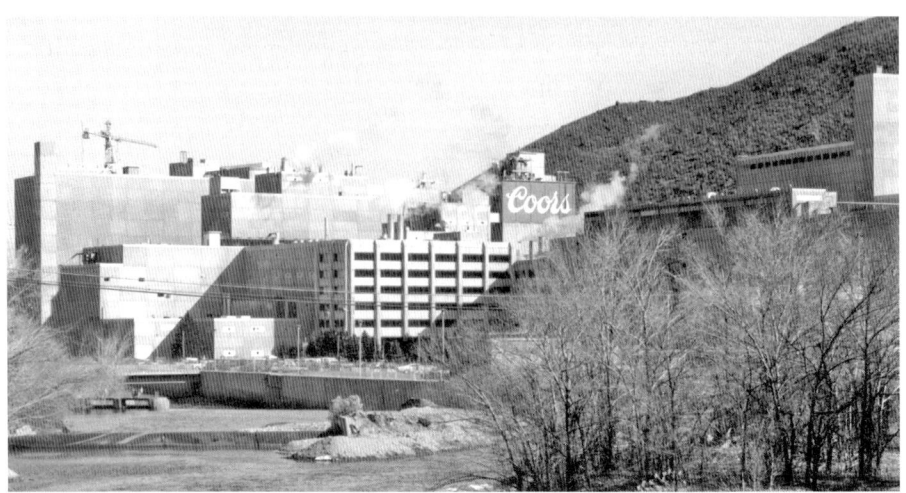

The Coors Brewery on Clear Creek, Golden, Colorado. *David L. Perry.*

Golden's newspaper, the *Colorado Transcript*, announced on November 12, 1873, "Another new and extensive manufactury is about to be added to the number already in Golden. Messers J Scheuler [*sic*] and Adolph Coors, of Denver, have purchased the old tannery property of C.C. Welch and John Pipe, and will convert it into a brewery." Coors moved quickly to convert the old tannery, and by February 1874, the new Golden brewery produced its first beer for sale. Adolph Coors himself carted the thirty-one oaken barrels of beer through town.

Coors was confident his new business was in the right place. The population of the Colorado Territory was growing fast. In 1870, the Colorado Territory had 39,864 people, but just five years later, the population had reached 135,300. When Coors founded his brewery in 1873, the city of Denver was only fifteen years old, but it already had seven small breweries. Golden had no breweries, was near important mining areas and was a point on the Colorado Central railroad that reached into gold and coal mining towns and to the growing cities of Boulder and Longmont. Shortly after its opening, the Golden brewery had throngs of visitors.

During its first year in business, the Golden brewery brewed 10 barrels of beer a day. Coors beer was taken to towns such as Denver and Blackhawk by horse and wagon. By comparison, two of the big American breweries at that time were producing 100,000 barrels of beer a year. Coors's business did so well in its first year that it began expanding. In the next few years, Coors constructed new buildings for a malt house, a bottling plant, an ice dam and a pavilion.

In 1874, a grasshopper plague destroyed many crops in the West. The publisher of Golden's newspaper suggested that hard-hit farmers consider growing barley instead of wheat because barley could be harvested earlier and there would be a demand for it in breweries. Some years later, Coors began using locally grown barley and eventually established his own malting barley growing program.

Adolph Coors also began to take a more active part in politics. He was chosen as a delegate to the state Democratic convention in Pueblo and appeared before the Golden City Council to protest an increase in retail license taxes. For the most part, Coors devoted his time and energy to his business rather than to politics, but he involved himself in local affairs in small ways. He was a member of the committee to raise money for a new railroad depot and was on the judging committee for Golden's Fourth of July firemen's races, where he offered twenty-five dollars' prize money and a box of beer to the winners of a tug-of-war contest.

Temperance and anti-temperance groups became active in the early 1880s. A number of cities wanted to prohibit the sale of alcohol. As early as 1845, the U.S. Supreme Court upheld using local option laws, so some villages, towns and even states were "dry," but as late as 1861, there were no liquor regulations in Colorado whatsoever. That started to change. By 1874, a Ladies Temperance Committee was asking saloonkeepers in Golden to voluntarily go out of business.

Most beer drinking in the 1880s and 1890s was done in saloons, and about 80 percent of Coors beer in the early years was sold in wooden kegs. Of course, some customers wanted to drink beer at home, so they got their beer by sending their sons to the saloon with a tin bucket rimmed with lard. The bartender would fill a bucket with beer, and the boy would carefully carry it home. The lard on the rim of the bucket kept the beer from foaming and spilling on the walk home. The quality of Coors beer attracted customers wherever it was available.

Having experienced some success, Adolph Coors was ready to establish his household. On April 12, 1879, Coors married Louisa Webber, daughter of the superintendent of the railroad maintenance shops for the Denver and Rio Grande Railroads. For years, Mrs. Coors fed her husband's brewery workers simple meals on the brewery grounds. Coors built a typical German beer garden next to the house. Coors entertained as many as eight hundred people at one time in the beer garden. Near the brewery grounds was a skating spot that Coors kept groomed and well lit for public skating. Business was good, and Coors was able to buy out his partner in 1880. Between 1880 and 1890, the brewery's output increased from 3,500 barrels of beer a year to 17,600 barrels a year. Adolph Coors's brother, William, had followed him out to the United States, and eventually he came to Golden to work for his brother in the Coors brewery.

By 1893, Coors and his wife had six children. Their three daughters, Louise, Augusta and Bertha, would all attend Wolcott School for Girls in Denver, while the three sons, Adolph, Grover and Herman, were all sent to Cornell University. All three boys returned to Golden to work in varying capacities in the brewery.

For his family, Coors built a large home surrounded by pine trees and lawns on the grounds of the brewery. The mansion had twenty-two rooms with Oriental rugs and handcrafted furniture. The library held books written by German authors. A chandelier was imported from Copenhagen, and a Steinway piano graced the music room. Dinner in the mansion was a formal affair. The white tablecloths were stitched from the fine linen bags in which hops were shipped from Germany to the brewery. Promptly at 6:25 p.m. each evening, the six children lined up behind their mother and father and filed into the dining room. Recalling this time period, their housekeeper said that the children followed their parents into dinner like "little ducks."

At the 1893 Chicago World's Fair, Coors beer won its first major award. Coors never rested on his laurels and always held firmly to three business beliefs. One was to pay and give fair treatment to the men who worked for him, another was to reinvest profits into the brewery to improve the product and the third was to devote hours of hard work to his business. This last tenet almost got him into serious difficulty at nine o'clock on the evening of June 14, 1897. Working alone in his office, Coors heard a knock on the door and opened it to find a man with a drawn gun. Slamming the door and dashing out the back, Coors rang the plant whistles. The cacophony brought a horde of residents and employees to the plant. The would-be robber left in a hurry.

The movement throughout the country to prohibit the sale of alcohol gained momentum. More and more cities were banning the sale of alcohol through local option laws. In 1907, Boulder was voted dry. A newspaper reported that just before the Boulder saloons closed, they were "patronized as never before, and hundreds of people carried away booze by the gallon." In 1908, Loveland voted itself dry. In 1909, the issue was put on the ballot in Golden, but the town voted to stay "wet." By the end of 1910, 78 million Americans lived in wet states and 13 million in dry states.

In 1912, when he was sixty-five years old, Coors appointed his son Adolph Jr. to be superintendent of the Coors Company. This period of growth and prosperity was coming to an end. The voters of Colorado prohibited the sale of alcohol in a law that went into effect on January 1, 1916, four years before national Prohibition took effect on January 16, 1920. The Coors brewery had to dump 17,391 gallons of beer into Clear Creek. Coors family lore says that Adolph Coors never tasted a glass of beer after that night of New Year's Eve 1915.

By the time of Colorado's prohibition, Adolph Coors Sr. had amassed a fortune of about $2 million, but rather than close his business during the seventeen years of prohibition that followed, he found ways to weather the difficult times. He already was active in industries outside the Golden brewery, including mining, real estate and a cement company. To keep the brewery going, Adolph Coors Sr. and Jr. needed to reduce costs and change products. The Coors family members cut their own salaries and diversified the business. Coors made a near beer called Mannah. This was produced like beer, but after fermentation, the liquid was sent through a still that condensed out the alcohol. This near beer could be sold as a drink, and the alcohol could also be sold to the government, which in turn sold it to drug companies and hospitals. Coors also made malted milk, perfected by Grover Coors, which it sold to candy companies and malt shops. Another new Coors division was devoted to fashioning scientific and chemical products made from porcelain.

After Prohibition ended in 1933, more than half of the brewing companies that had been in business in the United States never reopened. But the first year after Prohibition, the Coors brewery started production again and produced 136,000 barrels of beer. The Coors porcelain plant remained in business and continued to grow into one of the world's leading industrial and technical ceramic manufacturing companies.

Adolph Coors, however, did not live to see the end of Prohibition. He died on June 5, 1929, by leaping from the sixth floor window of the Cavalier Hotel in Virginia Beach, Virginia. He was eighty-three years old and had gone there to recover from the flu. There was much speculation over his death, with most believing that with his active work in the brewery ended, he felt ready for his life to end, too.

Adolph Coors Jr. took over full operation of the company upon his father's death. The family business continued to prosper, and by 1939, the Coors brewery was distributing its product beyond Colorado to many western states. In 1941, World War II broke out, and various industries faced significant shortages. Coors brewery won governmental consent to buy the supplies it needed by reserving one-half of its beer for the military. In 1959, the Coors brewery was the first to introduce all-aluminum beer cans, and with the advent of aluminum cans, the Coors brewery also popularized the idea of recycling.

Through several generations, the Coors brewery continued to prosper and to be a major force in the city of Golden. On the death of Adolph Coors Jr. in 1970, his sons, Joe and William Coors, took over management of the company. For the first time, in 1981, Coors began selling its product east of the Mississippi. Joe Coors's son in turn became CEO upon his father's retirement at the end of 1997, and other members of the family ran subsidiaries of the parent company.

In 1990, the Coors brewery was recognized as the third-largest brewer in America. In 2005, brewers Adolph Coors Company and Canada-based Molson Company merged into the Molson Coors Brewing Company. This combined company ranked fifth in the world in brewing volume. In 2007, Molson Coors merged with SAB Miller to become Miller Coors, the second-largest beer company in America.

In reflecting back on the life of his grandfather, Bill Coors said, "What did my grandfather believe in? I guess, above all, in the promise of the individual." Some people speak of the Coors "dynasty." That dynasty began with Adolph Coors, an immigrant from Germany with a dream of owning his own brewery. Despite enormous business obstacles, including national Prohibition, Adolph Coors, and his brewery, survived turbulent times and thrived as a significant force and major influence in Colorado

Otto Mears

1840–1931 • Poncha Pass

Ten-year-old Otto Mears stood on the deck as the ship pulled into the harbor at San Francisco in 1850. Excitedly, he looked down at the busy pier where crowds of people were waving and calling to passengers. He searched for his uncle's face. Otto had never met this uncle. How would they recognize each other? Would the man simply be looking for a small boy traveling all alone? Straining his ears, at one point Otto thought he heard someone calling his name. He looked quickly in that direction, but he saw no one looking for someone else.

Awkwardly, the boy jostled along with the others, watching everyone rush off the ship onto the dock to meet up with family and friends. Otto Mears stood there in the bustling crowd on the pier. He waited until the ship was empty and the dock was cleared of the crowds before he admitted to himself that his uncle was not coming to meet him. He was all alone in a new city. Who would have thought this small and frightened boy would not only survive but also eventually became a prominent man in the history of Colorado?

Otto Mears was born in the Kurland Province of Russia on May 3, 1840. Although his mother was a native Russian, his father was a British subject. Before Otto was four years old, his parents died, and he began living with a series of relatives in Russia, England and the United States. From an uncle in England, he was sent to New York and then off to live with another uncle in San Francisco.

At that time, travel across the continent was slow and difficult. It took several months for young Otto Mears to travel by ship from New York, cross the Isthmus of Panama on horseback and then sail up the coast of California, only to arrive and find no one at the dock to meet him in San Francisco.

Otto Mears asked everyone he saw for information about his uncle. Someone said they thought he had moved to Australia, but most had simply never heard of him. Whatever the case, Otto found himself entirely on his own in California. Desperate to earn enough to pay for room and board, Mears sold newspapers and took whatever other work he could find and managed to survive. In his teenage years, Mears traveled from one California gold camp to another, finding enough work to stay alive, but was never lucky enough to strike it rich.

Mears was twenty-one when the Civil War broke out. He enlisted in the First Regiment of California Volunteers and served in the Union army for three years. He fought along with Kit Carson in the Navajo campaign in New Mexico. Discharged in 1864 in Las Cruces, New Mexico, Mears moved to Santa Fe and for a time worked as a store clerk. Perhaps because he had been bounced around so much in his youth and had no real home or family to hold him in any one place, Mears soon drifted off to Colorado Territory.

Although he had never gone to school after age ten, Mears was bright, energetic, good with his hands and creative in solving problems. In 1865, he homesteaded a piece of land in the San Luis Valley. His plan was to grow wheat and grind it in a gristmill that he had built himself near the town of Conejos. He also hoped to cut trees in the area, knowing that lumber would be needed for houses for a growing population and to shore up mine tunnels. Since Fort Garland was nearby, Mears thought the government would be another likely market for lumber and flour.

By the time he had harvested a wheat crop and had flour to sell, the price being paid by the government for flour had plummeted. Mears was not one to give up. He learned of a shortage of both flour and lumber in California Gulch, a mining area close to the site where Leadville, Colorado, is now located. Although the mining camp was 140 miles away in mountainous country and it promised to be a difficult trip, Mears did not hesitate. He formed a wagon train and set off to sell his flour and lumber.

For a time, the wagons lurched along over well-traveled roads. Then the roads became worse as the wagon train twisted its way through the San Luis Valley and over Poncha Pass. By that point, the road was only a few scattered wagon tracks. Finally, the road ended, and there was nothing to follow but an Indian trail.

Mears looked up at the top of the mountain and knew that once they reached the other side, his wagon train would find a good market in

California Gulch. He didn't intend to let the lack of a road over a mountain stop him. He didn't forget this experience but came back in two years with picks, shovels and hardworking men from his wagon team. They dug a road where none had existed before. His wagon train made its way to the gold mining area where its load of goods quickly sold.

According to a popular story, another passerby on the Poncha Pass trail who saw Mears and his men working on the road was the former Colorado territorial governor William Gilpin. Impressed by the work that Mears and his men were doing, Gilpin made two excellent suggestions. He told Mears to continue building the road, making sure the grade would be gentle and suitable for a railroad bed, and he encouraged Mears to go on to Denver to charter his road, which would allow Mears to charge a toll for others to use it.

Mears followed through on both suggestions to build the first major toll road in southwest Colorado. In 1867, Mears started building at the town of Saguache and ran his road over Poncha Pass to connect with the road from Denver to the California Gulch gold mines. Mears built a tollgate at the pass to collect fees. It had cost Mears $14,000 to build his toll road, and he collected that amount back in just a few months because of heavy road traffic from miners on the way to strikes in Leadville. Otto Mears's hard work paid off. He was finally making money. In road building, he had found his calling.

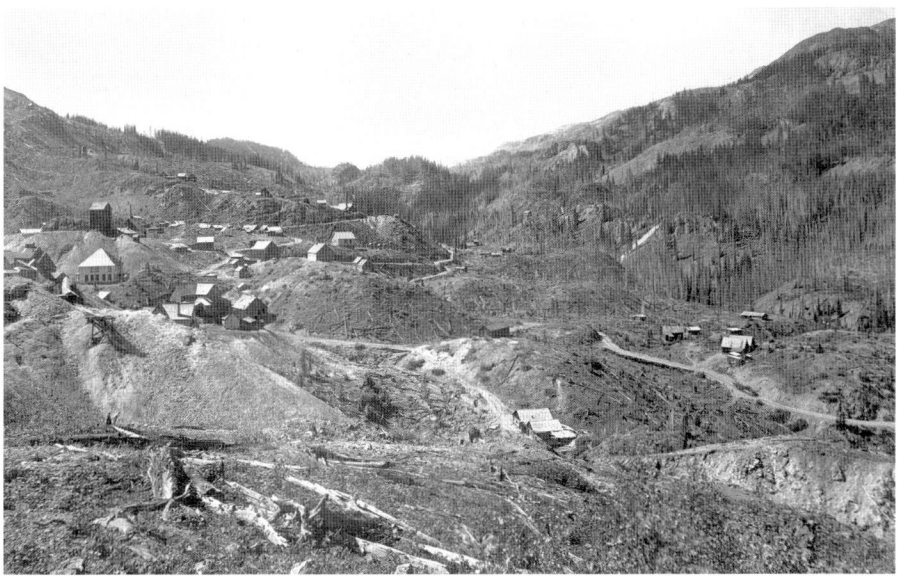

This image views some of Mears's great works up the canyon above Ironton toward Red Mountain atop the pass with the same name at 11,110 feet in altitude. *U.S. Geologic Service.*

Mears met and courted a girl from Granite, Colorado, whom he met there where he had his wheat milled to flour. They married on November 17, 1870. The couple lived in Saguache. An up-and-coming businessman, Mears suddenly found himself destined for a new role. He became a negotiator between Chief Ouray of the Utes and the United States government.

Back in 1868, the Utes had agreed to move from the San Luis Valley, which was becoming crowded with settlers, to a new reservation west of the Continental Divide. Then, to everyone's surprise, silver ore was discovered on the new Ute reservation, and miners rushed in to stake claims. To avoid conflicts between Native Americans and miners, the government decided to move the Utes again, but the tribe was not eager to move a second time.

When the Utes were ready to consider a new treaty, Otto Mears was selected to negotiate this second move. Mears met with Chief Ouray, and after that meeting, he proposed to the principal government negotiator that for the inconvenience of moving again the U.S. government should give the Utes $25,000 a year to move to the Uncompahgre Valley. An additional $1,000 a year would be paid to Chief Ouray. Though unhappy with the proposal at first, the government finally accepted this proposition. Otto Mears was sent with Chief Ouray to Washington, D.C., to meet the president, and the new treaty was ratified by Congress on April 29, 1874.

Mears had already learned that gold and silver strikes meant that towns would be built and roads would be needed, so he set about building another road. This one would connect the Ute Agency to the new town of Lake City. Eager to capitalize on this development, Mears organized the Lake City Land Company to boost settlement of the town. This turned out to be profitable. Within two years, two thousand people were living in Lake City.

His next venture proved risky. After Mears built a toll road to the Ute Indian Agency and brought the toll road from there to Ouray, he negotiated a contract with the government to deliver mail to Ouray three times a week. He was aware that a stiff penalty would be assessed if he failed to deliver, but Mears did not plan to fail. He built relay stations about twenty miles apart. He hired men to deliver the mail using horses and wagons. Mears had already thought ahead to a time when winter snow would make travel difficult. He had dog sleds ready to carry the mail through the snow.

This mail delivery system worked out well until the spring thaw turned the trail to mire, making it impossible for dog sleds or horses and wagons to negotiate the seventy-five-mile trip from Lake City to Ouray. Rather than paying a huge fine for failing to deliver, Otto Mears asked his men to carry the mail on foot. When they refused, he put on a backpack and walked the distance over about ten days to meet the government mail deadline. Mears learned from this experience. When his government mail contract was up, Mears did not renew it.

Mears's toll road over Poncha Pass continued to be profitable. In 1878, there were more silver strikes in Leadville. To feed the settlers, tons of produce were brought over Poncha Pass, and each wagon paid a toll to Otto Mears. When the rush began to Gunnison, Mears built yet another road. This one was constructed over 10,846-foot-high Marshall Pass. In time, Mears sold his Marshall Pass route to the Denver and Rio Grande Railway. This gave the Denver and Rio Grande a head start and allowed them to beat their rivals, the South Park and Pacific Railroad, into Gunnison.

In 1883, Mears built a road from Ouray to Ironton up the Uncompahgre Gorge. It was very expensive to build. His tollbooth over Bear Creek Falls was 274 feet above the canyon floor. Mears charged five dollars for a wagon team to use the road. Today, this route is Colorado State Highway 550, sometimes called the Million Dollar Highway. Some people say its name comes from the cost of rebuilding the road between 1921 and 1924, but others suggest the name refers to the value of mine tailings in the road itself.

Mears could see that what southwestern Colorado needed in the future was steam locomotives that could negotiate the mountains on narrow gauge tracks. Mears decided to use the roadbed of his toll road from Silverton to the Red Mountains for his first railroad. Mears organized the Silverton Railroad Company and began selling stock. Mears wanted to link Silverton to the mining camp of Ironton and haul ore from the Yankee Girl Mine in the Red Mountain Mining District.

Hand labor alone was used to complete the line between Ironton and Silverton by 1883. Tons of ore began to move from the Yankee Girl mines to smelters. Mears had a jeweler make railroad passes out of solid silver and gold to hand out to impress his investors and dignitaries.

Mears was making a name for himself in the Colorado Territory and was selected to serve on the Colorado Board of Capitol Managers. This group would go over plans, select architects and contractors and oversee the building of Colorado's state capitol in Denver. He served on this board from 1890 to 1917.

Mears started another ambitious railroad project in 1890 that he completed in 1892. He built the 172-mile Rio Grande Southern starting with connections with the Denver and the Rio Grande at Ridgway and then going over another old toll road. Then he built on to Durango and

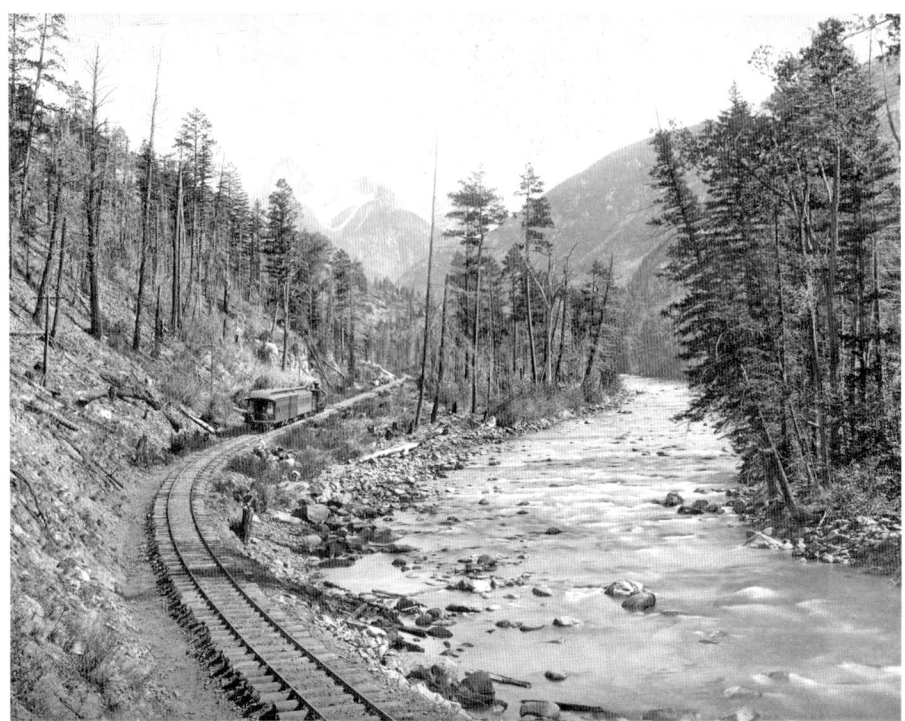

A railroad built by Otto Mears. *William Henry Jackson, 1843–1942, photographer. Library of Congress.*

into Telluride. The trestle at Ophir was so high that legend says frightened passengers were given the option of walking rather than riding over the chasm. The completed railroad was regarded as an engineering marvel.

Unfortunately, this railroad was never particularly profitable. The great silver crash that hit the United States in 1893 caused financial panic and ruined railroad building throughout the West. Many of the railroads, including the Union Pacific, Northern Pacific and the Santa Fe as well as Mears's Rio Grande Southern, went into receivership.

Mears left Colorado for a while in 1896 to take over the presidency of the Washington and Chesapeake Beach Railway in the East. Also during this time, he helped form the Mack Motor Company, which eventually went on to build huge Mack trucks. By 1907, however, Otto Mears returned to Colorado and bought a home in Silverton.

Mears looked back on a very productive career in Colorado. He had built 450 miles of roadway into almost every town in the San Juans, opening up the high mountains for the mining industry. He did this for the most part

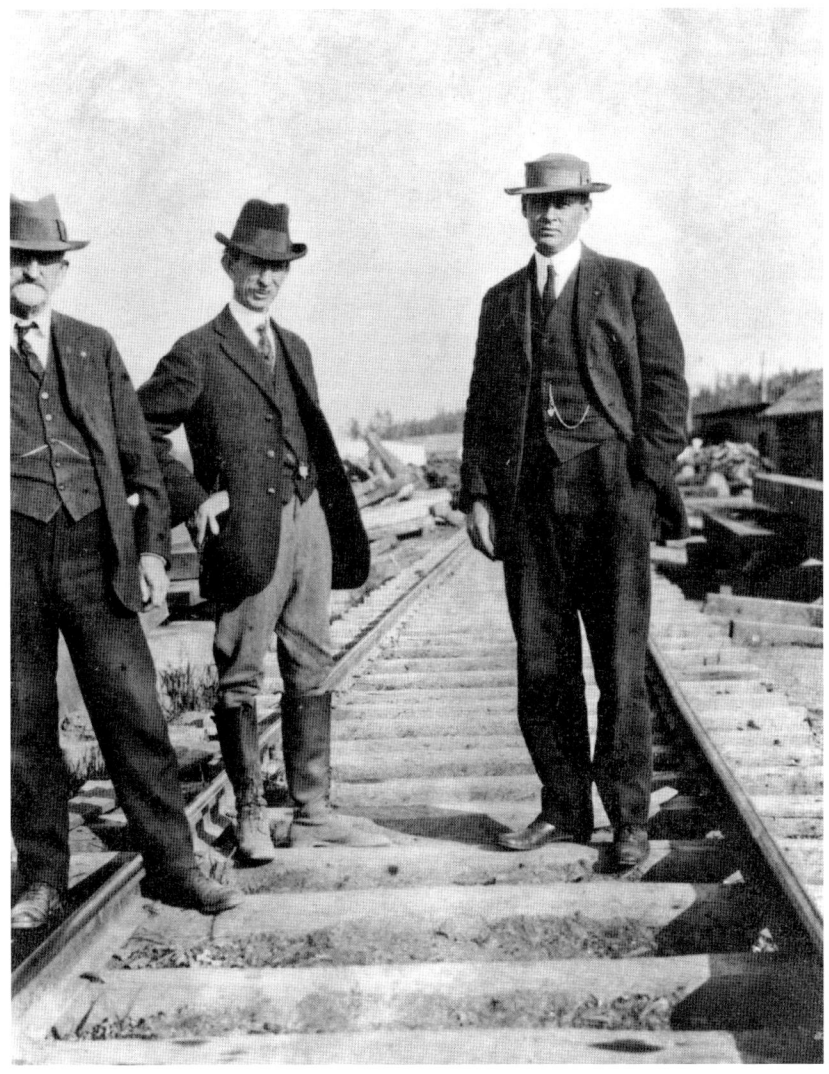

At the new railroad, *left to right*: Mr. Edes, Frank G. Carpenter, Lieutenant Mears (between circa 1900 and 1916). *Library of Congress.*

without government support, earning the nickname of "the Pathfinder of the San Juans."

Mears's wife, with whom he had raised two daughters, was now in failing health. They stayed in Silverton until 1917, when they decided to relocate to the milder climate of Pasadena, California. His wife, Mary, died three years later, but Mears remained in California until his own death in 1931.

A stained-glass portrait in honor of Otto Mears was placed in the senate chamber of the Colorado state capitol in Denver. At his request, a memorial service was held in Silverton, Colorado, and the ashes of Otto and Mary Mears were scattered over the site of the old tollgate on the Rainbow Route south of Ouray.

F.O. Stanley

1849–1940 • Stanley Hotel, Estes Park

It was June 1909. Freelan Oscar Stanley stood in the beautiful new music room and gazed with pride and satisfaction as a spectacular Steinway grand piano was carefully moved into place. The piano was a surprise gift for his wife, Flora, in honor of the opening of a luxury hotel that Stanley had just built in the tiny Colorado mountain town of Estes Park.

F.O. Stanley, who seldom used his name Freelan, was an expert violinist. Music had always been an important part of his life. But never in his wildest dreams, while growing up on a farm in New England, could he have predicted this moment. F.O. had transported this grand piano, which had accompanied such great singers as Enrico Caruso, Lily Pons and Marion Anderson, from a New York opera house to the rugged Rocky Mountains. It had come by train to Lyons, Colorado, and then had to be pulled by ox cart to Estes Park. For Stanley, securing this magnificent piano for Flora was but one more "impossible dream" come true.

F.O. Stanley had followed a long and fascinating path to the Rocky Mountains. Freelan Oscar Stanley and Franklin Edgar Stanley, identical twins, were born in Kingsfield, Maine, on June 1, 1849. Both teachers, their parents gave each of their seven children names from literature, science and religion. They named their first son Isaac Newton. Another son was called John Calvin, and the names of the twins were taken from a Sir Walter Scott novel. Family members usually called them "Freel" and "Frank." Their only daughter was called "Chansonetta," an adaptation of the French name for "little song."

Even as young boys, growing up in the western Maine Carrabassett Valley, the Stanley twins were "whittlers" and "tinkerers." Before they were five years old, their father had bought each of them a jackknife, and from pine and cedar, they made their own toys. By age nine, they were using a lathe to make spinning wooden tops that they sold to playmates. Both boys worked on the farm. F.O. followed a family tradition of violin making established by his grandfather, making his first violin at age sixteen. His twin brother also made violins but spent the bulk of his free time busily experimenting with new photography techniques.

Teaching appealed to the twins as a profession, so when they turned eighteen, they went to Western State Normal School in Farmington, twenty-four miles to the south, to become teachers. F.O. Stanley soon developed tuberculosis and left school for six months to recover. Once he was well again, he went back to school and graduated with the class of 1871. He went on to Hebron Academy and then to Bowdoin College in Brunswick, Maine, for one year. At Bowdoin, he participated in a student strike against a college requirement that all students drill and dress in military attire.

F.O. took a teaching job in Pennsylvania in 1874, and then he returned to Maine to teach in Mechanic Falls. There he met and married another teacher, Flora Tileston. Noticing that students at the school needed mechanical drawing tools, F.O. Stanley began tinkering again. He designed a set of drawing tools that fit in a wooden case and would sell for one dollar. By the early 1880s, he owned a factory and was successfully manufacturing and selling these mechanical drawing tools.

Meanwhile, F.E. Stanley, who had dropped out of Normal School, became a teacher/principal in North New Portland. There he met and married Augusta Walker, "Gusti." F.E. could not give up tinkering, either. After several years of teaching, he began experimenting with various photographic techniques. He secured a patent in 1876 for an airbrush technique. Next, he began coating his own glass photographic plates. By 1881, he had a successful dry-plate photography business and, soon after, had the largest photographic studio in New England.

After firing two plant managers at his dry-plate photographic plant, F.E. invited his twin brother to come join him in the business. The timing was right. F.O.'s drafting tool factory had recently burned down. So in 1884, the Stanley twins were united again as full partners in the Stanley Dry Plate Company.

The twins operated their photographic business in Massachusetts and made good profits. George Eastman approached them with an offer to buy them out. For a time, they resisted, but eventually they sold the business for a sizable fortune. One of the first things the twins did with their money was to buy a home for their widowed sister, Chansonetta Stanley Emmons, who had become one of the best photographers of her day.

Just because they had developed and sold a successful dry-plate photography business did not mean that the twins had stopped tinkering. An excellent opportunity arose when F.E.'s wife, Gusti, complained that she wobbled about too much when she tried to ride a bicycle. F.E. quickly promised her that he'd build something she could safely ride. Instead of making some simple attachment, like training wheels, to keep a bicycle steady, he decided to experiment with something much more complicated.

The two brothers turned their genius to designing one of the first cars. F.E. constructed a small, 350-pound prototype, for $500. The steam engine for this first car was built in Milton, Massachusetts. In September 1897, the brothers drove their new car down Maple Street in Watertown, Maine. The car was a two-seater and rode on spoked bicycle-like wheels. It was a clean and quiet machine with only muffled pumping sounds and the faintly audible whoosh of steam.

F.O. always insisted that building cars was only a hobby and that he and his brother had no intention of manufacturing automobiles. But almost before they knew it, they had purchased on old bicycle factory and began assembling parts for cars. Both brothers loved to race their cars, and they knew how to promote their business, too. In 1896, one of their cars won the hill-climbing contest at Charles River Park. In 1898, another of their early cars made news when it was timed at 27.4 miles per hour. With publicity and fame, one hundred orders for these cars came pouring in.

Turning out the same old car wasn't challenging enough for the twins, so they sold the manufacturing rights to A.B. Barber and J.B. Waller in 1898 for a quarter of a million dollars in cash. The new Locomobile Company began turning out more cars. The Stanley brothers agreed not to build any cars themselves for a year and also agreed to stay on for a year with the company and assist in the factory.

In August 1899, F.O. and Flora Stanley helped publicize the new company by agreeing to drive a little Locomobile to the top of New England's Mount Washington. It meant driving 4,600 feet to the summit, an eight-mile climb up a road of rough sand, gravel and rock with precipitous edges and a steep grade. After reaching the summit, they faced the dangerous drive back down—with primitive brakes. F.O. and Flora succeeded. Their feat made history and was broadcast throughout the world. By the end of the year, two hundred of these automobiles were running on the roads of Massachusetts.

After selling their original designs, assisting in the factory and promoting the Locomobile for a year, the Stanley twins kept tinkering. They made many improvements over their earlier inventions and soon designed new and better steam cars. The most popular of these was called the Stanley Steamer. A 1903 model sold for $750, which worked out to be $1 a pound. A demonstration ride with F.E. or F.O. was included. Another model was a speedy little roadster that in 1907 went an unbelievable seventy-five miles per hour.

The Stanley Steamer had some drawbacks. It could go only about fifty miles before it was necessary to add water. Starting up the car was a slow process, because it took ten to fifteen minutes for the water in the car to develop a head of steam sufficient to propel it. In the early 1900s, Henry Ford began making automobiles. These cars with gasoline engines did not have the two main problems of the Stanley Steamers. Ford's gasoline cars quickly became very popular, largely replacing steam automobiles.

When F.O. Stanley was fifty-four years old, his doctor confirmed that he had tuberculosis again and gave him only six months to live. Thinking that clean, high mountain air might prolong his patient's life, the doctor sent Stanley to live in a mountain cabin in the tiny town of Estes Park, Colorado, which had fewer than one hundred residents.

To reach their new home, Flora took a train from Denver to Lyons and a stagecoach to Estes Park. But F.O. decided to drive there in his own Stanley Steamer. Everyone he spoke with in Colorado thought that driving an auto up the rough, narrow road was insanity. Since no one wanted to go along, Stanley went alone and made the trip without trouble. Apparently Estes Park was exactly what F.O. Stanley needed. He made a miraculous recovery. Within three months, his weight had increased from 118 pounds to 147. Once again, F.O. Stanley was filled with energy and enthusiasm.

Stanley's wife suggested that they build a house, and this they did in 1906. They spent the next thirty-seven summers in a gracious home on Wonder View Avenue. But a mere house was not enough to occupy F.O. Stanley's energy. He had bigger plans. He wanted to build a luxury hotel in the middle of the Rocky Mountains, believing that guests from the East Coast would flock to it to enjoy the magnificent scenery. In the area of his home, Stanley purchased 1,400 acres of land from the Irish earl, Lord Dunraven, who had come to Estes Park area in 1872 on a hunting trip and ended up purchasing thousands of acres of land from homesteaders.

Later that year, Stanley started work on the hotel by investing $500,000 and hiring the Denver architect T. Robert Wieger. The majestic Georgian-

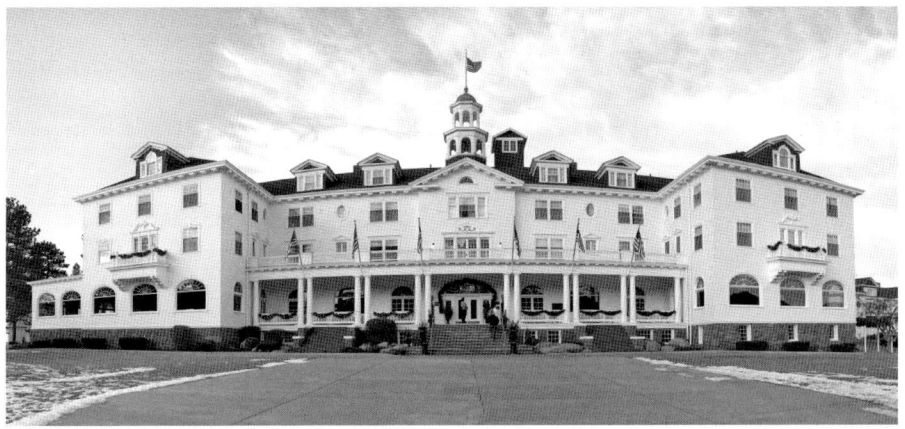

The landmark Stanley Hotel overlooks Estes Park, Colorado. *Brett Levin.*

style hotel was completed in 1909. Well ahead of its time, this hotel boasted running water, electricity and telephones in each of its 135 rooms. It had a one-hundred-foot long veranda with sixteen columns stretching between two wings. Tall windows took advantage of the mountain views. There was also a billiards room and the beautiful music room.

Building this large hotel in the mountains, located seventy-two miles from a city, was far from easy. Materials and supplies needed to be brought by horse and wagon from Lyons. Tremendous care was taken with furnishing each room. F.O. Stanley loved to play billiards and carefully planned the elegant billiard room with its dark wood paneling. Filled with light, the music room featured a view of Longs Peak out the window. Stanley also provided facilities for tennis and an eighteen-hole golf course.

Adjacent to the hotel was the Stanley Concert Hall, first used in June 1909 when the Colorado Pharmaceutical Association held its twentieth annual meeting in it. Stanley planned theater and art performances and dinner dancing. He even wrote music. One of the programs for the concert hall on August 18, 1940, listed "Original compositions—F.O. Stanley, played by the Stanley Ensemble quartet."

A first-class hotel must have a first-class kitchen. Stanley designed what may have been the first all-electric kitchen in the country. And he also designed a hydroelectric plant to supply the electricity not only for his hotel but for the whole town of Estes Park. Stanley knew exactly how to get his guests to the hotel from Denver. He used a fleet of his own Stanley Steamer automobiles to drive them up winding roads to the hotel.

As usual, F.O. Stanley was successful. The rich and famous flocked to stay at the Stanley Hotel. Guests included such well-known and diverse personalities as Teddy Roosevelt, John Philip Sousa and the Unsinkable Molly Brown.

Over the next ten years, the hotel thrived, and Stanley kept busy with many projects for the town of Estes Park. In addition to providing the hydroelectric plant, Stanley improved roads and gave land for a fairgrounds and a city park. He joined with others such as Enos Mills and Cornelius Bond in promoting a huge game refuge in the area, an idea that eventually evolved into Rocky Mountain National Park.

His twin brother, F.E. Stanley, was killed in an automobile accident in 1918. Shortly after that, F.O. Stanley sold their auto company. And in 1920, he sold the Stanley Hotel to the Rocky Mountain Transportation Company. F.O. and Flora Stanley returned to live in their New England home.

Though retired again, F.O. set up a partnership with his nephew, Carlton Stanley, in a violin-making business. F.O. provided the equipment and space, and Carlton did most of the work. While F.O. and F.E. had built only twenty-five violins in their lives—and these were always made for friends and family—Carlton produced and sold more than five hundred. They were considered exceptionally high-quality instruments that are prized by musicians and collectors to this day.

F.O. and Flora moved back to New England, but they continued to come and spend each summer in Estes Park until 1939, when Flora died. His long residence and devotion to the town caused F.O. Stanley to be known as the "grand old man of Estes Park."

Even though F.O. Stanley was expected to die of tuberculosis in 1903 at age fifty-four, he actually lived to be ninety-one years of age. He died in Newton, Massachusetts, on October 2, 1940, just ten days after returning home from a visit to Estes Park. Commenting on his death, the trustees of the Hebron Academy reported, "He planned always for tomorrow. He lived in the future tense."

Nikola Tesla

1856–1943 • Telluride, Colorado Springs

It was dusk in the little village of Smiljan, a rural area of Croatia, in 1859, and a three-year-old boy sat inside his house gently stroking the back of the family cat, Macak. The action of the boy rhythmically stroking the fur produced a shower of lively sparks of static electricity that could be seen and heard crackling in the quiet room. Excited by the tiny points of light he had produced, the boy asked what had caused the sparks. His father explained this was nothing but electricity, the same thing that he sometimes saw during a storm.

The boy's mother, alarmed and fearing he might cause a fire, asked the boy to stop playing with the cat. That child was Nikola Tesla, and many years later in his autobiography, he vividly recalled this formative incident. He remembered wondering, "Is nature a giant cat? If so, who strokes its back? It can only be God, I concluded. Day after day I asked myself what is electricity, and found no answer." Eventually, Nikola Tesla found many of the answers he sought as a child and became one of the world's greatest inventors. He lived much of his adult life in New York, but Tesla spent a year experimenting in Colorado Springs, and the first practical demonstration of the use of his technology that harnessed alternating current electricity was demonstrated in Telluride, Colorado.

Nikola Tesla was born in Croatia (then Austria-Hungary) at midnight on July 9, 1856, during a fierce thunderstorm. He grew up in a rural area. Tesla had a brilliant older brother, Dane, who was killed in a horse-riding accident when Nikola was only a child. By comparison to his brother, Nikola did not think of himself as a great student, but he knew from a young age that he wanted to be an engineer.

A well-educated philosopher, writer, poet and priest of the Serbian Orthodox Church, Tesla's father, Milutin, had decided this son would enter the clergy. He would hear no talk of any other career. As a child, Tesla was fond of reading, but his father would not permit him to do much of it, because he thought it would hurt the boy's eyes. In fact, his father hid the candles so that Tesla could not read at night. Unknown to his parents, the young boy obtained tallow, formed candles in tin cans and by their light he often read almost all evening long.

Tesla credits his father with teaching him to memorize long passages and to perform mental calculations. But it is from his mother that Tesla felt he inherited his inclination to invent. Djuka Tesla's family contained a long line of inventors. Her father and grandfather had invented a number of household and farm implements. In his autobiography, Tesla describes her as "a truly great woman of rare skill, courage, and fortitude." He wrote that she was an "inventor of the first order" who came up with all sorts of tools and devices.

After his brother's death, Nikola and his family moved to the nearby little city of Gospic. Almost immediately, young Nikola Tesla became a hero. He was only seven years old, attending a picnic and celebration on a Saturday to see the town's new firefighting equipment in action. When the apparatus was turned on, no water came from the hose. Nikola Tesla ran to the river, jumped in, swam to the hose and straightened out a kink in it so that water began pouring from the hose. When asked how he knew what was wrong with the hose, Tesla replied, "It just came into my head, and I knew what I had to do." Cheering firefighters carried the boy through town.

While attending elementary school in Gospic, Tesla became especially interested in water turbine engines and constructed several of these. His family recalled that after seeing a picture of Niagara Falls in one of his father's books, Tesla told his uncle he hoped to go there some day and carry out a plan he had of building a big wheel that would be run by the crashing waterfalls.

At age ten, Tesla entered what was called the Real Gymnasium, a sort of junior high school, which was well equipped with models of scientific apparatus, electrical and mechanical. He proved to be good at mathematics but poor at freehand drawing. After completing his course at the Real Gymnasium when he was fourteen years old, Tesla became very ill, a pattern of response to stress that he followed most of his life.

Once Tesla recovered, he was sent off to the Higher Real Gymnasium in Carlstadt, Croatia, where he lived with a relative. Considered a prodigy in math and physics, he completed the four-year program in three years with one of the highest averages in his class. At seventeen, Tesla turned toward serious invention. He went about this differently from most. He believed experimenting with crude ideas was a waste of energy, money and time. Why make endless drawings and models? Tesla said he could visualize in his mind the object he was trying to create and could change its construction, make improvements and even operate it, all in his mind. He insisted he could "rapidly develop and perfect a conception" without touching anything.

Now that he had graduated from high school, Tesla was dreading being sent off to study for the clergy because he still wanted desperately to be an engineer. Hoping to convince his parents to let him pursue a career in science, Tesla went home to talk with them. Cholera had struck his village, and he contracted the disease and became critically ill. During this long illness, Tesla pleaded with his father to allow him to study engineering. Reluctantly, his father agreed. In September 1875, at nineteen years old, Tesla entered the Polytechnic Institute in Graz, Austria.

During his three years at Graz, Tesla often studied from three o'clock in the morning until eleven o'clock at night. In his first year, he passed nine exams with the highest qualifications. He spent so much time in study that his professors worried about his health. Several of Tesla's professors took special notice and devoted extra time to him.

In physics class, during his second year, Tesla saw a horseshoe-shaped laminated field-magnet that stood over and around a cylinder tightly wrapped in wire. This new machine, a direct current generator, designed by Thomas Alva Edison, was impressing the scientific world, but the contact brushes used to provide current flowing in only one direction caused a lot of sparking. Tesla wondered if it was possible to operate a motor without brushes. His professor assured him it wasn't. In fact, he said, "Mr. Tesla may accomplish many great things, but he certainly will never do this…It is a perpetual-motion scheme, an impossible idea."

A bad period followed. Tesla briefly got involved with gambling, and he left school and worked for a year, living in a boardinghouse in Maribor, near Gratz. In September 1878, Tesla entered the University of Prague at age twenty-four. During the summer after his first year at the university, his father died, and Tesla found himself in need of a job. On learning in 1880 that the Central Telegraph Company in Budapest, Hungary, was hiring, Tesla went there hoping to be hired as an engineer. The project was still in the planning stages, but Tesla was hired on as a low-paid draftsman. His talents were soon recognized, and he was promoted to design a new telephone apparatus.

At this point, Tesla fell ill again. Doctors believed he was working too hard and not getting enough exercise. Tesla began taking long walks with a friend. One afternoon while walking in a city park, in what he describes as a "flash of lightning," Tesla saw the solution to his brushless current problem. Taking a stick, he drew on the sand for his friend the diagram that he would present six years later to the American Institute of Electrical Engineering.

Knowing that when an electric current is generated, a magnetic field is also created, Tesla realized there was a way to transform the magnetic field into a whirling rotating force. He would use an armature to create two or more alternating currents, out of step with each other. This would generate more electricity to go over a longer distance than direct current. In less than two months, Tesla came up with all the types of motors and modifications of the system that soon became identified with his name. Tesla accepted a position in the Central Telegraph Office of the Hungarian Government, where his talents were immediately recognized.

At twenty-six years of age, Tesla moved to Paris in April 1882. In addition to Serbian, he spoke French, English and German. He rented rooms on the edge of the Latin Quarter where many professors and students lived. Tesla soon settled into a routine. Up at five o'clock in the morning, he went to a bathing house to swim and then walked to the Continental Edison Company. Eccentric in the extreme, he counted each step he took as he walked to the factory. Since he liked things to be divisible by three, he always swam

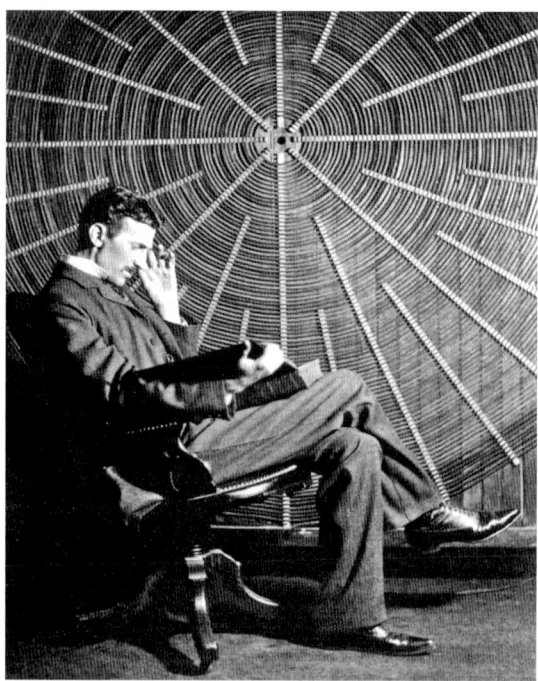

Nikola Tesla ponders a book while seated in front of a "Tesla coil" high-voltage transformer in his New York laboratory, 1896. *Originally published in "Tesla's Important Advances" in* Electrical Review, *May 20, 1896. Wikimedia Commons.*

twenty-seven laps of the pool. He disliked shaking hands and would not touch anyone's hair. He professed to have very sensitive hearing, stating that a fly landing on a table made a thud in his ear.

Tesla's boss, Charles Batchelor, was a close friend of Edison. Tesla kept busy traveling from one place to another in France and Germany, curing the ills of power plants. In his spare moments, he worked on developing his alternating current motor. Discouraged at not having the money to develop his new motor, Tesla took Batchelor's advice, along with a letter of introduction, and sailed off to the United States to meet Thomas Alva Edison.

Tesla arrived in the United States in 1884 and immediately went to work for Edison, but the two did not get along well. Edison said that Tesla was a "poet of science," whose ideas were "magnificent but utterly impractical." Tesla said of Edison, "His method was inefficient in the extreme." Tesla thought he had an agreement with Edison to be paid a $50,000 bonus if he could improve the dynamos that generated electricity for Edison's plants. Tesla did the work but was paid no bonus, so he quit. At twenty-nine years old, Tesla had little money and needed a job.

Some associates were eager for Tesla to form an electric company in his name, but they were interested not in alternating current but rather in improving the arc lamp for industrial and city lighting. The Tesla Electric Light Company was formed in 1885, and Tesla perfected a system of arc lighting in 1886 that was widely adopted for factory and municipal lighting. But investment money remained scarce for Tesla's alternating current idea.

A.K. Brown, manager of the Western Union Telegraph Company, loaned Tesla money and helped him form the Tesla Electric Company so that Tesla could begin building his motors. In 1887 and 1888, Tesla applied for and was granted more than thirty patents for original work. In 1889, the American Institute of Electrical Engineers invited Tesla to lecture on his alternating current system.

With this publicity, a "battle of the currents" started. Some, like Edison, believed in direct current and resisted changes. Others championed Tesla's alternating current theories. In 1889, an arrangement was made with George Westinghouse, a Pittsburgh inventor and businessman. Westinghouse would offer a contract that paid $1,000,000 in cash plus royalties for all the patents on Tesla's AC motors. Tesla accepted and went to work for the next year in Pittsburgh, where the Westinghouse Company was located. After a year, Tesla left, stating that he was tired of arguing with engineers about the capability of the machinery.

Independent at last with his own money, Tesla turned to his own work, creating a high-frequency alternating current transformer, which came to be called the Tesla coil. This device generated very high-voltage electrical discharges including artificial lightning and more practical applications. In 1891, Tesla became a U.S. citizen and was asked to give his second lecture before the American Institute of Electrical Engineers in New York, demonstrating a huge Tesla coil.

In the early 1890s, Westinghouse found his company in financial trouble. To save the company and his good friend, Tesla tore up his royalty contract with the company, which saved Westinghouse huge sums of money. It also meant that Tesla did not have the funds to support his own experimentation. Tesla's idea for alternating currents could prove a financial boon but still needed to be proven commercially feasible. The proving ground turned out to be the San Juan Mountains of Telluride, Colorado. The Gold King Mine was desperate for cheap energy. The owners asked Westinghouse in the spring of 1891 to come up with a plan to generate power from some other source than burning scarce wood or expensive coal.

In exploring the area, Westinghouse found that the San Miguel River falls 500 feet in less than a mile. Westinghouse moved quickly. He built a dam at the top of the cascades. He sold the Gold King Mine a Tesla AC generator, and by June, it was housed in a wooden shack next to a 320-foot waterfall and a new waterwheel. Three thousand volts of electricity traveled three miles on $700 worth of copper wire strung across the mountains to the mine's mill. At the mill, the current was changed by a transformer to power a one-hundred-horsepower single-phase Tesla motor. This simple system survived winter storms, winds and avalanches and was a commercial success.

Nikola Tesla never married, but he had a close relationship with Robert Underwood Johnson and his wife, Katharine Johnson. He often dined with them at their home, where he met writers such as Rudyard Kipling and Helen Hunt Jackson. Another of his friends was Samuel Clemens, known as Mark Twain. Once again, Tesla fell ill and, while recovering, made the decision to stop attending dinner parties and giving lectures and instead to devote his time to invention.

Tesla was in seclusion until February 1893, when he accepted an invitation to lecture at the Franklin Institute in Philadelphia. During his lectures, he was a striking figure dressed in a white tie and tails and wearing shoes with thick cork soles. At the institute, he proposed a new theory: that the upper layers of the atmosphere were charged with electrical energy. He believed that if the charged layers could be reached, sound waves, even the transmission of voices, could be sent and received. On a small scale, Tesla gave the first demonstration of wireless transmission, or radio. (Although Guillermo Marconi is widely credited with the invention of the radio, Marconi's patent application was denied since Tesla already owned the patent. This decision was eventually upheld by the Supreme Court, when in 1943 they named Tesla as the "primary inventor of radio.")

That same year, a world's fair opened in Chicago. The fairgrounds covered 686 acres of lakefront property, lit with electric lights. The Westinghouse company used the Tesla system of dynamos, transformers and motors to power the fair. When President Grover Cleveland turned on the lights, the resulting glittering "White City" provided the public with dramatic evidence of the advantages of alternating currents. The crucial advantage of alternating current over direct current electrical systems is that only with alternating current can voltage be changed by the use of transformers. High voltage is required to overcome the resistance of transmission lines, but lower voltage is needed for residential, commercial and industrial applications.

Not long after the fair, people in Upstate New York began to think about ways to utilize the power of Niagara Falls. Westinghouse won the contract to harness the power of the falls. Using the Tesla system, he built three generators to light up the entire Niagara Falls area in 1895, making true the dream Nikola Tesla had as a boy.

Tesla was busy experimenting again, this time in the field of resonance and vibrations. He built an oscillator that produced vibrations of varying frequencies. Tesla's New York laboratory building was made of steel, but it rested on a bed of sand. His latest experiments began to shake buildings in the neighborhood like an earthquake. The vibrations were so strong that after one experiment, Tesla's lab suffered a partly demolished wall and a door shaken off its hinges.

In March 1895, a fire broke out that destroyed Tesla's laboratory, including all his notes, books and equipment. He had little money left after having invested his funds in equipment. Edward Dean Adams, from the Niagara Falls project, invested money for Tesla to open a new laboratory. Here Tesla worked on radio and on robotics, or what he called "teleautomatics." In 1896, Tesla said, "I do not think there is any thrill that can go through the human heart like that felt by the inventor as he sees some creation of the brain unfolding to success…Such emotions make a man forget food, sleep, friends, love, everything."

In Madison Square Garden, he demonstrated a remote-controlled boat in a huge metal tank. In 1898, he filed the first patent for radio remote control

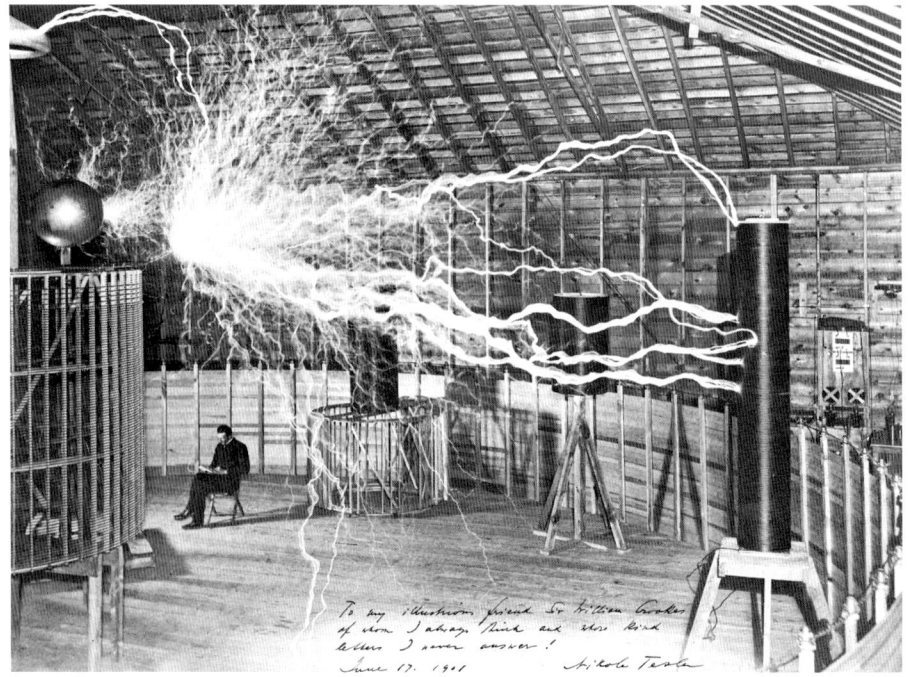

A double-exposure photograph shows both Tesla and an electrical discharge in his Colorado Springs laboratory, 1900. *Dickenson V. Alley, photographer,* Century Magazine. *Wikimedia Commons.*

of guided missiles. Tesla also invented a machine to harness solar energy. He told a *New York Times* reporter, "We are whirling through endless space with an inconceivable speed, all around us everything is spinning, everything is moving, everywhere is energy. There must be some way of availing ourselves of this energy more directly."

In 1899, Tesla received an offer from a patent attorney from the Westinghouse Corporation to leave New York City and set up a lab at the Colorado Springs Electric Company. Here he would be free to conduct major experiments without endangering lives and property. Tesla agreed and set off for Colorado. At the site, Tesla directed the carpenters who built his new laboratory and home, which were surrounded by a fence. Once it was ready, Tesla spent all his time in the lab.

One night in Colorado, Tesla witnessed a huge lightning storm where the bolts came in arcs rather than in straight lines. This discovery gave Tesla new ideas, one of which was how to send electric power over long distances without wires. He built the largest Tesla coil ever created, a twelve-million-volt machine that created sparks 135 feet long. One of his experiments with the new coil knocked out the generator at the Colorado Springs power station and set it on fire. The entire town lost power. The city was going to cut off the electricity to his lab, but Tesla convinced them to let him repair their generator at his expense and to continue giving him power.

While working late one night in his Colorado Springs lab, Tesla noticed regular sounds coming from his radio receiver. He thought a being on another planet was trying to signal Earth. Although scientists later discredited the idea that these were alien messages, Tesla was perhaps the first to receive and recognize radio waves in a regular pattern being given off by stars.

Tesla returned to New York and got enough investment capital to start building a new lab that he called Wardenclyffe on Long Island. There he hoped to construct a world communication center. It would house a huge transmitter capable of sending wireless messages around the world. Investors soon lost interest, and Tesla once again ran out of money. After creating a fantastic electrical display in the night sky at Wardenclyffe on July 15, 1903, Tesla closed up his lab and returned to New York City.

At his lab, Tesla built a mini-turbine only six inches long that he thought had great potential, but he could not interest investors. Then in 1915, at the age of fifty-nine, Tesla read on the front page of the *New York Times* that he, along with Thomas Edison, would be awarded the Nobel Prize in Physics for their work in electricity. He realized that this fame would allow him to again attract investors for his newest ideas, but he responded to the report by saying he had received no formal notification. A few days later, the official announcement named two British scientists as winners of the Nobel Prize for their research in the structure of crystals. Two years later, Tesla was persuaded to accept from the American Institute of Electrical Engineers the Edison Medal. Tesla was now sixty-two years old and living in a small room in a New York hotel. He continued to think of new designs, but investors were not interested, and World War I diverted all attention toward the war.

In 1926, a reporter writing an article asked Tesla to predict the future. Tesla said, "Before the end of this century, you will be able to communicate instantly by simple vest pocket equipment. We shall be able to witness and hear events; the inauguration of a President, the playing of a World Series game, the havoc of an earthquake, or the terror of a battle—just as though we were present." Tesla never ran out of ideas. Tesla also seemed to keep his inventions in perspective. He wrote, "These inventions of mine, however, were nothing more than steps forward in a certain direction. In evolving them, I simply followed the inborn instinct to improve the present devices without any special thought of our far more imperative necessities." In 1931, he published papers on generating electricity from seaweed and for building a steam plant that would run on geothermal energy.

Nikola Tesla died in his hotel room on January 7, 1943, at the age of eighty-six. Recognition followed. A New York City street is named after him, a commemorative stamp was issued in his honor, scholarships are awarded in his name, a school in Chicago was named after him, the international scientific unit for measuring magnetic fields is called the Tesla and the Nikola Tesla Award is given each year by the Institute of Electrical Engineers to the person who has made the most outstanding contribution in the field of electricity. The State of Colorado declared a Nikola Tesla Month in 1984 to mark the 100th anniversary of Tesla's arrival in the United States.

In writing about Tesla's scientific genius, Arthur Brisbane claimed, "Tesla lives his life up in the top of his head, where ideas are born." B.A. Behrend, a colleague of Tesla, said of his friend, "Were we to seize and eliminate from our industrial world the results of Mr. Tesla's work, the wheels of industry would cease to run, our electric cars and trains would stop, our towns would be dark, our mills would be dead and idle. So far-reaching is his work, it has become the warp and woof of industry."

Florence Sabin

1871–1953 • Central City and Denver

Each guest arriving for dinner in the Baltimore apartment was given a task and a way to contribute to the meal. The hostess, a popular researcher and teacher at Johns Hopkins Medical School, frequently invited small groups over for a meal. Often the meals were held late, after a Baltimore Orioles baseball game, for the hostess was a great fan of the team and hated to miss a game.

The guest list included some of her young laboratory students. Others were friends of hers and of her students whom she encouraged to bring along, including writers, painters, musicians and lawyers. Still others were medical colleagues. Each received a mealtime job. One set the table; another washed the fruit; others prepared vegetables or brewed the coffee. Dinner preparations, carefully organized by the hostess, moved forward smoothly in an efficient and orderly way.

A special task was that of cooking the steak. The person selected for this duty actually sat on the floor in front of the oven. He or she held a stopwatch in one hand and, in the other, a long-handled fork to turn the meat. The instructions were clear. The steak was to be turned in precisely three minutes, not a fraction of a minute earlier or later.

And after the food was prepared, it was passed around and enjoyed in the midst of stimulating conversation that might range from Oriental art to Shakespeare to politics. At the end of the evening, the guests helped with the cleanup, too. The dishes were not simply washed in soap and hot water; they were scalded. For after all, this dinner was being held in the home of a woman who became well known as a public health crusader, Florence Sabin.

Florence Rena Sabin was born on November 9, 1871, in Central City, Colorado. She was the second daughter born to mining engineer George Kimball Sabin and his wife, Serena, who was a schoolteacher. Florence's sister, Mary, was two years older. George Sabin had come west from Vermont in 1860 to try his luck in the Colorado mines. A few years later, he met another Vermonter, Serena Minor, who had arrived by stagecoach in 1867 to accept a position as a teacher in the nearby town of Blackhawk. They married in 1867, and for several years, the family lived in a small house perched on a steep hill in the little mining town, where Florence Sabin enjoyed playing and hiking in the mountains.

George Sabin managed a number of mines throughout the Rocky Mountains. After he bought a small mining company, he moved his family to Denver. It would be a home base from which he'd travel to various mines, and it provided more opportunities for the girls to attend school. It wasn't like moving to a big city because Denver was still a frontier town. Florence and her sister, Mary, watched horses and carriages going up and down and sometimes saw Arapahoes and Utes ride past their house through the streets of town to and from their Indian camp. The Sabin girls played in a huge vacant lot, overgrown with weeds, right across the street from their house. Many years later, this vacant lot became the site of the Denver courthouse.

Over the next few years, the Sabins added two more children to the family. A son, Richmond, was welcomed, but he died before he was one year old from a respiratory illness. Florence Sabin's mother died on Florence's seventh birthday, just two weeks after giving birth to another baby boy, named Albert.

For a short time after Serena Sabin's death, a nurse was hired to care for the baby while the two girls went to Wolfe Hall, an Episcopal boarding school in Denver. Now and then, for short periods, they were able to leave the school and visit their father at the Leadville mine. Then baby Albert died of pneumonia, and in 1880, George Sabin decided to send the two girls to live with his brother and sister-in-law, near Chicago.

Florence and Mary lived with their uncle Albert and his family for four years. Their uncle was a schoolmaster, and he encouraged the children to read and to study music. When a symphony came to Chicago, Albert Sabin bought tickets to take the entire family. In fact, for a time, Florence Sabin hoped for a career as a concert pianist. Her uncle encouraged this love of music and gave Florence her own piano.

One summer, when Florence Sabin was twelve years old, she and her sister were taken to visit the home of their paternal grandparents in Vermont. At the end of summer, it was decided that the girls would continue to live with their grandparents. Both Florence and her sister were sent to the Vermont Academy in Saxton's River. Upon the death of their grandmother, the girls continued in the school as boarding students.

At first, Florence Sabin pursued a career in music at the academy. Although she enjoyed playing, she had small hands and stubby fingers and eventually realized that she was not suited to excel in that field. If not music, then what should she study? Florence Sabin considered other possibilities. She knew that her great-great-grandfather had been a doctor, that one of her uncles was a doctor and that her father had studied for two years to be a doctor before he changed his mind and went off to the gold fields of Colorado. Medicine and the sciences appealed to Florence Sabin.

Florence Sabin gave up her hopes of a career in music and turned instead to the sciences. She found that she had a great aptitude for them. Sabin did especially well in the laboratory and was graduated with honors from the Vermont Academy in 1889.

Because she was two years older, Florence Sabin's sister was the first to enter Smith College in Northampton, Massachusetts, but Florence followed soon after her. At Smith, Florence Sabin concentrated her studies in mathematics and zoology. The school physician, Dr. Grace Preston, encouraged her to consider a career in medicine. Although most medical schools at the time refused admittance to women, Dr. Preston knew that a new school, Johns Hopkins, was being founded by a small group of wealthy women. A condition of their financial support was that females would be admitted. Dr. Preston encouraged Florence Sabin to be ready to apply for admittance as soon as the new medical school opened.

After graduating from Smith, Mary Sabin returned to Denver to teach. When Florence Sabin visited her father and her sister, she told them that she wanted to continue in school and study medicine. Unfortunately, her father had suffered some financial setbacks, and he explained that he could not afford to pay her tuition to medical school even if she could get admitted. In her final two years at Smith, Florence took jobs tutoring students and working at the library, saving her money and hoping that in time she would be able to save enough to pay her own tuition to medical school.

After graduating Phi Beta Kappa and receiving her bachelor of sciences degree from Smith in 1893, Florence Sabin went back to Denver to teach zoology and algebra at her former school Wolfe Hall. But she continued to dream of attending medical school. After two years of teaching in Denver, Smith College offered Florence Sabin a position as a substitute for a zoology professor on leave. She accepted this position and began to teach at Smith.

It quickly became evident that Florence Sabin was not only excellent in the laboratory, but she was a great teacher, too. She was known to tear up her notes after completing each lecture. She explained that this was to ensure she would read and rethink and study new material before giving that lecture again. Sabin's excellent teaching at Smith earned her a summer fellowship to work in the Marine Biological Laboratories at Woods Hole, Massachusetts, where she assisted on several projects and refined her skills with the microscope.

With the money she had earned from teaching, Florence Sabin could now afford to enter Johns Hopkins Medical School in Baltimore, Maryland. In 1896, at the age of twenty-five, she was accepted into the fourth class of students to attend the school. Female doctors and women in the medical field were still rare and often the object of jokes by male students. In fact, the women's dormitory at Johns Hopkins was referred to as "the Hen House."

As a first-year student at Johns Hopkins, Florence Sabin's fine work brought her to the attention of Franklin Paine Mall, a well-known professor and world-renowned anatomist. Professor Mall took a special interest in his new pupil and became her advisor and mentor. Mall was known for his unorthodox teaching methods. He posted a sign in his laboratory that said, "Your Body Is Your Textbook." Rather than relying heavily on textbook reading, Professor Mall encouraged students to carry out independent research on topics that he suggested to them. Professor Mall suggested a special project of study for Sabin when she was a sophomore. She researched the lymphatic system. Using colored dyes to work with lymph vessels from pig embryos, Sabin made considerable progress. As a second-year student, Sabin had the distinction of having a neuroanatomy article published in the *Johns Hopkins Medical Bulletin*. She occasionally made summer visits to German laboratories to learn new techniques in microscopy.

In her senior year, Sabin's project was to study the human brain. She developed a beeswax model of a newborn baby's brain. Professor Mall thought it was an exceptional piece of work. He secured the financing so that Sabin could take her model to Germany, where it could be copied and manufactured. Sabin's notes and drawings of her brain study were published in 1901, in her first book, *An Atlas of the Medulla and Mid-Brain*. This book and her model of the brain were used as references in medical schools all over the country for the next thirty years.

After graduating from Johns Hopkins in 1900, Sabin interned for a year working with patients in a hospital. Each intern was assigned to an experienced doctor, and Sabin got the coveted assignment to work with the well-known Dr. Osler. After her successful internship, during which she studied lymphatic channels, Sabin might have decided to be a practicing physician. However, she was offered a research fellowship to work in the laboratory with Professor Mall. He said that he thought only one in ten thousand students was meant to be a laboratory researcher and that Florence Sabin was one of these rare people. Sabin was happy to accept the fellowship because by this point, she knew that she preferred laboratory research to working with patients in the hospital.

In 1902, Sabin became the first female to join the faculty at Johns Hopkins, where she taught embryology and histology in the Department of Anatomy. She investigated the origin of blood vessels, cells and connective tissues. In her work, she also perfected a staining technique that allowed her to study living cells. Florence Sabin also continued a series of experiments to discover the beginning of the lymphatic system and how it worked. In 1903, there was considerable controversy in scientific circles about this work. Dr. Mall supported her findings. Sabin won a $1,000 prize for her research, which allowed her to travel to Europe for further study. On her return, she was promoted to associate professor of anatomy.

At this point in a successful career, Sabin hoped that she no longer would suffer slights and discrimination for being a woman in a man's field. In fact, she wrote, "Women get exactly what they deserve in this world, and needn't think they are discriminated against. They can have whatever they are willing to work for." Unfortunately, before long, she was to find this was not the case.

In addition to being a mentor, Dr. Franklin Mall and his wife were close friends of Florence Sabin. When Dr. Mall died unexpectedly in 1917, it was a great personal loss to Florence Sabin. Many, including Professor Mall's widow, thought Florence Sabin would be appointed as head of the Department of Anatomy. Everyone agreed she was the logical choice to replace Dr. Mall. But even Johns Hopkins was not ready to give such an important post to a woman. Instead of offering the position to Florence Sabin, it was given to a man—Dr. Lewis Weed, one of Sabin's former students.

Sabin's students were angered at her being passed over for this position, which they considered an injustice, and they wanted to stage a large-scale demonstration. Sabin persuaded them not to do so. Some suggested that Sabin should leave the school in protest, but she refused that course of action also. Sabin said she still had important research to carry out.

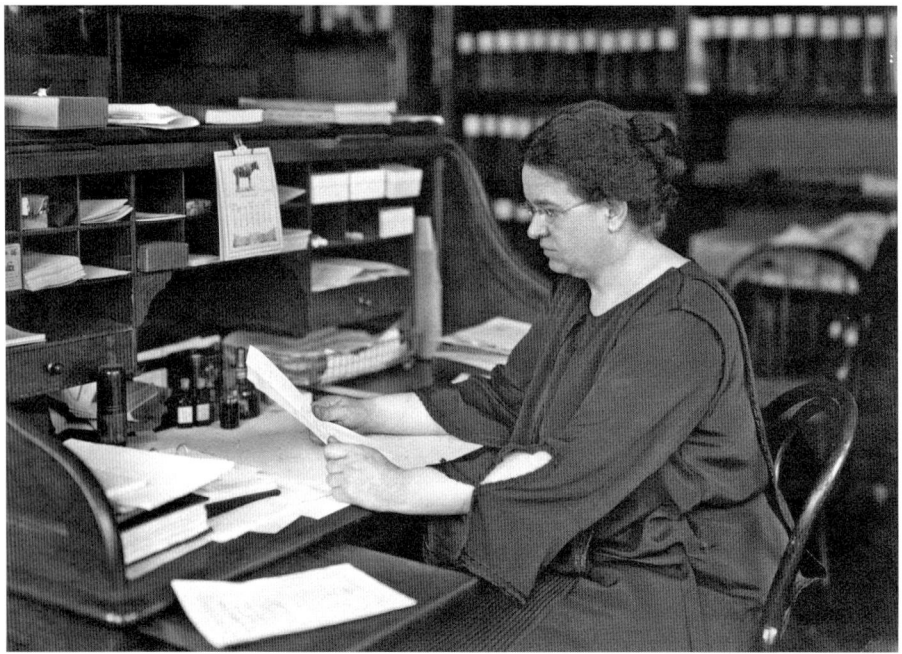

Florence Sabin works at her desk at Johns Hopkins University. *U.S. National Library of Medicine, NIH.*

Perhaps in recognition of the unfairness of their earlier action, Johns Hopkins offered Florence Sabin a significant but less important post. She became head of the Histology Department, studying the microscopic appearance of tissues. The appointment made her the first female to become a full professor at the school.

Once she was a full professor, with more money at her disposal, Sabin rented and shared a home for a period with an art teacher, Gabrielle Clements. During this time, she learned a good deal about sculpture, painting and drawing. Sabin also became friends with the writer Gertrude Stein and Stein's brother, who both sometimes came to Sabin's dinner parties.

Although her work in the laboratory prevented her from having the time to take a leadership role, Florence Sabin was active in the women's movement. She occasionally marched in demonstrations, and she participated in a letter-writing campaign to promote women's suffrage. Her humorous approach was evident when she named her first car "Susan B. Anthony," after the crusader for women's voting rights. With two of her friends, Sabin helped publish a weekly newsletter, the *Maryland Suffrage News*. Although they always appreciated her help, her cohorts in the movement felt that Florence Sabin's greatest contribution was by serving as a role model.

Florence Sabin continued her work and her research, focusing on the development of blood vessels and blood cells. She began receiving national and international attention. The *Pictorial Review*, a popular magazine, presented her with an achievement award of $5,000 in 1928 for the most distinctive contribution made by an American women to American life in the fields of art, science and letters. In accepting the award, Sabin said, "It matters little whether men or women have the more brains. All we women need to do to exert our proper influence is just to use all the brain we have."

Sabin was invited to Peking, China, to present a paper on her blood cell work. While there, she also advised the Chinese on ways to control malaria. In 1921, she was given the honor of introducing Marie Curie at a meeting of the American Association of University Women. She attended a dinner and was seated next to Albert Einstein.

Florence Sabin continued to excel in the laboratory and as a teacher, arguing that all teachers should carry out research. She was well known as one who took a genuine interest in her students and often brought them into her home for special events. Her teaching approach was much like that of her mentor, suggesting research topics for her students. Many of these students went on to achieve significant careers.

From 1924 to 1926, she served as the first woman elected president of the American Association of Anatomists. In 1925, Sabin became the first woman elected to the National Academy of Sciences for her significant scientific contributions. She was the first woman to be honored in the eighty-six years of the academy's existence.

Sabin left Johns Hopkins in 1924 to work at the Rockefeller Institute for Medical Research in New York City. They invited her to head the Department of Cellular Studies. Her acceptance made her the first woman appointed a full member of the Rockefeller Institute. In 1931, *Good Housekeeping* named her one of twelve most eminent American women. In 1935, she was awarded the M. Carey Thomas Prize, a $5,000 award from Bryn Mawr in "Recognition of Her Eminent Achievements."

At the Rockefeller Institute, Sabin specialized in a study of tuberculosis, a disease that at the time was the number-one cause of death in the United States, killing thousands of people each year. She studied the immune system and how white blood cells responded to infections. Her research revealed a good deal about the bacterium that causes the disease.

After reaching the age of sixty-seven, rules required that Florence Sabin retire from the Rockefeller Institute. She did so reluctantly because she felt she still had much work to do. Just before leaving New York, Florence Sabin was given a surprise farewell party. Three of her friends took her to a dining room high up in Rockefeller Center. The tables were arranged so that she moved from the head of one table to the head of another, enjoying one course with friends at each table. At the end of the evening, after hearing many accolades from her admirers, Florence Sabin spoke with great enthusiasm about her most recent work. And she did a surprising thing. She confessed that she'd just discovered that everything she'd been doing for the past four years was mistaken. But she smilingly insisted that negative results make as great a contribution to research as do positive results.

After Sabin retired from the Rockefeller Institute in 1938, she returned to Colorado to live with her sister, Mary, in Denver, Colorado. But Florence Sabin was not really ready to retire and was happy when, in 1944, Colorado governor John Vivian appointed her to head a public health committee. Apparently the governor did not expect much would happen with this committee led by a nice old lady. He was wrong.

Chairing the Post-War Health Planning Committee of Colorado, Florence Sabin investigated health services in the state, and she found some terrible conditions. There was a high tuberculosis rate, livestock infected with brucellosis and contaminated milk. The infant death rate from diphtheria was high. Enforcement of existing laws was rare, and funding in the entire field of public health was inadequate.

Sabin and her committee drew up a set of bills known as the Sabin Program. Sabin was not about to let this report gather dust in someone's desk drawer. She printed up and distributed copies of the committee's work and, when health bills were drawn up, actively campaigned for their passage in all sixty-three counties of the state of Colorado. Largely due to her efforts, six of these bills were passed into law in 1947. Her suggested reforms to public health included a stricter control of infectious diseases, ensuring the purity of milk and seeking sanitary methods of sewage disposal.

Sabin actively launched a vigorous campaign to clean up the city of Denver and to enforce health regulations, especially those dealing with restaurants and food supplies. She also urged the screening of the population for tuberculosis and syphilis. Under her leadership, within two years, the tuberculosis rate was reduced from 54.7 to 27.0 persons per 100,000. The syphilis rate per 100,000 people dropped from 700.0 to 60.0. In 1945, Sabin received the Trudeau Medal of the National Tuberculosis Association in recognition of her work.

Working with Colorado's new governor, W.L. Knous, Sabin also served as chair of an Interim Board of Health and Hospitals in Denver and then became manager of the Denver Department of Health and Charities until 1951. She cut in half the city's death rate from tuberculosis by having the city provide for free X-rays. When she received a salary from the City of Denver for her public health work, she donated it to the research program at the Colorado General Hospital. Eighty years old and retired, Sabin continued to go to the office almost daily to contribute to the effort and did not stop this practice until the winter before her death.

Sabin had a motto, placed on a bookplate, taken from Leonard da Vinci. It read, "Thou O God, dost sell unto us all good things at the price of labor." This summed up her strong belief that happiness and longevity were the result of working with enjoyment. A friend reported that after a dinner party, Sabin once commented, "It is now night, and I am glad. For soon morning will come and I can again open the door of my beloved laboratory."

Her hard work was recognized. Over her lifetime, fifteen colleges presented her with honorary degrees. In 1951, Sabin was presented the Lasker Foundation Public Service Award for the public health work she had pioneered in Colorado. That same year, the University of Colorado Medical School named its new biological sciences building in her honor. The following year, the American Association of University Women established the Florence R. Sabin Fellowship to support women doing research in the area of public health.

During her lifetime, Florence Sabin wrote one hundred scientific papers, several book chapters and two books, including a biography of her mentor at Johns Hopkins, Franklin Mall. Her lifetime of work was honored in one special way. The United States Congress passed a law allowing each state to place two statues in the National Statuary Hall of the United States Capitol. Colorado chose to place there a large bronze statue of Florence Sabin, created by Joy Buba. She is shown seated on a stool, with her arm resting on a book called *Colorado Health Laws*. Beneath the statue are the words "teacher, scientist, humanitarian." The statue was completed and dedicated in 1959.

A baseball fan all her life, Sabin died quietly at home on October 3, 1953, at age eighty-one, during a seventh-inning stretch of a televised baseball game between the Yankees and the Dodgers. Simple services were held at St. John's Cathedral in Denver. On the occasion of Sabin's death, Denver's mayor, Quigg Newton, said, "Dr. Sabin was one of the greatest persons I've ever known. She was learned, she was wise, she was humble. She loved the world and every living creature in it."

Enos Mills

1870–1922 • Rocky Mountain National Park

I s it uphill both ways?" eight-year-old Harriet Peters asked famed naturalist and guide Enos Mills. He had been describing to friends his climb up gigantic Longs Peak, which jutted toward the clouds in the rugged Rocky Mountains. He smiled and gently replied that while the trail went both up and down, it was indeed a very long and difficult climb. He promised to take his little neighbor, though, when she was old enough.

And so it was that in September 1905, when Harriet was eight years old, she and Enos Mills climbed the famous peak that towers 14,255 feet into the sky. Mills had never taken anyone so young up the mountain before, but he knew little Harriet could do it. Indeed, she did, making observations and asking questions all along the way. On the "home stretch," the last bit of the climb to the top, where for safety reasons many adults crawl on the ledge at the edge of a precipice, Harriet walked along, swinging her arms as she went and humming softly.

Perhaps her wonderful, confident spirit of adventure is what led Enos Mills to comment in his book *Adventures of a Nature Guide*, "Of the two hundred and fifty-odd trips which I made as a guide to the summit of this great, old peak, the trip with Harriet is the one I liked best to recall." Little Harriet was but one of countless visitors Mills introduced to the wonders of what was to become Rocky Mountain National Park.

By the time of his death, Enos Abijah Mills had become known as one of the most important naturalists in the country, a man who was often referred to as "the father of Rocky Mountain National Park." But his early life

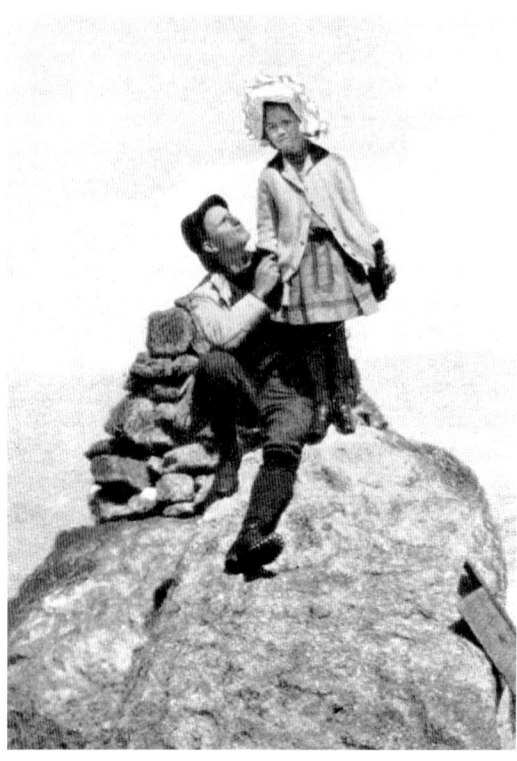

Enos Mills on top of Longs Peak. *From* Wild Life on the Rockies *by Enos Abijah Mills.*

certainly gave no hint of this future. In 1857, Enos A. Mills Sr. married Ann Lamb, and they, along with other family members, moved to the Kansas Territory. Enos Mills Jr. was born on April 22, 1870, on a farm in Linn County, Kansas. He suffered from an allergy to wheat, which made him a sickly child with many serious digestive problems. In spite of frequent illnesses, he loved being outdoors, and he was also an avid reader.

Enos Mills's mother, father and many of his other relatives had visited Colorado during the gold rush of 1859. They had loved the rugged mountains and the clean air. Remembering the Rockies, his parents encouraged Enos at age fourteen to leave Kansas because of his poor health and go to live with relatives in Colorado. His family thought that the new area might be a healthier environment for him.

All alone, Mills walked to Kansas City about sixty-five miles away, stopping and earning his keep by doing chores on farms along the route. He took a job as a baker's helper to earn the train fare to Denver. Once in Colorado, he first went to Greeley to visit his elder sister, Belle. Then he moved in with his cousin, the Reverend Elkanah Lamb, who ran an inn for guests near the foot of Longs Peak.

In the summer of 1884, Mills worked on Lamb's ranch. Clearly, life in Colorado agreed with him. He grew strong and healthy working on the ranch in the mountain air. During winters, he'd earn a little money doing odd jobs for other ranches and hotels, always saving plenty of time for reading and being outdoors observing nature.

Although Enos Mills's love of the Estes Park area was not confined to any one mountain, lake, pass or meadow, gigantic Longs Peak seemed to have an almost magnetic pull on him. He grew to love and know it in every season of the year. In 1885, at age fifteen, Mills made his first ascent of Longs Peak. When he was sixteen, Mills built himself a homestead cabin near the peak's base, where he lived in summers. He soon joined Elkanah Lamb and Lamb's son, Carlyle, as a professional guide for tourists who wished to climb the mountain.

During his lifetime, Mills estimated that he climbed the peak forty times by himself and made another three hundred trips to the top guiding others. Mills made the climb in all seasons and weather conditions, including one trip when the winds were blowing at 170 miles per hour. He is credited with making the first winter ascent of the mountain in 1903.

When guiding others, Mills shared his extensive knowledge of animals, trees, rocks, soil and glaciers. He was an enthusiastic hiker who sometimes walked thirty miles a day and often went off hiking for three weeks at a time. Whenever he went into the wilderness, he carried with him a notebook for making observations, and he packed fifteen pounds of raisins for provisions.

From 1887 to 1901, Mills worked in the winters at the Anaconda Copper Mine in Butte, Montana. In Butte, he had access for the first time to a library. As a constant library patron, he came in contact with members of the University Club who invited him to their gatherings. Soon Mills joined a writers' group. Mills also had the opportunity to attend plays, musicals and lectures.

When a fire closed the copper mine in 1889, Mills decided to do a little traveling. On a trip to San Francisco, California, that year, Mills met the famous naturalist John Muir. Muir admired the young man and encouraged him to write and speak about conservation of our natural resources. Enos Mills needed little urging to become active in the emerging conservation movement, and he started writing about his wilderness experiences. In 1905, his first book was published. It combined local history, poetry and stories of Longs Peak. Eventually, fifteen more books would follow.

Mills spent part of the next decade traveling. He journeyed to Alaska, went to the World's Fair in Chicago, and visited Europe. But he kept returning to Estes Park. There he would spend weeks at a time watching and tracking animals and studying their habits.

Enos Mills also became a correspondent for Denver newspapers, contributing articles on scenery and wildlife. His photographs often accompanied these writings. Mills also included human interest items. He rode to the various resorts in the area and reported on which prominent people were visiting. In any way he could, Mills encouraged people to come visit and get to know Colorado.

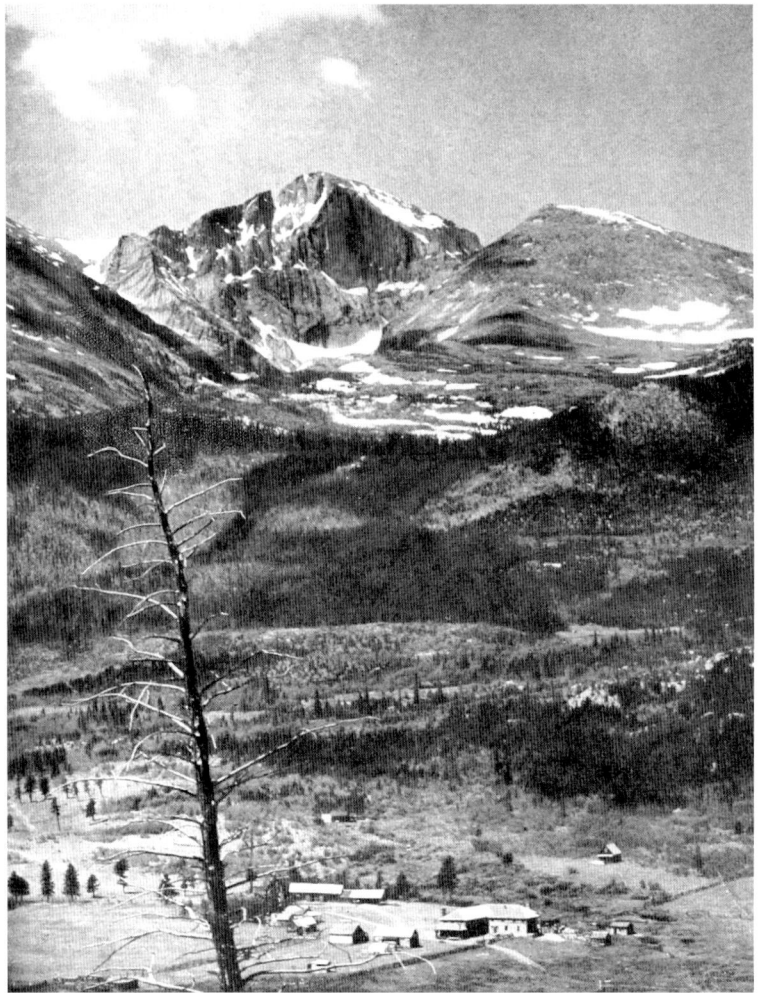

Longs Peak from the east. *From* Wild Life on the Rockies *by Enos Abijah Mills.*

In the summer of 1891, Mills worked as a surveyor in Yellowstone National Park. He found it to be a beautiful spot that reminded him of his own Colorado home. He thought that the gorgeous area of Colorado where he had built his cabin also deserved to be preserved so that it could be enjoyed by future generations. Mills became not only a passionate admirer of nature but also a passionate campaigner to preserve it.

Mills knew that the tourist industry was growing in Colorado. So that same year, with money he had earned and saved, Mills bought the Lamb

214

Ranch from his relatives. He expanded it, first calling his place Longs Peak House and then naming it Longs Peak Inn. Mills spent much of his time there, providing activities for tourists, including bird-watching, nature walks, climbing and hiking. He also tried to convert tourists to his views of protecting nature. One of the signs posted in the forest near his lodge read, "SPARE THE FLOWERS! Those who pull flowers up by the roots will be condemned by all worthy people."

In the 1890s, Enos Mills was often invited to lecture throughout the state. One of his frequent topics was "Our Friends, the Trees." He explained how trees conserved rainfall, prevented soil erosion and tempered the climate. Soon he was traveling throughout the country. In Washington, one of his audience members was President William Howard Taft, who refused to leave the lecture to keep another appointment until Mills had finished speaking.

From 1902 to 1906, Enos Mills was the Colorado State Snow Observer. His job was to measure snow depths to help predict the amounts of the spring and summer runoff.

A friend gave Mills a gift in 1902. It was a border collie pup named Scotch. The dog became a faithful companion. A frequent guest at Longs Peak Inn wrote of the dog, "Scotch was no less the host than his master." The little dog defended the chickens against coyotes, was always ready to play ball and often joined guests on hikes. He is credited with saving the life of a solo climber who arrived at the summit of a mountain late in the day and lost her way back down in the dark. Scotch stayed huddled close to her and kept her alive during a freezing night. At dawn, after a rescuer arrived to help her back down, Scotch ran home to have breakfast.

President Theodore Roosevelt was an ardent conservationist and recognized how helpful Mills could be to his cause. He created for Mills the position of government lecturer, and Mills worked in this position from 1907 to 1909. In one seven-month period, he delivered 125 lectures in thirty-six different states. By that time, Mills had authored several books on nature and the value of preserving land for future generations. Always extremely involved in his nature projects, there is a story about Mills that says that once, when President Roosevelt sent for him to come to Washington, D.C., Mills replied, "I am too busy to come."

In June 1906, while Mills was off giving one of his lectures in St. Paul, he learned that the main building of the Longs Peak Inn had burned to the ground. Mills immediately set about rebuilding, using boulders and fire-killed trees from the surrounding mountains. He also added a nature museum. Carpenters followed Mills's plans and created something new and artistic in rustic architecture. In the middle of a living room, as a decoration, he placed a gigantic mass of tree roots.

Enos Mills wrote a letter in 1908 to H.N. Wheeler, local head of the national forest, to support a proposed one-thousand-square-mile game refuge that was being promoted by Freelan O. Stanley, Cornelius Bond and other businessmen in the Estes Park area.

The game refuge plan eventually gave way to the idea of creating a national park, and Mills became a strong voice in speaking out to create Rocky Mountain National Park. His knowledge of nature, his enthusiasm and his willingness to convince others made him ideally suited for this task. In 1909, Mills proposed that six hundred square miles around the Longs Peak area be set aside as a national park. He wrote thousands of letters on behalf of the creation of the park, he spoke to magazine and newspaper editors, he gave countless lectures and he lobbied in Washington, D.C.

Mills enlisted the efforts of Congressman Edward Taylor of Glenwood Springs to help him. A bill was introduced calling for the establishment of the Estes National Park and Game Preserve. Later, in 1911, the name of the proposed national park was changed to Rocky Mountain National Park.

The first bill introduced in Congress to create the park failed. So did the second bill. Mills mustered more supporters. At the hearing for the third bill, in addition to Mills, three past, present and future Colorado governors all testified in support of the bill. Although the size of the park had been cut to 358.5 square miles, the bill creating Rocky Mountain National Park was finally signed in January 1915 by President Woodrow Wilson. (The Never Summer Range was added to the park in 1929.) At the park dedication services on September 4, 1915, as master of ceremonies, Mills said, "In years to come when I am asleep forever beneath the pines, thousands of families will find rest and hope in this park, and on through the years others will come and be happy in the splendid scenes that I helped save for them."

In 1916, a visitor arrived in Estes Park. Ester Burnell came from Des Moines, Iowa, to the Rocky Mountains on a vacation trip with her sister. Burnell had been educated at the Pratt Art Institute and worked as an interior designer for Sherman Williams. She and her sister first stayed at Lester's Hotel four miles north of Estes Park. Their cabin was a primitive one of half board and half canvas. Like other tourists, they roughed it while enjoying the wonderful scenery. Then Burnell went to stay at Enos Mills's Longs Peak Inn. Fascinated with the work of this naturalist and the beauty of the area, Burnell did not return home at the end of her vacation. Instead,

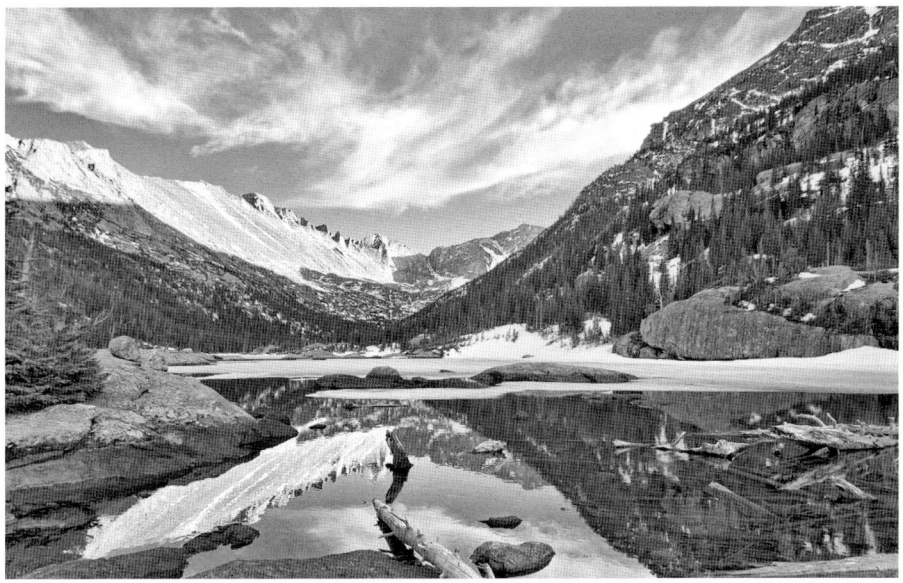

Mills Lake early spring sunset. *Steven Bratman.*

she stayed on as a part-time secretary for Enos Mills. She took to life in the backcountry and was soon climbing mountains and guiding tourists.

In 1918, when Burnell was twenty-eight years old and Enos Mills was forty-eight, they married. The following year, they had a child named Enda. The little family enjoyed a brief and happy time. When Enda was only three years old, Enos Mills made a trip to New York. While there, he was in a subway train collision in which he suffered broken ribs and a punctured lung. Mills traveled home and came down with the flu and was also suffering from abscessed teeth. On September 22, 1922, he suffered a heart attack. At the age of fifty-two, Enos Mills died in his home near the foot of Longs Peak. He was buried at a grave site near his cabin.

Many features today in Rocky Mountain Park bear Mills's name, including Mills Lake, Mills Glacier and Mills Moraine.

Enos Mills is fondly remembered for his hard work in the creation of Rocky Mountain National Park. An editorial in the *Denver Post* congratulating Mills for his efforts notes, "Others have helped, to be sure, but it was by Enos Mills' persistent labor that they were made supporters of the movement. So let Colorado take off its hat to Enos Mills, who has nationalized Colorado's scenery, in which every citizen is a stockholder and dividend participant."

In 1973, Enos Mills's homestead cabin in Estes Park was placed on the National Register of Historic Places. It is still open to visitors today as a museum, run largely by his daughter, Enda; his granddaughter, Elizabeth; and his great-granddaughter, Eryn, all of whom grew up sharing Mills's love and respect of wilderness.

Bibliography

ZEBULON PIKE

Bueler, Gladys R. *Colorado's Colorful Characters*. Boulder, CO: Pruett Publishing, 1981.

Carter, Carrol Joe. *Pike in Colorado*. Fort Collins, CO: Old Army Press, 1978.

Coues, Elliott, ed. *The Expeditions of Zebulon Montgomery Pike*. Vol. 1. Mineola, NY: Dover Publications, 1987.

Hollon, W. Eugene. *The Lost Pathfinder: Zebulon Montgomery Pike*. Norman: Oklahoma University Press, 1949.

Orsi, Jared. *Citizen Explorer: The Life of Zebulon Pike*. Oxford, UK: Oxford University Press, 2014.

Pierce, Dale. *Wild West Characters*. Phoenix, AZ: Golden West Publishers, 1991.

Terrell, John Upton. *Zebulon Pike: The Life and Times of an Adventurer*. New York: Weybright & Talley, Inc., 1968.

Wibberly, Leonard. *Zebulon Pike: Soldier and Explorer*. New York: Funk & Wagnalls Company, 1961.

STEPHEN LONG

Bueueler, Gladys R. *Colorado's Colorful Characters*. Boulder, CO: Pruett Publishing, 1981.

Evans, Howard Ensign. *The Natural History of the Long Expedition to the Rocky Mountains*. New York: Oxford University Press, 1997.

Goodman, George J., and Cheryl W. Lawon. *Retracing Major Stephen H. Long's 1920 Expedition: The Itinerary and Botany*. Norman: University of Oklahoma Press, 1995.

Haltman, Kenneth. *Looking Close and Seeing Far: Samuel Seymour, Titian Ramsey Peale, and the Art of the Long Expedition, 1818–1823*. University Park: Pennsylvania State University Press, 2008.

James, Edwin. *Account of an Expedition from Pittsburgh to the Rocky Mountains*. Ann Arbor, MI: University Microfilms, Inc., 1966.

Kane, Lucile M., June D. Holmquist and Carolyn Gilman, eds. *The Northern Expeditions of Stephen H. Long: The Journal of 1817 and 1823 and Related Documents*. St. Paul: Minnesota Historical Society Press, 1978.

Nichols, Roger L., and Patrick L. *Halley Stephen Long and American Frontier Exploration*. Norman: University of Oklahoma Press, 1995.

Viola, Herman J. *Exploring the West*. Washington, D.C.: Smithsonian Books, 1987.

Winchester, Simon. *The Men Who United the States: America's Explorers, Inventors, Eccentrics and Mavericks, and the Creation of One Nation, Indivisible*. New York: Harper Collins, 2013. Kindle Edition.

JAMES PIERSON BECKWOURTH

Bonner, T.D. *The Life and Adventures of James P. Beckwourth*. New York: Arno Press & New York Times, 1969.

Canby, Tom. *Legends of the West: A Collection of U.S. Commemorative Stamps*. Kansas City, MO: U.S. Postal Service, 1993.

Hafen, LeRoy R. "The Last Years of James P. Beckwourth," *Colorado Magazine* (State Historical Society of Colorado), August 1928.

———. *The Mountain Men and the Fur Trade of the Far West*. N.p.: Arthur H. Clark, Co., 1965.

Shepard, Betty, ed. *Mountain Man, Indian Chief: The Life and Adventures of Jim Beckwourth*. New York: Harcourt, Brace & World, Inc., 1968.

Wilson, Elinor. *Jim Beckwourth: Black Mountain Man, War Chief of the Crows, Trader, Trapper, Explorer, Frontiersman, Guide, Scout, Interpreter, Adventurer, and Gaudy Liar*. University of Oklahoma Press, 1972.

THE BENTS

Bacon, Melvin, and Daniel Bligen. *Bent's Fort, Crossroads of Cultures on the Santa Fe Trail*. Palmer Lake, CO: Filter Press, 2002.

Blassingame, Wyatt. *Bent's Fort: Crossroad of the Great West*. Champaign, IL: Garrard, 1967.

Halaas, David Fridtjof, and Andrew E. Masich. *Halfbreed: The Remarkable True Story of George Bent, Caught between the World of the Indian and the White Man*. Cambridge, MA: Da Capo Press, 2004.

Lavender, David. *Bent's Fort*. New York: Doubleday & Co., Inc., 1954.

Simonetta, Sam, and Linda Simonetta. *Trappers, Trains and Mining Claims*. Boulder, CO: Pruett Publishing, 1976.

U.S. Department of the Interior. *Bent's Old Fort: Official Map and Guide*. Washington, D.C.: National Park Service, 2002.

Whitely, Lee. *The Cherokee Trail: Bent's Old Fort to Fort Bridger*. Boulder, CO: Johnson Publishing, 1999.

Chief Black Kettle

Greene, Jerome A. *Washita: The U.S. Army and the Southern Cheyenne, 1867–1869.* Norman: University of Oklahoma Press, 2004.

Hatch, Thom. *Black Kettle: The Cheyenne Chief Who Sought Peace but Found War.* Hoboken, NJ: John Wiley & Sons, 2004.

Hoig, Stan. *The Sand Creek Massacre.* Norman: University of Oklahoma Press, 1961.

Schultz, Duane. *Month of the Freezing Moon: The Sand Creek Massacre, November 1864.* New York: St. Martin's Press, 1990.

Scott, Bob. *Blood at Sand Creek: The Massacre Revisited.* Caldwell, ID: Caxton Printers, Ltd., 1994.

Jim Bridger

Alter, J. Cecil. *Jim Bridger.* Norman: University of Oklahoma Press, 1925.

Brininstool, A.E., and Grace Raymond Hebard. *Jim Bridger: "The Grand Old Man of the Rockies."* N.p.: Amazon Digital Services, January 2015. Kindle Edition.

Gowans, Fred R., and Eugene E. Campbell. *Fort Bridger: Island in the Wilderness.* Provo, UT: Brigham Young University Press, 1975.

Hollihan, Tony. *Mountain Men, Frontier Adventurers Alone Against the Wilderness.* Alberta, CA: Folklore Publishing, 2004.

Magorian, James. *Mountain Man.* Lincoln, NE: Black Oak Press, 1976.

Vestal, Stanley. *Jim Bridger: Mountain Man.* New York: William Morrow & Co., 1946.

Kit Carson

Abbot, John S. *C. Christopher Carson, Familiarly Known as Kit Carson, Pioneer of the West.* N.p.: Amazon Digital Services, 2013. Kindle Edition.

Blackwelder, Bernice. *Great Westerner: The Story of Kit Carson.* Caldwell, ID: Caxton Printers, 1962.

Estergreen, M. Morgan. *Kit Carson: A Portrait in Courage.* Norman: University of Oklahoma Press, 1962.

Guild, Thelma S., and Harvey L. Carter. *Kit Carson: A Pattern for Heroes.* Lincoln: University of Nebraska Press, 1984.

Hafen, Leroy R., ed. *Fur Trappers and Traders of the Far Southwest.* Logan: Utah State University Press, 1997.

Quaife, Milo Milton, ed. *Kit Carson's Autobiography.* Lincoln: University of Nebraska Press, 1966.

Sides, Hampton. *Blood and Thunder: The Epic Story of Kit Carson and the Conquest of the American West.* New York: Doubleday, 2006.

Vestal, Stanley. *Kit Carson: The Happy Warrior of the Old West.* Boston: Houghton Mifflin, 1928.

UNCLE DICK WOOTTON

Bradley, Glen D. *Winning the Southwest: A Story of Conquest.* Chicago, IL: A.C. McClurg & Co., 1912.

Carter, Harvey L. "Dick Wootton." In *The Mountain Men and the Fur Trade of the Far West.* Vol. 3, edited by LeRoy R. Hafen. Glendale, CA: A.G Clark, Co., 1966.

Conard, Howard Louis. *Uncle Dick Wootton.* Edited by Milo Milton Quaire. Lincoln: University of Nebraska Press, 1980. First printed in Chicago: W.E. Dibble & Co., 1890.

Hafen, Leroy R., ed. *Fur Trappers and Traders of the Far Southwest.* Logan: Utah State University Press, 1997.

Simonetta, Sam, and Linda Simonetta. *Trappers, Trains and Mining Claims.* Boulder, CO: Pruett Publishing, 1976.

JOHN H. GREGORY AND GEORGE A. JACKSON

Beadle, J.H. *Western Wilds and the Men Who Redeem Them.* Cincinnati, OH: Johns Brothers & Company, 1881.

Brown, Robert L. *The Great Pikes Peak Gold Rush.* Caldwell, ID: Caxton Printers, Ltd., 1985.

Denver Public Library. http://history.denverlibrary.org/research/fiftyniners/J.html.

Jackson, George A. *Jackson Diary of '59.* Idaho Springs, CO: Placer Inn, 1929.

RootsWeb. http://freepages.history.rootsweb.com/~cescott/jhgregory.htm.

Voynick, Stephen M. *Colorado Gold: From the Pike's Peak Rush to the Present.* Missoula, MT: Mountain Press Publishing Co., 1992.

CHIEF NIWOT (LEFT HAND)

Coel, Margaret. *Chief Left Hand.* Norman: University of Oklahoma Press, 1981.

Lambert, Julia S. "Plain Tales of the Plains." *Trail* 9 (1916): 20.

Trenholm, Virginia Cole. *The Arapahoes: Our People.* Norman: University of Oklahoma Press, 1970.

Ubbelohde, Carl, Maxine Benson and Duane A. Smith. *A Colorado Reader.* Boulder, CO: Pruett Publishing, 1982.

JOHN LONG ROUTT

Bueler, Gladys R. *Colorado's Colorful Characters.* Boulder, CO: Pruett Publishing, 1981.

Clearfield, Elaine Arams. *Our Colorado Immortals in Stained Glass.* Denver, CO: Mountain Bell, 1986.

Lohse, Joyce B. *First Governor, First Lady: John & Eliza Routt of Colorado.* Palmer Lake, CO: Filter Press, 2002.

Routt, John. *Inaugural Address of John L. Routt to the Eighth General Assembly of the State of Colorado, January 1891.* Denver, CO: Collier and Cleavland Lith. Co., State Printers, 1890.

Voight, Robert Charles. *The Life of John Long Routt*. Greeley: Division of Social Studies, The Graduate School, Colorado State College of Education, 1947.

James Nugent and Lady Isabella Bird

Bird, Isabella. *A Lady's Life in the Rocky Mountains*. Norman: University of Oklahoma Press, 1960.

Canning, Anne Smedley. *Early Estes Park*. Denver, CO: Dingerson Press, 1990.

Dunning, Harold Marion. *The Life of Rocky Mountain Jim (James Nugent)*. Boulder, CO: Johnson Publishing, 1967.

Jessen, Kenneth. *Estes Park: A Quick History*. Estes Park, CO: First Light Publishing, 1996.

Mills, Enos A. *The Story of Early Estes Park*. Estes Park, CO: Temporal Mechanical Press, 1905.

Perry, Phyllis J. *It Happened in Rocky Mountain National Park*. Guilford, CT: Two Dot/Globe Pequot, 2008.

———. *Postcards of America: Rocky Mountain National Park*. Chicago: Arcadia Publishing, 2008.

Helen Hunt Jackson

Bueler, Gladys R. *Colorado's Colorful Characters*. Boulder, CO: Pruett Publishing, 1975.

Danneberg, Julie. *Women Writers of the West: Five Chroniclers of the American Frontier*. Golden, CO: Fulcrum Publishing, 2003.

Jackson, Helen Hunt. *A Century of Dishonor: A Sketch of the United States Government's Dealings with Some of the Indian Tribes*. Norman: University of Oklahoma Press, 1995.

———. *Ramona*. New York: New American Library, 2002.

Mathes, Valerie Sherer. *Helen Hunt Jackson and her Indian Reform Legacy*. Austin: University of Texas Press, 1990.

May, Antionette. *Helen Hunt Jackson: A Lonely Voice of Conscience*. San Francisco, CA: Chronicle Books, 1987.

West, Mark I., ed. *Westward to a High Mountain: The Colorado Writings of Helen Hunt Jackson*. Denver: Colorado Historical Society, 1994.

The Tabors

Bancroft, Caroline. *Augusta Tabor: Her Side of the Scandal*. Boulder, CO: Johnson Publishing, 1955.

Karsner, David K. *Silver Dollar: The Story of the Tabors*. New York: Crown Publishers, 1932.

Moynihan, Betty. *Augusta Tabor: A Pioneering Woman*. Evergreen, CO: Cordillera Press, 1988.

Riley, Glenda, and Richard W. Etulain, eds. *Wild Women of the Old West*. Golden, CO: Fulcrum Publishing, 2003.

Smith, Duane A. *Horace Tabor: His Life and the Legend*. Boulder: Colorado Associated University Press, 1989.

Temple, Judy Nolte. *The Mad Women in the Cabin*. Norman: University of Oklahoma Press, 2007.

Wood, Richard E. *Here Lies Colorado: Fascinating Figures in Colorado History*. Helena, MT: Farcountry Press, 2005.

CHIEF OURAY AND CHIPETA

Becker, Cynthia, and P. David Smith. *Chipeta: Queen of the Utes*. Montrose, CO: Western Reflections Publishing Co., 2003.

Blackhawk, Ned. *Violence Over the Land*. Cambridge, MA: Harvard University Press, 2006.

Herrow, Victoria. *Political Leaders and Peacemakers*. New York: Facts on File, Inc., 1994.

Houston, Robert B., Jr. *Two Colorado Odysseys: Chief Ouray, Porter Nelson*. Lincoln, NE: iUniverse, Inc., 2005.

Smith, P. David. *Ouray: Chief of the Utes*. Ouray, CO: Wayfinder Press, 1990.

Wood, Richard E. *Here Lies Colorado: Fascinating Figures in Colorado History*. Helena, MT: Farcountry Press, 2005.

WILLIAM JACKSON PALMER

Abbot, Carl, Stephen J. Leonard and Thomas J. Noel. *Colorado: A History of the Centennial State*. Boulder: University Press of Colorado, 2005.

Anderson, George Laverne. *General William Jackson Palmer: Man of Vision*. Colorado Springs: Colorado College Studies, No. 4, 1960.

Fisher, John Stirling. *A Builder of the West: The Life of William Jackson Palmer*. N.p.: Arno Press, 1981.

Lowry, Thomas P. "William J. Palmer: Forgotten Union General of Americas's Civil War." *Civil War Times*, September 2007.

Ubbelohde, Carl, Maxine Benson and Duane A. Smith. *A Colorado History*. Boulder, CO: Pruett Publishing, 2001.

Wilcox, Rhoda Davis. *The Man on the Iron Horse*. Manitou Springs, CO: Martin Associates, 2000.

DAVID H. MOFFAT

Bollinger, Edward T. *Rails That Climb: A Narrative History of the Moffat Road*. Golden: Colorado Railroad Museum, 1979.

Bollinger, Edward T., and Frederick Bauer. *The Moffat Road*. Athens: Ohio University Press, 1981.

Boner, Harold A. *The Giant's Ladder*. Milwaukee, WI: Kalmbach Publishing, 1962.

Griswold, P.R. *David Moffat's Denver, Northwestern and Pacific: The Moffat Road*. Denver, CO: Rocky Mountain Railroad Club, 1995.

Mehls, Steven F. *David H. Moffat, Jr.: Early Colorado Business Leader*. New York: Garland Publishing, Inc., 1989.

Mehls, Steven F. "Success on the Mining Frontier: David Moffat and Eben Smith—A Case Study." In *Essays and Monographs in Colorado History* edited by David N. Wetzel. Denver: Colorado Historical Society, 1982.

Casimiro Barela

Barela, Casimiro. *Return Trophies of Mexican War!* Denver, CO: Smith-Brooks Printing Co., 1899.

Fernandez, José Emileo. *The Biography of Casimro Barela*. Albuquerque: University of New Mexico Press, 2003.

Hunt, Inez. *The Barela Brand*. Colorado Springs: Colorado Public Schools, 1971.

Monnet, John H., and Michael McCarthy. *Colorado Profiles*. Niwot: University Press of Colorado, 1996.

Simonetta, Dave, and Linda Simonetta. *Trappers, Trains and Mining Claims*. Boulder, CO: Pruett Publishing, 1976.

Adolph Coors

Banham, Russ. *Coors: A Rocky Mountain Legend*. Lyme, CT: Greenwich Publishing Group, 1998.

Baum, Dan. *Citizen Coors: An American Dynasty*. New York: William Morrow, 2000.

Bellant, Russ. *The Coors Connection: How Coors Family Philanthropy Undermines Democratic Pluralism*. Boston: South End Press, 1991.

Kostka, William, Sr. *The Pre-prohibition History of Adolph Coors Company, 1873–1933*. Golden, CO: Adolph Coors Co., 1973.

Krajeski, Anita. *Coors Taste of the West*. Des Moines, IA: Meredith Publishing Services, 1981.

Otto Mears

Hunt, Inez, and Wanetta W. Draper. *To Colorado's Restless Ghosts*. Denver, CO: Sage Books, 1960.

Kaplan, Michael. *Otto Mears: Paradoxical Pathfinder*. Silverton, CO: San Juan County Book Co., 1982.

Monnett, John W., and Michael McCarthy. *Colorado Profiles: Men and Women Who Shaped the Centennial State*. Niwot: University Press of Colorado.

Simonetta, Sam, and Linda Simonetta. *Trappers, Trains and Mining Claims*. Boulder, CO: Pruett Publishing, 1976.

Strong, William K. *The Remarkable Railroad Passes of Otto Mears*. Silverton, CO: San Juan County Book Co., 1988.

F.O. Stanley

Canning, Anne Smedley. *Early Estes Park*. Denver, CO: Dingerson Press, 1990.

Davis, Susan S. *The Stanleys: Renaissance Yankees, Innovation in Industry and the Arts*. New York: Newcomen Society of the United States, 1997.

Jessen, Kenneth. *Estes Park: A Quick History*. Fort Collins, CO: First Light Publishing, 1996.

Karwatka, Dennis. *Moving Civilization: The Growth of Transportation*. Ann Arbor, MI: Tech Directions Book/Prokken Pub., 2003.

Pickering, James. *Mr. Stanley of Estes Park*. Boulder, CO: Stanley Museum, Inc., Johnson Printing, 2000.

Tessendorf, K.C., and Gloria Kamen. *Look Out! Here Comes the Stanley Steamer*. New York: Atheneum, 1984.

Nikola Tesla

Bueler, Gladys R. *Colorado's Colorful Characters*. Boulder, CO: Pruett Publishing, 1981.

Cheney, Margaret. *Tesla: Man Out of Time*. New York: Barnes and Noble Books, 1993.

Cheney, Margaret, and Robert Uth. *Tesla: Master of Lightning*. New York: Metro Books, 1999.

Dommermuth-Costa, Carol. *Nikola Tesla: A Spark of Genius*. Minneapolis, MN: Lerner Publications, 1994.

Jonnes, Jill. *Empires of Light: Edison, Tesla, Westinghouse and the Race to Electrify the World*. New York: Random House, 2003.

Seifer, Mark J. *Wizard: The Life and Times of Nikola Tesla, Biography of a Genius*. New York: Kensington Publishing Corporation, Citadel Press, 1998.

Tesla, Nikola. *My Inventions: The Autobiography of Nikola Tesla*. New York: Cosimo Classics, 2007.

Tesla, Nikola, with additional material by David Hatcher Childress. *The Fantastic Inventions of Nikola Tesla*. Stelle, IL: Adventures Unlimited, 1992.

Florence Sabin

Bluemel, Elinor. *Florence Sabin: Colorado Woman of the Century*. Boulder: University of Colorado Press, 1959.

Bobonich, Harry M. *Pathfinders and Pioneers: Women in Science, Math and Medicine*. West Conshohocken, PA: Infinity Publishing, 2008.

Campbell, Robin. *Florence Sabin: Scientist*. Chelsea House Publishers, 1995.

Downing, Sybil, and Jane Valentine Barker. *Florence Rena Sabin: Pioneer Scientist*. Boulder, CO: Pruett Publishing, 1981.

Flanagan, Mike. *Out West*. New York: Harry N. Abrams, 1987.

Hunter, Shaun. *Leaders in Medicine*. New York: Crabtree Publishing Co., 1999.

Kubie, Lawrence. "Florence Rena Sabin, 1871–1963." *Perspectives in Biology and Medicine* 4, no. 3 (Spring 1961). Chicago: University of Chicago.

Bibliography

Phelan, Mary Kay. *Probing the Unknown: The Story of Dr. Florence Sabin*. New York: Thomas Y. Crowell Company, 1969.

Reynolds, Moira Davison. *American Women Scientists: 23 Inspiring Biographies, 1900–2000*. Jefferson, NC: McFarland & Company, 1999.

Zach, Kim K. *Hidden from History: The Lives of Eight American Scientists*. Greensboro, NC: Avisson Press, 2002.

Enos Mills

Canning, Anne Smedley. *Early Estes Park*. Denver, CO: Dingerson Press, 1990.

Drummond, Alexander. *Enos Mills: Citizen of Nature*. Boulder: University Press of Colorado, 2002.

Fielder, John, T.A. Barron and Enos Mills. *Rocky Mountain National Park: A 100 Year Perspective*. Englewood, CO: Westcliffe Publishers, 1995.

Frank, Jerry J. *Making Rocky Mountain National Park: Environmental History of an American Treasure*. Lawrence: University Press of Kansas, 2013.

Hawthorne, Hildegarde, and Esther Burnell Mills. *Enos Mills of the Rockies*. Boston: Houghton Mifflin, 1935.

Jensen, Kenneth. *Estes Park: A Quick History*. Loveland, CO: First Light Publishing, 1966.

Mills, Enos A. *Adventures of a Nature Guide*. Friendship, WI: New Past Press, 1990.

———. *The Rocky Mountain National Park*. Boston: Houghton Mifflin, 1932.

———. *The Story of Early Estes Park*. Longs Peak, CO: Temporal Press, 1905.

Perry, Phyllis J. *It Happened in Rocky Mountain National Park*. Guilford, CT: Globe-Pequot Press, 2008.

Rinehart, Frederick R., ed. *Chronicles of Colorado*. Niwot, CO: Roberts Rinehart Publishers, 1993

Stansfield, John. *Enos Mills, Rocky Mountain Naturalist*. Palmer Lake, CO: Filter Press, 2005.

Wild, Peter. *Enos Mills*. Caldwell, ID: Boise State University Western Writers Series, 1979.

Index

About the Author

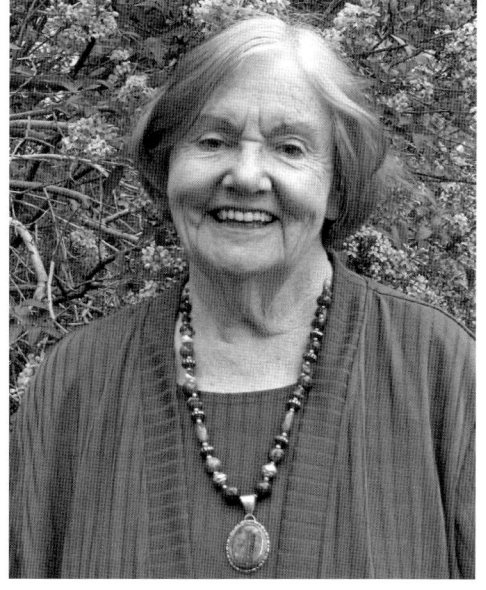

Phyllis Perry was born in a small gold mining town in northern California. After graduating from the University of California–Berkeley, she and her family moved to Boulder, Colorado, where she held a number of positions in the Boulder Valley Schools, including teacher, principal and director of Talented and Gifted Education. She also earned her doctorate from the University of Colorado.

Perry is an award-writing author of more than eighty books for children and adults. She has published seven books about Colorado, including two about Rocky Mountain National Park, which she and her photographer husband, David, visit frequently. She is a member of the Colorado Authors' League and of the Society of Children's Book Writers and Illustrators. You can learn more about her and her books by visiting her website at www.phyllisjperry.com.

Visit us at
www.historypress.net
···
This title is also available as an e-book